THE SHADOW COMMANDER

THE SHADOW COMMANDER

SOLEIMANI, THE U.S., AND IRAN'S GLOBAL AMBITIONS

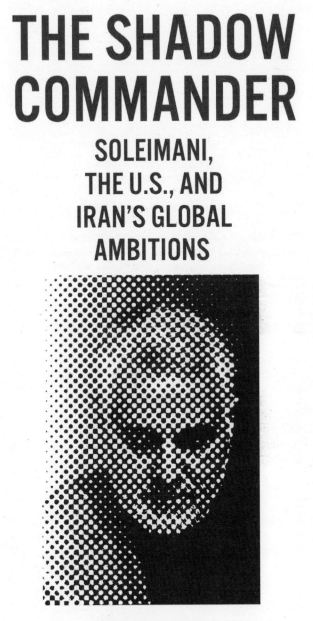

ARASH AZIZI

ONEWORLD

A Oneworld Book

First published by Oneworld Publications in 2020

Copyright © Arash Azizi 2020

The moral right of Arash Azizi to be identified as the author
of this work has been asserted by him in accordance with
the Copyright, Designs, and Patents Act 1988

ISBN 978-1-78607-944-2
eISBN 978-1-78607-945-9

Map © Erica Milwain

Typeset by Hewer Text UK Ltd, Edinburgh
Printed and bound in Great Britain by Clays Ltd, Elcograf S.p.A.

Oneworld Publications
10 Bloomsbury Street
London WC1B 3SR
England

Stay up to date with the latest books,
special offers, and exclusive content from
Oneworld with our newsletter

Sign up on our website
oneworld-publications.com

To Tehran and Kerman; Haifa and Jenin;
Baghdad and Aleppo; Erbil and Kuwait

For if there is hope, it's in the cities we love

Contents

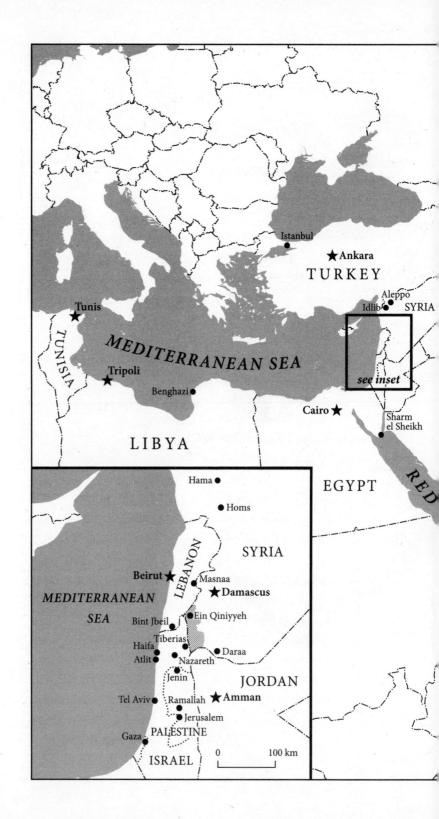

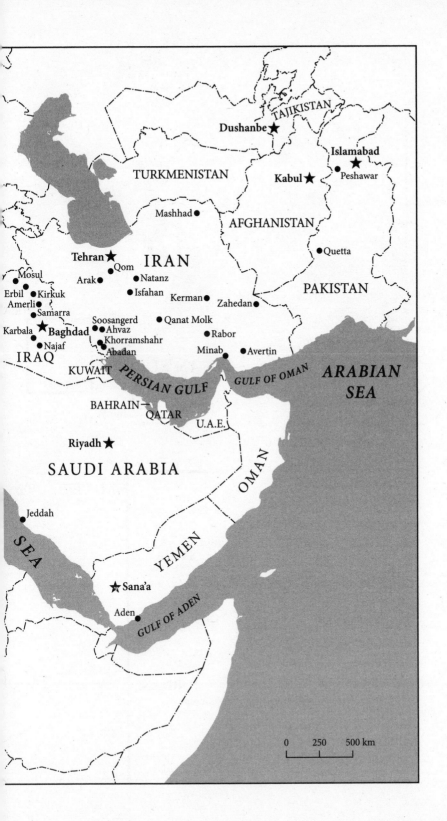

Introduction

#WorldWarIII

When the ominous hashtag started trending globally, it was evening in New York on January 2, 2020, and already the morning after in the Middle East. The new decade was off to a stormy start.

The social media craze had been caused by an American drone strike on Iraq's capital, Baghdad. Killing military opponents in the Middle East was hardly a rare event but this wasn't just any strike—and the main man it had killed wasn't just any opponent. At around 12:47 A.M. local time, US Predator B drones fired several missiles at two vehicles leaving Baghdad International Airport. They killed ten people in the convoy, including the top intended target, Iran's Major General Qassem Soleimani. Initial rumors about his death were confirmed when pictures were published of his severed arm, his *digitus medicinalis* adorned with a signature amulet ring. Soleimani was gone.

The world panicked and many didn't know how to react. Like a mythical bandit in a folktale, Soleimani had been larger than life. The commander of the Quds Force—the external operations branch of Iran's Islamic Revolutionary Guards Corps (IRGC)—ruled over a global army of tens of thousands of Shia Muslim fighters. He moved seamlessly across borders, as if he could be present in more than one place at the same time. The shadow commander had been a man without a shadow. But now he was merely a mutilated corpse.

His last hours fit his reputation. Barely seven minutes prior to his death, he had touched down in Baghdad on a flight from Damascus. Shortly before, he had been in Beirut, the gorgeous Mediterranean port and one of at least five capitals in which Qassem was among the most powerful men.

The decision to assassinate Soleimani counted as bold and reckless by any standard. Not since 1943, when the Americans shot down the plane carrying Marshal Admiral Isoroku Yamamoto of the Imperial Japanese Navy, had the United States killed such a high-ranking military official. President Donald Trump had made up his mind a few days before at his Mar-a-Lago resort, where he spent New Year's Eve conferring with his top cabinet members, including CIA director Gina Haspel, who raised eyebrows by advocating for the action. A few hundred kilometers to the west, across the Florida peninsula, United States Central Command headquarters in Tampa hatched the plans. The operation came a few days later. It was a devastating success.[1]

The world now held its breath for what was to come next. The 82nd Airborne Division sent thousands of its soldiers to the region, the largest such expeditionary action in years. The British Royal Navy started escorting ships in the Persian Gulf. From Mexico to Nigeria to Thailand, police forces were alerted to be prepared for the consequences. In Brazil, a social media panic erupted, with users worried that Iran might mistakenly retaliate against the entire Americas.

Soleimani's demise stunned the world. Who was this commander?

* * *

Qassem Soleimani hadn't always been a name to be reckoned with. When he was born in the Iran of 1956, few in his small mountain village could have predicted the emergence of a global military celebrity from their midst.

How had it come to this? How was it that a boy from the margins of Iranian society rose to become a commander feted by thousands and feared by many more? This is the central question at the heart of this book. I tell the story of a man and his rise to power; of how his world changed and how he changed his world. We must therefore begin at the beginning. Years before Qassem became a commander, he was a young man on the periphery.

Chapter 1

A Life on the Margins

A foreign traveler to Iran once retold the story of an encounter somewhere in the borderlands of the country. Meeting a local villager, he
spoke of his love for Iran, whereupon the startled villager asked: "Where
is Iran? I know all the villages in this area and we don't have any with
such a name." We don't know how much truth there is to this apocryphal
tale but it illustrates a point about life on the margins of the Iranian
plateau.[1] The great urban jewels of Iran have long seduced many a visitor
but the people of its pastoral and rural borderlands have been something
of a silent majority, a mystery or a danger: now castigated as disloyal
subjects who don't belong, then lauded as heroic keepers of the marshlands and guardians of the nation. This is tribal Iran.

The tribes of Iran are diverse and changing in their ethnicity, language,
religion, and mode of life. Their fortunes rise and fall with the tides of
history and events near and far. One event that affected them all was the
rise to power, in the 1920s, of an ambitious young monarch named Reza
Pahlavi. Backed by many of the country's modernizing intellectuals who
were disillusioned with the chaos that had followed the ups and downs
of the Constitutional Revolution of 1905–6, Reza wanted a centralized
and effective state and had to wage war against anything that stood in his

way. The nomadic tribes definitely made the list and many of the nation-alist intellectuals, opposing what they perceived as tribal backwardness, were enthusiastic about taking them on. Lacking permanent settlements, the tribes often migrated seasonally, taking their massive tents with them. They were equipped with their own arms, and consequently the state apparatus had limited penetration into the lives of tribal peoples. They spoke a variety of languages: some Persian or a close sibling, Lori, but many Turkic Azeri, Kurdish, Arabic, or Balochi. If Reza Shah wanted to build his centralized state, he had to suppress the tribes. And so he did. Traditional clothes and the black tents were banned, tribal confed-erations were broken and many tribes were forcibly settled. The process of forced settlement came to be known by a Turkic term, *"takhte qapu,"* which simply means "building a wooden gate," seen as the most conspic-uous sign of a resettled tribe. The term still disturbs many and tribal histories still speak with fear and trembling of the young monarch's campaign of terror against them.

Reza had gone on the record describing the tribal peoples as "illiter-ate, unproductive, abnormal tent-dwelling savages, left in their primitive state for too long."[2] The young monarch wasn't alone. Ignorant of the cosmopolitan histories of these tribes, the country's literati held similar conceptions. In the southern province of Kerman, not far from the waters of the Persian Gulf, the tribes hadn't played the pivotal role that their counterparts had elsewhere in Iran. They weren't kingmakers, allies of revolutionaries, or armed accomplices to foreign governments, but they had the most colorful mercantile history. The provincial urban center of Kerman sat not far from Bandar Abbas, the old port on the Persian Gulf which got its current name when the forces of Shah Abbas defeated the Portuguese in 1622, reconquering it after a century of European domination. Kicking out the Portuguese didn't lead to autarky: English, Dutch, and Portuguese merchants continued to pass through southern Iran and each tribe in Kerman boasts its own stories of interac-tions with the European merchants and empires.

By 1956, when our story begins, years of central state oppression had taken their toll. The tribes of Kerman province were no longer the inter-national mercantile interlocutors of the past and now languished on the margins of power and wealth in modern Iran. The forced settlement program was to intensify around this time. The province's most valued commodity, wool, particularly from the soft and fluffy hairs closest to a mammal's skin (known as down hair, ground hair or undercoat), had seen a drop in price.[3] Successive years of bad droughts had led to animal deaths. The tribes were devastated and struggled to find new avenues for livelihood: Girls would be raised to take part in the intensive and artful labor of producing the famed Kermani carpets for the markets, while young men would learn to drive, to become truckers perhaps, connecting central and southern Iran to the ports on the Persian Gulf via the roads that the new shah of Iran, Reza's son, Mohammad Reza, was busy building. Not everybody chose such noble callings. Some held on to their rifles, hiding them from the central government, practicing road robbery or engaging in petty crime.

In the county of Rabor, a few hours' drive away from the city of Kerman, lies the small village of Qanat Molk with a population of a few dozen families. Rabor has something in common with many locales around the world: villages in Jordan hosting forcibly settled Bedouin, hill towns in Southeast Asia home to sedentarized populations whose nomadic lives cannot be tolerated by modern states. The people of Qanat Molk claimed common descent from a particular sub-tribe. They almost all shared the same last name: Soleimani, that is, people of Soleiman (the biblical Solomon), the mythical king of the Jews in whose magical qualities Muslims believed as fervently as their Abrahamic predecessors.

The Soleimanis' presence in Kerman dated back to the eighteenth century when they had chosen to settle there on their way back from the Indian subcontinent where they had fought under the command of the legendary Persian king Nadir Shah. Or so they claimed. This gave them seniority over the many tribes that had been displaced in the previous few decades or during the tumult of the nineteenth century.

The village boasted beautiful walnut trees which the local lore claimed as the oldest in the world. But there was little to mark it beyond the local level. In 1956, even the county seat of Rabor, less than ten kilometers away from Qanat Molk, was yet to be founded. That would happen only in 1962 by bringing together five smaller locales. There was no industry or factories—nor is there today. No significant site of the kind that brought tourists in droves to the neighboring Fars province, to see beauties such as Persepolis or other ruins of the ancient Persian empires. No grand historical character, no famed Persian poet, no notable scientist of the golden age of Islam had ever emerged from this marginal part of Kerman.

But that mattered little to the many who loved their part of the world. Qolam Ali, who grew up in the 1960s in the nearby village of Nosratabad, just a stone's throw from Qanat Molk, is full of fond memories. "The harsh winters bothered us but the temperate spring and summer were so heavenly," he says. "The walnuts were famous but we had so much more. Apples, pears, and even some exotic fruits, believe it or not. We even had our own olives, rumored to have come from Lebanon."[4]

Qolam well remembers Nosratabad's village head, Khosrow, or *kadkhoda* Khosrow, to use the Persian prefix. The retired Khosrow still summers in Nosratabad while living in the nearby town of Jiroft. In the late 1950s, he had a close friend in Qanat Molk, Hassan Soleimani.

Born in 1922 into a small landowning family of peasants, Hassan had worked on his family's fruit gardens all his life. *Kadkhoda* Khosrow remembers him as a hardworking and humorous man, just as he appears in a video interview from decades later.[5] He had his first child at a relatively late age, being thirty-three when, in 1955, he and his wife, Fatima, had a daughter. Their first son arrived the following year. Like many Persian Muslims, they picked an Arabic name for him. The boy was to be called Qassem, Arabic for "divider" and the name of a rare son of the Prophet Mohammad (who had many daughters but no son who survived to adulthood). More to the point, Qassem was the name of a great-grandson of the Prophet, born to Imam Hassan, the Second Shia Imam. Hassan of Qanat Molk now had his own Qassem, just like Imam Hassan of 1,400 years before.

It was this son, Qassem, who would change the fate of this little village and much beyond. He would give this part of Kerman its first real celebrity, the first local boy who would make it. He'd be feted and known not only in the provincial center, Kerman, but in Tehran and the ancient Arab capitals that Qanat Molkis had only heard about in stories: Damascus, Beirut, Baghdad. He'd even be welcomed and honored in Moscow, then one of the two superpower capitals of the world, and his image would appear on countless magazine covers the world over, causing fear and loathing in lands far from the pleasant walnut trees of central Kerman.

The village saw dividends from this rise to power of the little boy who became Major General Qassem Soleimani. Helped by the general, Qanat Molk would get amenities sooner than other villages. It would boast a workshop to produce herbal medicine[6] and a massive mosque, partially built by the proud father himself. Until his death in 2016 at the age of ninety-five, Hajj Hassan Soleimani was to never leave his small village of 300 families or so. "One feels better in one's homeland," he said in a video interview with a Kermani outlet a few years before this death. Qanat Molk, with its pleasant cool breezes and sturdy walnut trees, was as good as one could wish for in a "homeland." Today he is buried there, next to his wife, who predeceased him by a few years. But the small village has entered the annals of history, due to the deeds of their first son.

The general never lost touch with this corner of the world. He'd visit as often as he could. His career would have been nothing without the sons of the area that flocked to join the military force he built in the 1980s to fight against the Iraqi invasion. One wonders how the family of Ebrahim Araste, for example, thinks of General Soleimani. Born in 1971 in the village of Mohammadabad, Ebrahim went to Qanat Molk, three kilometers away, for part of his schooling. Like many local boys, he worked hard to help his family from an early age. Life in Mohammad Abad was even harder than in the relatively rich Qanat Molk. The Shah's grandiose development projects were yet to bring running water to the village and Halime, Mohammad's mother, sometimes accompanied by her daughters, had to walk to a stream nearby, even in the dead of winter, to wash clothes and dishes and bring water back, just like Victor Hugo's fictional Cosette a century and a half before her. In his early teens Mohammad, who couldn't bear to see his mother go through this, took action. He managed to find a water pump in Qanat Molk and, not having the means to hire a car or get help, brought back the heavy piece all by himself, walking the three kilometers to Mohammad Abad. Like any good family of farmers, the parents hoped to rely on such a hardworking son for years. But this wasn't to pass. In 1987, in the fields of Shalamcha, on the Iranian-Iraqi border and not far from the port city of Basra, Ebrahim was killed by an Iraqi bullet, one of the up to 65,000 Iranians who died in the disastrous Iranian siege of Basra. His grave is there in Mohammad Abad today but it is empty as his body has never been found. He was all of fifteen years old.[7]

Mohammad was one of the many Kermanis mobilized by General Soleimani to fill the ranks of the Islamic Republic, a regime built in the name of the people of the margins. Before giving these people anything, the republic needed them to perform that age-old duty: dying for the nation. This is one thing Qassem would turn out to be very good at: mobilizing people to fight and die. What he started with the tribal Kermanis, he'd repeat with astonishing success in lands far from his marginal home village. But before he could get there, he had to get out of Qanat Molk.

* * *

Qassem was born into an Iran run by a man around the age of his father. Born in 1919, Mohammad Reza Shah Pahlavi was the first son of Reza, that very ambitious monarch who had brutalized the Iranian tribes to build his modernizing state. Reza's project and ambitions were typical of the statesmen of the region. He followed the lead of Mustafa Kemal Atatürk of Turkey and Amanallah Khan of Afghanistan, heads of states which, like Iran, had the rare distinction of being non-European realms never to be colonized. Reza particularly cherished the reform model of Atatürk. The two had met in Reza's first and only foreign trip during his reign, a state visit in 1934 to Turkey. In time away from interpreters, Reza had tried to converse with Atatürk in what he knew of the Turkic dialects of his native northern Persia but didn't have much success as Atatürk's Anatolian Turkish, soon to become a standardized language, shorn of its Arabic and Persian loanwords, was quite different. This symbolized the distance between the two men. Atatürk had been a general in the armed forces of a grand empire, the Ottomans; had fought in a world war; had defeated the British and French (under the leadership of the UK's First Lord of the Admiralty, Winston Churchill) on the hills of Gallipoli. He had lived in Bulgaria and had seen something of the world. Reza had had to build his military career during Iran's worst times of chaos, following the dying days of the Qajar dynasty when the country was falling prey to

Russia and Britain's "Great Game" in the region. The intrigues of London and Moscow called the shots in Iran before Reza rose to power thanks to a UK-backed coup in 1921. The British had liked his military discipline—the only field in which he had some talent. Iran's new strongman flirted with republicanism before helping to replace the Qajars with a new dynasty with himself as the founding king. Taking the ancient Persian name Pahlavi, the uncouth general from a humble background sought entry into the annals of the Iranian dynasties.

Atatürk had inherited something of the impressive Ottoman state and traditions whereas all Reza got was the remnants of the weak Qajar regime. He also had the support of at least some of the intellectual and political elites of the Persian Constitutional Revolution of 1905–6, ranging from liberals to social democrats, but he was quick to suppress them. Like many a military man, Reza soon grew tired of his intellectual supporters. By 1941, when he was overthrown by the Anglo-Soviet invasion of Iran due to Allied worries about the country falling to Hitler's Germany, much of what the Iranian historian Touraj Atabaki was to call "authoritarian modernization" had failed to stick.[8] Compared to Atatürk's Turkey, Reza created much more chaos and disharmony with far fewer results to show for it.

In 1941, as he departed Iran for a fatal exile in British-held realms (Mauritius, then South Africa), Reza gave the reins to his Swiss-educated 21-year-old son, Mohammad Reza. The young Shah was initially overshadowed by the country's raucous tribes, skilled politicians, and political parties, chiefly the communist Tudeh Party, in the only democratic period in Iran's history. The democratically elected parliament occasionally returned communist MPs and cabinet ministers. It also became the base of power for Iran's progressive prime minister, Mohammad Mossadeq. Backed by communists and a mass movement on the streets, Mossadeq took on the most powerful empire of his world, the British, but ended up becoming the first casualty of the world's newest imperial power. In 1953, the United States helped the British organize a coup, overthrow Mossadeq, crush the communists and all other political parties, and put an end to Iran's twelve-year experience of democracy. The young Shah, now thirty-three years of age, had a new lease on life. No longer an overshadowed monarch, he was well on his way to

n all-powerful autocrat like his father. In 1958, after a
ıst-backed revolution overthrew the young monarchy in his
ɔoring Iraq, the Shah's fears grew and he cracked down further.
ɹe once vibrant parliament became a pliant rubber-stamp assembly,
divided into two groups famously known as the "Yes" and "Yes, Sir"
parties. The Shah emerged to become a seminal figure in the colorful
tapestry of the global Cold War.

Iran had been central to the Cold War since day one. Historian Bruce
R. Kuniholm even claimed that the "war" had started in the Near East,
with the Soviet-US face-off in Iran being a big part of the story.[9] Iran was
to be a theater of the Cold War throughout its entire duration and though
they might not have known it, the lives of the people of Qanat Molk, too,
were deeply affected by the ebbs and flows of that global conflict. The
Cold War made lives of people around the world interconnected but in
deeply unequal waves. The decisions of a relatively few people in the
swing states of the United States could change the lives of millions
around the world, including the unsuspecting farmers of Qanat Molk. In
the 1960 US presidential elections, John F. Kennedy, a young senator
from the state of Massachusetts, surprised the world by defeating the
Republican governor of California, Richard Nixon. Who would have
known that the people of the Midwestern state of Missouri would vote
for a yuppie Boston Catholic? Although Barack Obama came close in
2008, to this day no other northern Democrat has ever carried Missouri.
But on that fateful day of November 8, 1960, decisions by people like the
farmers in the almost all-white Osage County of Missouri affected the
fate of the world. The Soleimanis of Qanat Molk, Kerman might not have
known of Frankenstein, Missouri but such small communities were
interconnected in the context of the global Cold War.

President Kennedy had promised to change the way the US fought the
Cold War. In 1958, a political novel by Eugene Burdick and William
Lederer symbolized Kennedy's problem with the Cold War policies of his
Republican predecessor, Dwight Eisenhower, the man who had approved
the 1953 coup that ended democracy in Iran, three years before our
Qassem was born. Burdick and Lederer had both served in the navy
during the Second World War, with the latter rising to become an impor-
tant captain in the Pacific theater. They were now both disillusioned with

the US backing of tinpot dictators in the Southeast Asia they had so valiantly fought to free from fascist Japanese aggression in the war. The novel was called *The Ugly American*. It was set in the imaginary country of Sarkhan, described as somewhere akin to Thailand or Burma and obviously meant to represent that festering sore of the Cold War, Vietnam. Senator Kennedy loved the book so much that he sent a copy to all his colleagues in the Senate. The cinematic version, starring Marlon Brando, had to wait until 1963 but the book was already a phenomenon, ultimately selling four million copies, and might have had something to do with average Americans in places like Missouri turning to Kennedy. Americans don't usually care much about foreign policy. Did they want the "Quiet American" the world knew to turn so quickly to an "Ugly American"?

Kennedy's message was clear. If the US wanted to reduce communism's popularity in the Third World, it had to stop backing repressive dictators and instead give the people what the communists were promising them: development and jobs. In office, President Kennedy would make this something of a priority. In 1961, he launched the Peace Corps, a significant volunteer program which sent young Americans around the world. The Peace Corps Americans were to be the ultimate counter-image of the "Ugly American" Brando portrayed in 1963: ambassadors of economic development and even justice.

Early in his post-coup rule, the Shah was more pliant to Kennedy than he would be to his successors. Thus when the liberal president pressured him to be more democratic and progressive, he gave in. But, like other liberal presidents before him, the young Bostonian was quick to find out that grandiose visions outlined on the pages of the New York journal *Foreign Affairs* were not always easy to translate into policy, least of all in the rocky waters of the Cold War. In 1961, under pressure from Kennedy, the Shah appointed the reform-leaning, American-educated Ali Amini as prime minister. As ambassador to the US in the post-coup years of 1955 to 1958, Amini had been so close to Washington as to irk the insecure Shah, who recalled him home. As a prime minister enforcing Kennedy's agenda, he was never to have the full cooperation of the Shah and the imperial court. Amini also failed to get any backing from the supporters of Mossadeq and the Iranian opposition, who considered any collaboration with the US-installed Shah as political suicide, a sin they were not prepared to commit. Amini's premiership failed miserably and, a year later, he was replaced by Asadollah Alam, his opposite in every imaginable way. Alam was a grand landowner from northeastern Iran who considered himself a humble and obedient servant of the Shah. With Alam at the helm, and Kennedy out of the reckoning after his tragic assassination in 1963, the Shah had the chance to offer his own version of state-led development — one more attempt to bring happiness to people and stave off a communist revolution.

What would this all mean for the people of Qanat Molk and Qassem's family? How would lives change in this corner of Kerman province? Although his opponents would come to caricature him in that way, the Shah was no corrupt and nasty Cold War dictator like François Duvalier or Ferdinand Marcos. He saw himself not as a hidebound reactionary but as a revolutionary and even a socialist who knew his people's interests better than the communists ... and better even than his people themselves. And therein lay the problem. Writing sweepingly about different regimes around the world, anthropologist James Scott would come to criticize "seeing like a state," in other words implementing state-led plans from above that were well-meaning but rarely took into account the priorities of the people they wanted to help.

In 1963, the benevolent autocrat of Iran declared the principles of his "Revolution of Monarch and the People," nicknamed the White Revolution to differentiate it from the Red Revolution it was meant to prevent. Not for the first time the establishment decided to counter the opposition by adopting its agenda. Didn't the old Prussian Otto von Bismarck introduce social reforms to stem the rise of German Social Democrats, the party meant to work for the ideas of Karl Marx and Friedrich Engels? The Shah's "revolution" had nineteen principles which read like the agenda of a progressive party. It planned to nationalize the jungles and waterways of the country, give workers a share in factories, introduce female suffrage (a proposal of the communist Tudeh in the 1940s), bring about free education and social insurance for all, and send young teachers and doctors around the country as part of "the Knowledge Corps" and "the Health Corps." Most consequential for our story and for the course of Iranian history was the very first item on the agenda. The White Revolution pledged to bring about "land reform and annulment of the master-subject relationship." The Shah hadn't declared his revolution from a farmers' congress for nothing. He knew that his agenda for change would live or die according to how it touched the lives of farmers, the majority of Iranians.

Land reform had long been the bugbear of progressives and reactionaries alike. The plans that the Shah introduced were even more far-reaching than those of his socialist arch-nemesis in the region, President Gamal Abdul Nasser of Egypt. Large landowners held more than fifty percent of Iranian land at the time. They often controlled the lives of "their" peasants, calling the economic and political shots in the country. Just a few years before, an attempt by the Shah's agriculture minister, Jamshid Amoozegar, to bring a land reform bill to the parliament had been defeated by strong representation from the landed interests there. This time around, the Shah brought back Hassan Arsanjani, the most dynamic minister of Amini's cabinet. The forty-year-old Arsanjani had translated Montesquieu's *Persian Letters* in his teen years and had been elected as a MP by the people of Gilan, located on the Caspian coast and perhaps Iran's most progressive-leaning province. His appointment was alarming to the landowning class and a most obvious sign that the Shah was serious about land reform. In the power struggle that ensued, Arsanjani was forced to shelve his radical plans and found that most familiar fate of those who lose in politics: He was quietly dispatched to be Iran's ambassador to Rome.

The half-hearted land reform that followed brought more chaos than relief. The episode has been a heated subject of debate in Iran and an inspiration to many novelists who have chronicled the lives from below, missed by those who "saw like a state."

Hassan Soleimani lived one of those lives. When Qassem was born in 1956,[10] his family barely owned any land. The White Revolution was to give them land and could have made them lifelong devotees of the Shah, Light of the Aryans, the successor to Cyrus the Great, a man who had come to help those on the margins. But its botched implementation meant that the Soleimanis went from being a landless family to one that was heavily indebted, a sign of deep shame and trouble in their surroundings. Reza Shah had caused the tribal make-up of the area to collapse with his forced resettlements. Shah the son had created another round of chaos, despite his best intentions. The old habits of villagers, disdain and suspicion toward the city and the center, had been doubly vindicated.

Qassem grew up with a father who had to live with debt and could not provide for his family the way he wanted. A bright kid by all accounts, he was intelligent enough to continue his studies and even go to a university. But like many a poor man's son, he needed to work. He did odd construction jobs from his early teens, sojourning around the province in the summers. In 1970, at the age of fourteen, he finished primary school. He was able to go to Rabor to finish high school and get the desired diploma, a rarity known to open many doors. The White Revolution hadn't helped his father become a sustainable farmer but the massive state built by the Shah would find Qassem a reliable source of income. The high school diploma was to prove useful. The Iranian state kept expanding as the Shah, drunk on the astronomically high oil prices in the aftermath of the Yom Kippur War of 1973, grew more confident about his grandiose plans. He now claimed to have sighted the gates of the Great Civilization soon to be reached by Iran. For the teenage Qassem, the Great Civilization meant a steady job. In 1975, at the age of eighteen, he found employment with the Kerman water organization as an aide in the public relations department. The new job necessitated a move to the city of Kerman, center of the province and several hundred kilometers away from home.

Like many villagers before him, Qassem was taking the first step in broadening his horizons: a move to the city.

Chapter 2
A Young Man in the City

With a population of around 140,000, Kerman in 1975 was no metropolis. It wasn't one of the ten largest cities of Iran and even some less-populated cities were more open and lively than this caravan town in the middle of the grand Iranian desert. This wasn't Tehran with its museums and restaurants, Mashhad with its ever-growing population, or even the nearby Shiraz with its charming gardens and tourist sites. Still, compared to Qassem's little village, where even electricity was a luxury, Kerman was a new world, a window into the bustling times later fabled as the Long Global Sixties. The world was changing in every way and young people were at the forefront of that change. Established politics and social mores were coming under challenge everywhere, and the Iran of the 1970s was no exception.

Qassem hadn't moved to Kerman alone. Excited by his new job in the provincial capital, some of his family members joined him for this new chapter. Closest among them was Ahmad Soleimani, born around the same time as Qassem in the same village. He wasn't his brother, as many mistaken accounts would later claim, but a first cousin. But Qassem loved him like a brother. Few people would play a more decisive role in his life in this period. Unlike Qassem, Ahmad was religious and had some interest in politics. It was for him to pester Qassem and others about all that was going on around the country, things not known to most people in Qanat Molk.

As the eldest son in the family, Qassem had done his younger brother, Sohrab, a big favor by taking him to Kerman. In 1977, at the age of thirteen, Sohrab went to join Qassem, who, with his salary from the water organization, was starting to live a modest life. Despite the salary, the going was rough. Sohrab, Ahmad and Qassem, together with another cousin, lived on Kerman's Nasseriye Street in a rented room, owned by an old lady named Assiyah. Sohrab remembers those days with excitement. In Qanat Molk, construction or agriculture were the only real avenues open to a teenager like him. In a city like Kerman, the young Soleimanis could experience so much more and Sohrab didn't need to worry about working as Qassem insisted on him pursuing his studies for as long as he could. The new world of Kerman was theirs for the taking.

In Kerman's ancient bazaar, there was a two-storied cafe serving Persian saffron ice cream and the Kermani version of the sorbet *faloodeh*, much less well known than its famous sibling from Shiraz. There, the Soleimanis would see young unmarried men and women going out and exchanging letters and promises. Many of these youngsters went to Kerman University (KU). KU had opened its doors in 1975, accepting ninety students. The founders of the university, Alireza Afzalipoor and Fakhere Saba, came from a world virtually alien to the young men of the Soleimani tribe. Afzalipoor was a French-educated chemist who had made his money by trading electronics. After finishing his studies in Bordeaux and Lille, he returned to Iran in 1938 to do what many virtuous Iranians thought proper: serve the country after a stint abroad. Philanthropy was the name of the game. Afzalipoor had married Saba, a beautiful soprano who was at the forefront in Iran of the opera world, then a most glamorous Western import. In the 1960s, Saba enchanted Tehrani audiences with her performance as Suzuki the maid in Puccini's *Madama Butterfly*, an oriental tale, told by an Italian, reverberating in another corner of the orient.

Iran was by no means a regional pioneer in this field. Almost a hundred years before any opera would be staged in Iran, Egypt's Khedive Ismail had ordered the building of an opera house in Cairo to celebrate the opening of the Suez Canal in 1869. Designed by Italian architects Avoscani and Rossi, Cairo's opera house was the first in Africa and the Middle East. In 1939, when Mohammad Reza married the Egyptian princess Fawzia and brought her home, she complained about how backward Iran was, putting a chip on the shoulder of the Iranian monarch and those like Afzalipoor who wanted to tell their colleagues in places like Lille and Bordeaux that Iran was in no way inferior to any European nation.

But could a nation have an opera house but no proper sewerage system? Maybe it was a question of that kind that led to Saba quitting the stage at the height of her career to team up with her rich husband in supporting philanthropic development in places such as Kerman. Young teachers and civil servants there, as in other parts of the country, were increasingly political and critical of the Shah, his American backers, and his grandiose regime. In 1975, the monarch had stunned the country by rejecting his previous aversion to one-party states. He now banned all political parties except for his newly founded Resurgence Party (RP), which was to be the only legal party in the country. Anybody who didn't like things could leave, the Shah said. Like many a state party, the RP opened offices all over the country, including in Kerman.

As Qassem was working on that other important and crucial national task, building and maintaining a water and sewerage system, he encountered many new worlds in Kerman: people who went to a university cofounded by a soprano, and people who critiqued the order of priorities; "yes men" of the country's only legal party, and those who denounced it. But unlike what the revolutionary histories would later claim, this wasn't necessarily a sharply divided country. It didn't feel like a place pregnant with revolution. For the vast majority of Kermanis, the Shah was a fact of life, here to stay, as permanent as his piercing eyes that gazed at the populace from portraits hung in every shop.

The 1970s were an exhilarating time. Decades later, Iranians in New York would indulge in fantasies of the era by holding "Tehran Disco" nights at premier clubs in the world's most exciting city. Many non-Iranians attended, which suggests that the allure of Seventies Iran had something to offer New Yorkers of the twenty-first century. Iranians of all generations since then have had and still have a liking for the cultural products of that exciting era. In the Kerman encountered by the Soleimanis, older people might recite the popular songs of such Persian divas as Delkash or Marzieh. Some of these songs were based on the medieval poetry of Persian bards such as Hafiz and Saadi, who hailed from nearby Shiraz, where their mausoleums had been developed as tourist sites that must have made Kerman jealous. Others would be based on the work of new songwriters such as Shahyar Ghanbari or Iraj Janati Ataei, who created some of the best masterpieces in the history of their mother tongue. There was something for everyone. The perennial Persian "sad boys" might take to the songs of Dariush, who took the traditional dignified sulking in Iranian culture and made it into material for romantic songs. Dariush's vaguely worded critical songs irked the authorities a little and became favorites for those who, like their counterparts around the world, were revolting against the status quo. Many more might put their phonographs to use by playing records from Gogoosh, the most explosive talent of the era, a sex symbol and the shining star of the Iranian entertainment scene. In the traditional restaurants of Kerman (more or less the only type available), Iranian banquet cuisine, kebabs with rice, butter, and tomatoes, was served. There were no live appearances by popular crooners such as one could expect in bigger cities like Tehran, Isfahan, or Abadan, but, if you were lucky, you could be entertained by a most soulful Balochi performance with instruments native to southeastern Iran.

Even the relatively small Kerman had many trappings for those interested in fruits of the modern Iran. Not far from Kerman was the port of Bandar Abbas, where the middle class might go for holidays. Very few Kermani women would dare to don swimsuits, even of the conservative, long-tunic type. But everyone could flock to the port markets where dhows from the nearby Arab trading nations such as Kuwait and the newly formed United Arab Emirates would bring foreign goods of all sorts.

On television, many were glued to series such as *Morad the Electrician*, telling the tale of a nomadic caricature of a troubadour who fixed electrical goods instead of playing music. The protagonist fell in love with Mahboobe, played by the stunning actress Negar, the youngest in a family of seven daughters who could only marry after all the elder sisters did; this was a difficulty close to the heart of many young Iranian men struggling with building a family life in these new times. Schoolchildren like Sohrab were benefiting from the free compulsory education of the White Revolution, at least if they didn't have to work to help their poor families. They could take part in exciting activities such as chess competitions. The winners would go to other cities such as Yazd (as at least some from Sohrab's school did) and Tehran, and maybe even foreign countries.

Teenagers flocked to libraries like the massive private one endowed by Mohammad Hossein Meymandinejad, a local poet and writer who had risen to head Tehran University's faculty of veterinary sciences in the 1940s and had now come to give back to his hometown. Left-leaning and Shah-skeptic teachers might guide youngsters to literature that, while legal, was a code for progressive politics and opposition to the US-aligned Shah. Some Kermanis of the time remember reading the writers of the previous generation, the pioneers of modern Persian prose. Popular was Sadeq Hedayat, known for writing what many considered the first Persian novel, *Blind Owl* (1936), and for acerbic criticisms of Islam which had irked many. Another popular Iranian writer was Mohammad Ali Jamalzadeh, old enough to remember the revolution of 1905–6 and long since living in self-imposed Swiss exile. A young bookworm might pick up Victor Hugo's *Les Misérables*, in the highly questionable but very readable translation by Hoseinqoli Mostaan, who made his name as Hugo's translator but was once embarrassed when it turned out he couldn't hold the simplest French conversation in real life. The more politically minded might read socialist writers such as the Kurdish-Turkish Aziz Nesin or the American Jack London, far enough from the context of immediate Iranian politics to evade the censors.

On the cinema screens, the most controversial pastime of the era, shunned and banned by many families, Kermanis enjoyed US classics such as films by Charlie Chaplin or Iranian ones with the sex symbols of the era: actor-crooners such as Mohammad Ali Fardin, who played a perennial chivalrous lover, or Pooran, who sang her own songs, such as a Persian rendition of "Bint Chalabiya" by the famous Lebanese singer Fairuz. The first rows of cinemas were reserved for rowdy urban toughs known as *laat o loot*. With their black-rimmed hats, donkey jackets and

white shirts with the top buttons open, they mixed traditions of neighborhood chivalry with devotion to Shia Islam and the local mosques,
and looked up to the screen heroes such as Fardin or especially Naser
Malak Motiee, Iran's answer to Cary Grant. Women might sometimes
attend the cinema, mostly with families or with their fiancés, sitting in
the back rows.

Where did Qassem Soleimani fit in this world of seventies urban Iran?
Which public places did he frequent and what were his circles? The hagi-
ographic accounts of the future war commander don't tell us this but he
surely experimented with some of these with the curiosity of a young
man in a new city. Some of his choices, and his future developments,
show that he had some affinity with the *looti* crowd. But more than
movies, music or novels, an import from an industrial country did much
to shape this period of his life. However, it was an import not from the
West, but from the Far East.

After its defeat in the Second World War and the subsequent occupation by the Allies, Japan had re-emerged as an industrial nation and
wooed the world with its soft power. Japanese martial arts, as they fit the
orientalist fantasies of discipline, were quick to gain popularity around
the world. Few knew that the most celebrated of these "Japanese" arts
had been foreign to Japan itself not that long ago. Karate had developed
in the Ryukyu Kingdom, an archipelago with its own indigenous peoples
and traditions and its own independence until it fell to Japanese control
in the late nineteenth century. The martial art that came to be known as
a quintessential Japanese cultural export only came to Japan in the twentieth century. In the postwar years, with the spread of martial arts movies
and ideas about Japanese discipline, karate found many enthusiasts
around the world. On this front, Iran was in tandem with Europe. In the
1960s, just when karate clubs were starting to spread in Europe, Farhad
Varaste, an Iranian who had studied physical chemistry in Switzerland
before getting a PhD in political science from the University of Michigan,
came back to Iran. In lieu of the habitual Western imports, he brought
with him his love for karate. He opened the first karate class in his father's
basement and dedicated his life to the spread of the sport. Established in
1972, his karate academy was the first in Iran, and a year later, Iran had
a national karate team which played in a world championship in Paris,

gaining a bronze and a ranking of fifth worldwide. Varaste was so successful that by 1976, Tehran came to host the European Karate Championships, the first of only two occasions on which the contest has been held outside Europe.

Martial arts have long appealed to those in pursuit of martial professions. Military veterans were a natural constituency. Among the students of Varaste who became missionaries for karate was an army officer named Hashem Vaziri. He had gotten to know the sport in the 1960s but in 1971, after resigning from the army, he dedicated most of his life to the art he had learnt from his master. He had first established a club in Khorasan province in the northeast, home to Iran's second biggest city, Mashhad. Around 1975, just when Qassem moved to Kerman, Vaziri ended up in the city and established a very successful club there. Kerman was to become a hub for Iranian karate, producing a disproportionate number of the national champions in the sport.

Like many a Kermani *looti*, Qassem frequented the gym. Whatever feelings of rural inadequacy he may have had around the other aspects of Kermani life and his fellow civil servants in the water organization, they evaporated in the gym. Under the weights, he, with muscles that had worked on construction jobs since his early teens, was everybody's equal if not superior. He went several times a week, making the local gyms of Kerman a hub of his life. In addition to the modern gym at the Kerman Workers' Club, Soleimani also worked out at two local *zoorkhanes*, Jahan and Atayi.[1] Centers for traditional Iranian ritual athletics, *zoorkhanes* taught wrestling alongside the ethics of Persian chivalry. Like every other aspect of Iranian life, these supposedly ancient centers had also been touched with Western imports. Qassem watched as some young men practiced boxing there. Ali Akbar Pooriani was one such boxer. In later years, he would become a close military companion of Soleimani and his deputy as the head of a brigade.

But Qassem never got to like boxing. His serene and quiet attitude was a much better fit for another import. As Vaziri recruited in the local gyms for his nascent karate club, he found his perfect match. Kermani karate had found a most enthusiastic student and Qassem had found a pursuit that gave his life meaning, perhaps more than any other thing he had ever done. Contrary to what his hagiographies later claimed, he is unlikely to have gotten a black belt. Had it not been for the subsequent events, he might have ended up like Vaziri, known for spreading the gospel of karate and its theatrics. But there was another hub to Soleimani's life in Kerman and, as it turned out, that proved more consequential.

* * *

Scholars of the Iranian revolution of 1979 have often looked back at the Iran of the 1960s and 1970s to seek signs of the movement that would come to bring about a revolution that shocked the world and surprised just about every observer. Where had this revolution come from? Where was it hiding among the cinema-going crowds and mosques filled with young men who would ask for forgiveness for all the alcohol they had drunk the previous night? Deterministic accounts, lamenting the disruptions that the Islamic Republic brought to Iranian society, read like whodunits. Each has a favorite actor to blame for what came to pass. Did the nineteen-year-old Qassem Soleimani of 1975, or those in his Kermani circles, know that a revolution would overthrow the imperial kingdom of Iran in four years and that their lives would be so intimately tied to this revolution? It is unlikely that they even dreamed of such things.

This or that teacher or civil servant sympathized with the old communist Tudeh Party or the brave urban guerrilla organizations that had succeeded it. But most Kermanis went about their lives unaffected, without much sense of the impending revolution's gathering storm until it engulfed the nation and brought down the seemingly all-powerful Shah in a masterful final blow in February 1979.

In the mid-1970s, the movement of revolutionary clerics, with their charismatic leader Ayatollah Khomeini, who was in exile in Najaf, Iraq, had one big advantage over all other groups. Whereas the Shah's stringent anti-communism had brought massive repression on all communist groups, the clerics had nationwide networks of mosques that were much harder to crack down on. Yes, the Shah and his fearsome secret police, SAVAK, did suppress the Khomeini-supporting clerics but these were relatively mild constraints and allowed the clerics to persist in their activities. Kerman province presented some of the leading lights of this clerical movement: Ayatollah Rafsanjani would rise to become one of

Khomeini's closest clerical lieutenants and a founding father of the Islamic Republic, while Kerman-born Ayatollah Movahedi Kermani, whose father had been a well-known orator in the Kerman of the Reza Shah years, was among the founders of Tehran's Militant Clergy Society, the closest thing to a political party for Khomeinists. SAVAK had banned him from preaching in Kerman.

Qassem wasn't particularly religious but where else would an ambitious young man who didn't quite match with the Jack London-reading crowd fit? Taking the lead from his cousin Ahmad, who had been a regular at the mosque ever since they came to Kerman, Qassem started going to the mosque too. He briefly worked at a hotel, and often cycled to the mosque with the owner's son, another regular at the mosque, on cheap second-hand bicycles they had acquired.

The Khomeinist clerics had formed a nationwide movement whose partisans circulated around the country. In the old caravan city of Kerman, known for its conservatism, some of the out-of-province clerics did the most to kindle the fire of the movement. SAVAK's tactics of banishing the clerics it persecuted to places far from their hometowns inadvertently helped. It was thanks to SAVAK that Kermanis got to enjoy the presence of Mohammad Mofateh, a luminary of the clerical movement who held a PhD in philosophy. In 1969, he had been forced to stay in Kerman. His rousing speeches in the city ended up recruiting many a young Kermani.

It was another out-of-town cleric who came to shape Soleimani's life in ways he didn't anticipate. Born in a village in northeastern Khorasan, Seyyed Reza Kamyab was a *hojjatoleslam* (a level below an ayatollah) from a clerical family. Following the clerical path of social mobility, he had left the local seminary in Gonabad, the nearest town to his village, for the provincial center of Mashhad, Iran's holiest city. Mashhad was the hometown of some of the leaders of the revolutionary movement. No less a figure than Ali Shariati, the Sorbonne-educated, charismatic orator and theoretician of the emergent leftist Islamism, hailed from the city. A lesser-known and younger figure in Mashhadi opposition circles was Ali Khamenei, a young cleric characterized by his ambition and love for literature. Kamyab had met Khamenei when both were involved in organizing relief in the aftermath of the 1978 earthquake in Tabas,

Khorasan province. Recruited into the revolutionary underground, Kamyab was sent sent to the difficult province of Kerman, where much of the local clergy was too loyalist to the crown and the indigenous revolutionaries such as Rafsanjani and Movahedi were too well known to SAVAK to operate freely.

In the Muslim holy month of Ramadan in 1977, Kamyab gave one of the most memorable speeches of his life. The rising economic difficulties of the country and an apparently wobbling Shah had given the revolutionary movement a new lease of life. As the Khorasani cleric attacked the Shah and his White Revolution, the young civil servant of the water organization, the new karate athlete, confused in an emergent urban Iranian society that didn't have an easy place for the likes of him, took heart. Qassem Soleimani would later say: "My revolutionary struggles began when I heard a speech by Martyr Kamyab."[2]

But were there many "revolutionary struggles" to speak of? When the Shah left Iran, in the earliest days of 1979, Qassem was twenty-two. By all accounts, he had been mostly focused on his job and his love for karate.[3] He spent much more time at the gym than he did at the mosque. He wasn't a political activist by any stretch of imagination. But the revolution would come to engulf everybody.

The year 1978 had started auspiciously for the Shah. US president Jimmy Carter visited Iran for the New Year holidays, stressing his alliance with the Shah and calling Iran "an island of stability." A few days after he left, an article, signed with a pseudonym but approved by the Shah, appeared in Tehran's semi-official *Ettelaat* newspaper. It attacked the unholy alliance of the "Red and Black Colonialists." With the classic conspiratorial tone of authoritarian regimes it claimed that communists of the Tudeh Party (the Red Colonialists) were allied with the feudal landowners (the Black Colonialists), united in their hatred for the White Revolution. It also involved the favorite bogeyman of Iranian conspiracy stories, the British (in reality, now a fading empire). Ayatollah Khomeini had been the focus of the article, painted as a Machiavellian figure who had gotten British help during his years in India. Worse, it said that his black turban (denoting his descent from the Family of the Prophet) was fake as he was really an Indian infidel and an agent of the British. For many, this was the worst insult imaginable.

Two days later, the holy city of Qom, the seat of the main Shia semi-nary, saw a demonstration brutally put down by the authorities. At least six men were killed. Even the sleepy old Kermanis had to react. Clerics organized a prayer strike, refusing to lead communal prayers, shutting down the center of community life for most people. Mass mourning ceremonies were held for those killed in the Qom crackdown, on the fortieth day after their "martyrdom," as stipulated traditionally. More people were killed in these ceremonies and a new cycle of mourning and killing resulted. Before long, Kerman was to have its own martyrs.

A river of blood now separated the Shah from his people. Though very few knew it, the majestic King Sun was on his last legs. In less than 400 days, the Shah would be gone from Iran, destined to die shortly thereafter in exile just like his three immediate predecessors. A new Islamic republic was to replace a 2,500-year-old tradition of monarchy, giving birth to a platypus of a creature never before encountered in the annals of history. For people from the margins, this was a new opportu-nity. The revolutionaries had spoken in *their* name and on *their* behalf. As the revolutionary republic made a clarion call to them to bolster it against its internal and external opponents, young women and men like Qassem took the hint. Now was the time to make history, to be part of something bigger than the tribe or the village, bigger than the world of karate even. Qassem had not helped make the revolution but the revolu-tion was sure to help make him.

Chapter 3
To Guard a Revolution

The evening of February 11, 1979, in Kerman wasn't that special to Farid. A high school student who took karate classes just like Qassem, he didn't care much for the tumultuous events that had catapulted Iran to the top of world news. His Imperial Majesty, the Shah of Iran, had left the country in January but his portrait still hung in many, if not most, shops in Kerman. Just ten days earlier, an Air France flight from Paris had brought home the Shah's arch-nemesis, Ayatollah Khomeini. The 76-year-old cleric had shown a steely determination that broke the will of the famously arrogant monarch. Now he had to face Shapoor Bakhtiar, a French-educated social democrat whom the Shah had appointed as prime minister just before leaving the country. Bakhtiar had long been an opponent of the Shah and a leading member of the National Front, the banned opposition party founded by Mossadeq. But the party quickly expelled him once he was heading the new government. Credible figures couldn't risk being seen anywhere near his cabinet since that meant serving at the pleasure of the departed Shah. The revolutionary movement had conquered the streets and it was to accept no compromise. The Shah had to go. The monarchy had to go. Everything had to change.

On his arrival, Khomeini spoke to the millions of cheering supporters gathered in Tehran's grand cemetery and its surroundings. He promised to "slap the government in the mouth" and appoint a new one.

But what did all this mean to the people of Kerman, a thousand kilometers away from the capital? Once more, power changed hands in Tehran, and Kerman had to follow. Yes, Kermanis had also fought and died in the revolutionary movement. Yes, some from the province were among the leading lights of the revolution, not least the young and talented cleric Akbar Hashemi Rafsanjani, who hailed from a pistachio-growing family and was famous for—uncharacteristically for Iranian men—lacking facial hair. Yes, Kerman's police chief had been mysteriously assassinated a couple of weeks before. Yes, even Farid's mother had deep affection for Khomeini, though this was due less to his politics than to the black turban he wore, denoting his status as a *seyyed*, a descendant of the Prophet Mohammad and thus bearing miraculous charismatic qualities; these same qualities led her to join many Iranians in claiming to have spotted a likeness of the Ayatollah on the moon.

But most people in Kerman had more immediate concerns. "On that day, February 11, I remember we had caught a chicken with a few friends," Farid remembers. "In the chaos of those days, somehow a chicken coop had been left without care and all the chickens had fled. All we cared about that day was how to skin and grill a chicken! Who cares about this shah or that ayatollah?"[1]

Farid and his young friends might not have cared but the Ayatollah had surprised the world. How could a previously little-known cleric bring down one of the closest allies of the United States? Why had the Shah's massive army, fifth biggest in the world, not intervened? How could so many people be devoted to an exiled cleric? In the world of the Cold War, was he truly independent, as he claimed, from both Moscow and Washington? Theorists of revolution threw their hands in the air. Western-educated social scientists wondered if Muslim societies could be understood through their schemas. Orientalists summoned all their learning to understand this most unprecedented phenomenon. French thinker Michel Foucault rushed to Iran to celebrate this enchanted, spiritual revolution. Eric Hobsbawm, the dean of Marxist historiography, would come to call this "a social revolution in the Name of God."

It wasn't God but humans who had brought down the Shah. The rise of Khomeini seemed to suggest that "great men" did, after all, make history. Yet on February 11, 1979, the final blow to the *ancien régime* didn't come by order of Khomeini or any of the many men and few women who surrounded him in his makeshift compound in the Alavi school in Tehran. Rather, in actions that mesmerized many observers, swarms of people attacked government buildings around the country. The all-powerful army had declared its neutrality. It would no longer shoot at its people. The Shah's praetorian force, the Eternal Guards, had briefly fought back but they were no match for the people.

The last crucial building to fall was that of the national broadcasting service, whose employees were on strike. The broadcaster Ahmad Kasila, sympathetic to the revolution, now went on air to speak the words that would soon reverberate around the country and around the world: "This is Tehran. The true voice of the Iranian nation. The voice of the revolution. Today, with the chivalrous efforts of the nation, the last fortress of despotism fell down."

In Kerman, the revolution was to be bloodless. About ten kilometers from the town lay the barracks of Sarasiab. Founded in 1933, they were one of the oldest barracks anywhere in Iran and had once hosted a cavalry unit. Since 1965, they had housed a training unit, full of young cadets who sympathized with the revolution, at least for the moment. On the evening of February 11, pro-revolutionary crowds, who had gathered in the city's mosques, went down to the barracks holding bouquets of flowers and trays of Kermani pastries. Neither side wanted a fight. The commander of the barracks came out to meet the people and congratulate them on the victory of the revolution. It wasn't so much a surrender as an acceptance of the call of the revolution. In the preceding month, the Shah's statues had come down in many cities across the province. American experts working in Kerman's copper mines had fled and the revolutionaries had burnt down the offices of the secret police, SAVAK. SAVAK's building in the ancient city of Bam had been turned into a hospital. The defeat was now complete. Kerman, too, no longer belonged to the realms of His Imperial Majesty.

Revolutions often worry religious minorities, as they rarely fare well in upheavals, and Kerman was a city full of non-Muslims. They had even more reasons to worry about a revolution led by a Shia cleric. But in Kerman, even some non-Muslims supported the revolution. On January 18, a number of young Persian Jews went to the central mosque holding up pictures of Khomeini and declaring their solidarity with the revolution. Some might have worried about their fate now that the Shah had fled but at least a few were stalwart supporters of the revolution, not least those who sympathized with the Communist Party. A day later, the Zoroastrians, followers of an ancient Iranian religion predating Islam by centuries, declared their own solidarity with the revolution with a mass gathering in Kerman's main stadium. Less than a month later, when the final blow arrived on February 11, everyone seemed (more or less) enthusiastic about the revolution. Portraits of the Shah quickly came down and even people who, like Farid, hadn't cared much for politics saw their lives transformed. The old regime was gone and an air of optimism could be felt everywhere. No dream was too big and a new revolutionary government would give people everything they had been denied.

"I started going to the mosque because that's what everyone my age did," Farid remembers. "We didn't care about politics but politics cared about us. The revolution was to do everything for us. But we had to defend it first. We had to guard it."

* * *

A revolution is a mass phenomenon, a "forcible entrance of the masses into the realm of their own destiny"[2] in Leon Trotsky's memorable description of the 1917 Russian Revolution. But the number of people who make a revolution and deliver its victory is always infinitely smaller than the number mobilized and propelled into action by the forces it releases. Young Kermani men like Qassem and Farid had had next to no role in the events that led to February 11, 1979. But the new republic that sprung out from that revolt would touch their lives. Thousands of men and women had made the revolution but the revolution would make new lives for tens of millions.

The streets of Iran in the days following February 11 were filled with hundreds of armed men, and some women, involved in a deadly struggle to shape the revolution. In the two preceding decades, many an armed group had fought the Shah in urban and rural skirmishes. They had all failed. Their core members now either languished in the prisons of the Shah or hobnobbed in the cafes of Paris and Beirut. Some had taken to battlegrounds far from home, fighting the British-backed sultan of Oman or training in the Palestinian camps of the Levant. The revolution opened the prison gates and allowed the exiles to come back. Gone were the days when the revolutionaries had to recruit members carefully, under the watchful eye of the Shah's secret police. Tens of thousands of young men and women were now thirsty for new causes. They filled the ranks of the many groups who all fought in the name of the revolution. In the next three years, the struggles of these forces with one another determined the course of the revolution—and that of Iran and its nascent Islamic Republic.

* * *

The revolution was led by a broad anti-Shah coalition under the leadership of Ayatollah Khomeini, who, with his mystical air, was ambiguous enough to become a focal point for groups with widely divergent politics. There were old leftists and new leftists. Some adhered to Moscow, others to Beijing or Havana. There were Islamists of all colors. They had their own guerrillas but also Muslim modernizers in suits and ties, haughty intellectuals, and the revolutionary clerics who despised the quietism of their conservative predecessors.

Now that the Shah was gone, who would rule? What kind of a system would replace the monarchy? And what would be the role of the Grand Ayatollah who had united the rowdy coalition on the path to 1979? These were the burning questions of the day.

The first in line were the Muslim modernizers. The interim government appointed by Khomeini was led by Mehdi Bazargan, a bespectacled, energetic 71-year-old Muslim intellectual. Born in Tehran in 1907, Bazargan had been a junior member of the Mossadeq government prior to the 1953 coup. In the heady days of the 1940s and 1950s, the mainstream of Iranian politics belonged either to the communists, with their mass mobilization of workers, students, and intellectuals, or to the traditional Western-educated liberals. Bazargan belonged to a minority of thinkers who prioritized their Muslim identity and believed that an Iranian democratic movement needed to be Islamic if it were to suit the conditions of a Muslim nation. Together with his like-minded modernizing Muslim intellectuals, Bazargan wrote books that sought to bring Islam in conformity with the modern sciences. They were eager to prove that Islam wasn't an outdated schema or a reservoir of reactionary mullahs who were clueless about the quickly changing world around them. A graduate of thermodynamics from Paris's prestigious École Polytechnique, Bazargan referred in his books to both the holy Quran and the principles of modern engineering, explaining one by means of the other in a hodgepodge of rhetorical gymnastics that confounded many readers. In the 1960s, as the world burnt in the fire of revolt and revolution, Bazargan and his comrades founded the Liberation Movement of Iran (LMI), a specifically Muslim component of Mossadeq's movement.

Back in the 1960s, Bazargan and his comrades had been no stone-throwing rebels. They were mostly genteel statesmen who had held government positions a few years before and hoped for a return to power. But the CIA-backed coup of 1953 had brutally pulled Mossadeq down and the Shah had shown that he knew no compromise. He threw Bazargan and his comrades into jail in 1963, just as he prepared to launch his White Revolution. Prison has a way of radicalizing movements and the hammer blow of events pushed the LMI to the left. In his trial in 1964, Bazargan faced the judge and said the words that would ring in many ears for many years: "We are the last people who have engaged in political struggle constitutionally and we expect the judge to point this out to the higher-ups."

It wasn't just domestic repression that radicalized Bazargan and his comrades, but also the way the global winds were blowing. In Egypt, a popular new president, Gamal Abdul Nasser, had overthrown the monarchy, nationalized the Suez Canal, fought off the Israelis, the British, and the French, and held up the banner of the revolutionary Arab movement, inspiring many Iranians in the process. In the political theater of the Middle East, the rousing cry of Nasser and his Arab radical comrades was in sharp contrast to the established monarchies of Iran and her Arab neighbors like the Saudis and the Jordanians. In Iraq and Syria, revolutions and coups did away with the *anciens régimes* while radical forces of Arabism, Baathism, and communism competed for power.

Even more inspiring for the Iranian radicals were the struggles of the Palestinians and the Algerians. The two umbrella organizations running those national liberation movements—the Palestinian Fatah and the Algerian National Front for Liberation (FLN to use its French abbreviation)—both used Islam as a unifying identity. In the 1960s, as the youth of the world wandered from one movement to another in their search for a viable emancipatory alternative, Fatah and the FLN showed that a mixture of Islam and national liberation could be the answer. Moreover, the FLN had actually won, kicking the French out in 1962 and establishing a new revolutionary Arab republic on the Mediterranean. Algiers became the Mecca of revolution, attracting not only guerrillas from across the Muslim world but also the Black Panthers from the United States. Muslim revolutionaries in Iran had long suffered from a massive insecurity complex when faced with their Marxist rivals. The "comrades" could point to the glorious examples of victorious socialism in the Soviet Union or China, or in the younger revolutionary republics of Cuba and Vietnam. What did the Islamists have, given the collaboration of many clerics with the Shah in 1953, given the insular nature of Shia seminarians who cared more about the correct religious ruling for how the devout are to clean themselves after defecation than about the complexities of the economy, politics, and revolution? Algeria and Palestine showed that Islam could be a framework for a revolution and for a government, even if this was a vague and mostly cultural Islam.

Inspired by the Algerians, one Iranian intellectual in Paris did more than anyone to popularize this notion of a revolutionary Islam. Born in the northeastern Khorasan province in 1933, Ali Shariati hailed from a clerical family. His father, Mohammad Taqi, had left behind the seminary and the clerical garb to enroll at a university and engage in publishing. He saw this as a more effective way of countering the influence of communism and other non-Islamic ideas. In the 1940s, he founded the Center for Publication of the Islamic Truth (CPIT), a lone voice against the dominance of communist and secular ideas in Mashhad, the provincial capital. Shariati had been a comrade of his father's from an early age, joining the CPIT in 1948 at fifteen. But he was to go way beyond his father, offering a revolutionary and anti-clerical reading of Islam that electrified an entire generation of nascent Islamist revolutionaries. The publisher's son did so well in university that he got a scholarship to go to France in 1959. Once there, Shariati was quick to join an FLN cell. He wrote for its paper in French and was even briefly jailed. Seduced by the revolutionary Paris of the 1960s, Shariati read Jean-Paul Sartre and Frantz Fanon, whose *The Wretched of the Earth* he helped publish in Persian. Upon his return to Iran in 1964, he was abruptly arrested and sent to jail. Once freed, he became a professor of history at Mashhad University. His real popularity came in 1968 when he started his regular lectures at the Hosseyniye Ershad, a mosque in Tehran that doubled as a community center. The Hosseyniye became renowned for Shariati's bewitching speeches. He was a master orator whose skillful mixing of Islamic history with the radical vocabulary of the Sixties captured the hearts of many Muslim youngsters.

Shariati was able to make revolutionary icons of Shia figures of the early Islamic era, figures whom most Iranians knew intimately but only as bygone historical characters. In the colorful pantheon of revolutionary Islam created by the eloquent Shariati, Imam Ali, the cousin and son-in-law of the Prophet Mohammad, became a mystical militant figure who had slain the enemies of Islam and shunned the palatial ways of the monarchies of his time in favor of an ascetic and just Islam. His austere capital in Kofa, Iraq, was contrasted with the silk-wearing Islamic rulers in Damascus who had inherited the imperial ways of the deposed Byzantines and Persians. Imam Hossein, Ali's son, became a soldier for truth who had risen up against an unjust king and paid for this with his life, meeting his death on the plains of Karbala in 680. Zeynab, Ali's daughter, was a revolutionary orator who had avenged her martyred brother by eloquently defending his cause at the court of Yazid, the unjust caliph who had killed him. Just as the Iranian Marxists had learnt how to popularize the complex ideas of Marx and Engels, Shariati offered a popularized version of revolutionary Islam that could appeal to the everyday mosque-goer. He spoke of a Red Shiism of Ali and Hossein, which he counterposed to the Black Shiism of the ruling monarchy and its complicit clerical allies. In one of his most popular lectures in 1971, Shariati talked about visiting sites of world civilization such as the pyramids in Egypt or the Great Wall of China, only to realize they had all been built by slave labor of the people whom Shariati called his "brothers." "I realized: These all had been built on the back of my brothers' bones," he said. Such simple messages circulated among the Muslim youth, who accessed them not only by personally attending the lectures but also via cassette tapes sent around the country and the pamphlets legally published by the Hosseyniye Ershad.

Shariati's mixture of Fanon and iconographic Islam made many Marxist intellectuals laugh. But the Islamists were proud of him. The Marxists had had their many intellectuals, writers, and poets, foreign and domestic, and now the Islamists had their worthy counterpart. The revolutionary clerics were careful not to endorse his eclectic ideas (not least his anti-clericalism) but were happy to get any help in their ideological battle with the Marxists. Shariati's anti-communism also meant that the Shah's secret police did less to harass him. As scholars such as the sociologist Ali Mirsepassi have shown, in those days the Shah himself sponsored a project of nativism meant to dispel both liberal democracy and Marxism as Western fallacies unsuited to Iranian soil.[3] Both the Shah and the clerical leaders would come to change their minds about Shariati, aware that his electrifying ideas could end up destroying not communism but the very institutions of the monarchy and the clerical establishment. But Shariati didn't live to see them off in political battle. In 1977, shortly after arriving in the British port of Southampton to start a period of exile, he died of heart failure. His legacy was up for grabs.

The LMI, of which Shariati had been a member, was only too happy to be associated with the popular ideologue. Only fourteen years after Bazargan gave his warning in 1964, the Shah was gone and Mossadeq's ex-minister was ordered by Ayatollah Khomeini to form a new government. For centuries, the Iranian chief ministers had served at the pleasure of their monarchs. Bazargan was the first one to be appointed by a revolutionary cleric who got his legitimacy from a mass revolution, the first non-monarchical head of government who had to partake in building a republic from scratch. He filled his cabinet with his LMI comrades, who were of the same disposition for the most part: Muslim, educated, nationalistic, in love with Mossadeq. They had earned their revolutionary credentials. Chief among them was Ebrahim Yazdi, a 48-year-old professor of chemistry who had spent most of the past two decades in the United States, ending up in Houston, Texas, where he ran a local mosque and acquired American citizenship. But Yazdi led a double life, far away from Houston. When Bazargan was being tried in 1963, Yazdi was in Cairo seeking funding and military training from the Nasser government.

Men like Bazargan and Yazdi had sold Khomeini to the world as a Gandhi-like figure who would bring freedom and democracy to Iran. What was left unspoken was that they hoped to be the Nehrus to Khomeini's Gandhi. The crafty Indian intellectual Jawaharlal Nehru had run India's first independent government while Gandhi held no executive power. The ambitious men of the LMI imagined something similar for the Iran of 1979. The old Ayatollah would go to the holy city of Qom and become a harmless figure while these Muslim modernizers would rule the country. After all, they had administrative experience and revolutionary credentials. What could possibly go wrong?

* * *

Old Marxists loved to say that, in the final analysis, the state consists of armed bodies of men.[4] In early 1979, many competing groups of armed men controlled the streets of Iran, only some of whom were under any supervision by Bazargan's interim government. During the tense final days of the monarchy, Iran had effectively had two governments, one headed by the exiled Shah and Bakhtiar, the other by Khomeini and Bazargan. After the victory of the revolution, power diffused further. Iran now had multitudes of mini-governments, each vying for its own power and its own vision for the grand revolution whose victory on February 11 had been unplanned and unexpected.

But there was still one man who unquestionably commanded the loyalty of the masses. Ayatollah Khomeini knew that his word counted and he was initially careful not to appear partisan. On February 12, Khomeini gave his first commands as the founding father of the new revolutionary regime. He asked people to avoid "sabotage, theft, and arson" and "any un-Islamic and inhumane behavior." He implored the masses to trust the interim government, headed by Bazargan, to provide law and order. A day later, on February 13, he issued a special message asking people to give up the arms they had gained during the days of the revolution. The arms were to be deposited "to the care of a special committee appointed by the prime minister [Bazargan]," either directly or via imams at local mosques. "Dear people of Iran, Islamic soldiers of the Hidden Imam," the harrowing last lines of Khomeini's message read, "do not let the arms be passed on to the opponents of Islam. Do not give an inch to the enemies of God and the nation."

Khomeini, then, was asking for power to be passed on to Bazargan's government and the network of mosques that were to be its backbone. All other groups were to be subordinated to them while a new regime was to be built. But could the suit-wearing cabinet of the liberal Engineer Bazargan (as he was affectionately called) work effectively with the revolutionary clerics?

* * *

It didn't take long for Bazargan and his ministers to find out that they were in government but not in power.

On March 30 and 31, less than two months after the downfall of the old regime, a referendum was held with a simple question: Did the people want an Islamic Republic of Iran? There had been proposals that maybe an "Iranian Republic" or an "Islamic Democratic Republic" would be more appropriate but Khomeini had quashed all such notions.

"'The Islamic Republic,' not one word more or less," the Grand Ayatollah said, with his characteristic stubborn insistence. Khomeini's intransigence was backed by his network of clerics around the country, men who had never been in formal politics before and whose main political association was running the web of mosques which had been indispensable to the revolution. The Shah had banned all opposition political activity but he hadn't been able to shut down the mosques. They had thus become the cells of an unofficial yet powerful nationwide political party. Lenin would have been proud.

In Kerman, like in other Iranian cities, millions went to the polls on March 30. Ali Khamenei, a loud and somewhat flamboyant cleric from Mashhad, happened to be in town. He had earlier spent a good number of years in Kerman, having been forcibly deported from Mashhad and sent to the southern province by the Shah's secret police. That day, Khamenei was among the thousands in Kerman who voted "Yes" to the Islamic Republic. The final results would show a 99.31 percent affirmative vote nationwide. "The pagan regime is forever buried in the ash heap of history," Ayatollah Khomeini declared in a triumphant message to the people.

The Islamic Republic had now been born and plans were duly set in motion to elect an assembly, to draw up a constitution, and to erect governing institutions. But before jurists and MPs, clerics and Marxists, liberals and socialists could haggle over their divergent visions, power had to be won on the streets.

On February 13, the very day Khomeini issued his message, revolutionary committees formed around the country, tasked with gathering arms from the people and making sure the interim government was faithful to the revolution. The haphazard process meant that the committees included many dubious elements. People in Kerman, as in other places, remember the local tough boys using them as an excuse to settle old grudges that had nothing to do with the revolution. Khomeini was urged to introduce order into the committees by putting them under a national leadership. But should the committees be run by the interim government of Bazargan or should the mosques who had gathered the guns have a role?

If anybody had cared to study Ayatollah Khomeini's writings, as opposed to the carefully calibrated statements he made to the foreign press in the months leading to the revolution, they would have had no doubt as to the form of government he favored. In early 1970, he had given thirteen lectures from his base in the holy city of Najaf in Iraq, in which he espoused a radically new political theory, unknown to preceding scholars of Islam, Shia or Sunni. Transcribed and edited into readable Persian, the lectures were published as a pamphlet in Beirut under an obscure title that would have meant little to the vast majority of the readers, *Welayat al-Faqih* (The Guardianship of the Jurist). For Khomeini, a man heavily steeped in poetical traditions of Islamic mysticism, governance was to belong to a clerical jurist who would be a "guardian" in the absence of the Hidden Imam. According to Shia doctrine, the Twelfth

Imam of their faith had gone under occultation and his messianic return, together with Jesus Christ, was going to usher in the end of times. As scholars such as Vali Nasr would later argue, Khomeini's new model for governance owed more to Plato's *Republic* than to the Quran or the Islamic tradition. In simpler words, he wanted nothing less than to be a philosopher-king.

Initially, it was a low-ranking, liberal-aligned cleric, Hassan Lahooti, who was tasked with heading the nationwide network of the revolutionary committees. But one man opposed this appointment. Born in northeastern Iran in 1920, Ayatollah Morteza Motahari was one of the highest-ranking pro-Khomeini clerics. He had distinguished himself by not only serving at the seminary but also teaching in Tehran University's theology department. He headed the Revolutionary Council, something of a cabinet for Khomeini and a shadow government to Bazargan's. Motahari was a major public intellectual during the Pahlavi years and was perhaps best known for having loudly opposed Shariati due to his "eclecticism."

In the tumult of the early days of the revolution, decisions were taken by sudden and random interventions. One man could make history. When Motahari went to see Khomeini in his school compound, the great leader was meeting Bazargan's cabinet ministers and his LMI comrades. "Could I see you in the other room for a minute?" Motahari asked. In the other room, Motahari warned his old master that the LMI were "dangerous people" and that Lahooti was too close to them. To give him the committees was to put the interim government and its men in suits in charge of everything. Instead, the committees were to be given to a different cleric: Ayatollah Mohammadreza Mahdavi Kani.[5]

Unlike clerics such as Motahari, Khamenei, or Rafsanjani, the 47-year-old Kani was little known among the masses. Hailing from a farming family in the countryside near Tehran, he had spent his entire life in the world of religion, running a mosque in Tehran's Ferdowsi Square from 1963. He had joined the movement early on and had been imprisoned several times, but he was more of a cleric than a politician—a quality that appealed to Khomeini. The conservative Tehrani cleric had no time for the revolutionary excesses of 1979 Iran. He opposed the usurpations of property that were happening all over the country. To put someone of his temperament in charge of the revolutionary committees was a calculated decision by a sage like Motahari, who hated nothing more than the excesses of the Shariati-reading crowd.

Kani himself would later wonder how he came to hold this position. "How could someone like me be in charge of the police forces of the revolution?" he asked. "I hadn't even done my military service and didn't know how to hold up a gun. My spirit was that of a seminary student, my interest was in culture." Iranian historian Serge Bareghian would later come to call Kani the Georges-Jacques Danton of the Iranian revolution, a bulwark of statist conservatism among rebels and radicals.[6] Kani's opponents at the time attacked him as pro-capitalist and pro-American.

For the people on the streets, and even for historians since, Kani's appointment did not appear as a key event. But it was right here, on March 1, 1979, even before the referendum was held and the Islamic Republic declared, that the revolution faced an early turning point. The clerics decided to stake their claims to power. Whether Khomeini was Gandhi or not, these clerics were not going to let the tie-wearing Nehrus run the new revolutionary Iran. They hadn't endured years of humiliation, prison, and torture to go back to their mosques when the long-awaited victory arrived. They wanted the sovereignty of God and the rule of their own, not the liberalism of Bazargan or leftist eclecticism of Shariati. They wanted the rule of Islam, *their* Islam, not the rule of technocrats, not the return of the usual men of politics with their open contempt for the mullahs. And those who had studied that little pamphlet of Khomeini's, or, better yet, sat to listen to his long lectures in Najaf, knew that the Imam of the revolution was on their side. It might take some time but the clerics would come to rule.

It wasn't just the clerics and the politicians who were vying for power. The various socialist and Islamist guerrilla groups that had fought the Shah for more than a decade now filled the streets. What they had learnt in the battlegrounds of Oman and the military camps of Syria found new use in revolutionary Iran. In Turkmen-majority northeastern Iran, the largest new left grouping, the Iranian People's Fedai (devotee) Guerrillas (IPFG), formed a radical autonomous shadow government consisting of a series of elected councils, partially inspired by the neighboring Soviet Turkmenistan. In the western Kurdistan region, on the border with Iraq, local Kurdish groups with a history of militancy and various shades of socialism effectively took matters into their own hands. Much larger than all the other guerrilla groups was the People's Mojahedin Organization of Iran (PMOI), formed by young activists who had split from the LMI and were inspired by Shariati. Under the charismatic leadership of the thirty-year-old Masood Rajavi, recently released from jail, the PMOI offered an exhilarating mix of revolutionary Islam and socialist militancy attractive to hundreds of thousands. The PMOI's armed militias, which had been always rejected by Khomeini and most other leading clerics, were a power to be reckoned with. The visions of such revolutionaries couldn't be more different from the capitalist-oriented and socially conservative outlook of Kani. They wouldn't give up without a fight.

Defenders of Khomeini soon found out that they could not solely rely on the mosque-based committees to defend their revolution against domestic and foreign threats. The philosopher-king needed his own men with arms.

A few such groups had already been established and started to rival one another. Having lost the committees, the liberal-aligned Lahooti got an order from Khomeini to head a group of armed men, based in Tehran's Abbasabad Barracks. He brought together a number of Bazargan-aligned men to lead a new outfit. A few kilometers to the west, a different group of armed men occupied a police building. This group was headed by a most remarkable young cleric. The 35-year-old Mohammad Montazeri was the son of a leading ayatollah. A restless revolutionary activist, he had spent years abroad, involved in a gamut of adventures ranging from undergoing military training in the Palestine Liberation Organization (PLO) camps in Lebanon to securing funding from his major Arab sponsor, Libya's Muammar Gaddafi. Two other similar Islamist armed militias formed in Tehran: One was run by the men of the Islamic Nations Party (INP), founded in 1962 by a band of audacious youths inspired by Nasser's rhetoric; the other was founded by a group of rivals to the PMOI who were soon to coalesce into the Islamic Revolution's Mojahedin Organization (IRMO).

None of the Islamist guerrilla groups had been as theoretically or militarily sophisticated as their leftist rivals, the PMOI and the IPFG. If they were to successfully build the new regime, they needed to band together. The push for unity came from an unlikely agent: the 39-year-old activist Mohsen Rafiqdoost—aptly known as Mohsen the Chauffeur—who drove Ayatollah Khomeini around on the day of his historic return to Tehran on February 1. In a crowd full of well-read activists used to giving mini-lectures on the Vietnam War or the Sino-Soviet split, Mohsen was a doer not a talker. A working-class Tehran boy through and through, he had dropped out of high school and dedicated his life to helping with the logistics of the anti-Shah movement. He had first fallen in with the PMOI, helping them get arms from Lebanon, but had subsequently joined the more conservative Islamist crowds when the PMOI drifted too close to Marxism.

After the revolution's victory in 1979, Rafiqdoost was based in Khomeini's makeshift compound in the Alavi school, an epicenter of the nascent revolutionary order. He ran the logistics there and helped confiscate the property of the fleeing officials of the former regime. When Lahooti was tasked with forming an armed guard, the Khomeinist clerics asked Rafiqdoost to go join his outfit and be their eyes and ears. He became a founding member of that group and its head of logistics.

There was irony in the story of four different guards groups. Only one had authority from Khomeini and that was the one led by Lahooti, which was supposed to run under the supervision of the interim government. The other three groups were more Khomeinist, more doctrinaire, and more revolutionary, but they had no authority from their Imam. Rafiqdoost could help fix all of this. No one could mistake him for a liberal and yet he was a leader in the liberal-aligned Lahooti group.

Rafiqdoost had a solution. He called a meeting with representatives of the other groups: Montazeri; the INP's Abbas Agha Zamani, known by his *nom de guerre* Abu Sharif, a guerrilla recognizable by his massive bushy beard and a veteran of years of shuttling between armed camps of the Palestinian Fatah in Lebanon and a mysterious existence in Pakistan; and the IRMO's Mohammad Borujerdi, an unknown 25-year-old who was soon to become an early martyr of the Islamic Republic. With Rafiqdoost himself standing for the Lahooti group, each of the four groups now had a representative in the room. They could have engaged in the popular activity of those heady days: debate and discussions about the "stage of the revolution," "the balance of forces," and "the tasks of the revolution." But Rafiqdoost didn't have time for any of that. He locked the door and pulled out his .45-caliber automatic Colt.

"There is someone here from all four groups and we all have the same goal, which is to create a force to guard the revolution," Rafiqdoost said. "You have no legal basis. Our order comes from the Imam, who has allowed us to operate under the interim government." Unlike when he was associating with the intellectuals close to the government, Rafiqdoost knew he was faced with three devout Muslims with unwavering loyalty to Khomeini. They grumbled. How could he want them to remain committed to a prime minister like Bazargan, who was already cozying up with the Americans? Rafiqdoost reassured them that if they united, they would be the ones holding the real power, not the cabinet men.

"If we don't get somewhere in this meeting, I'll kill you three and then myself," he told them. It was an offer they couldn't refuse. They got a piece of paper and wrote twelve names on it, three from each of the four groups. The new group was to be called the Islamic Revolutionary Guard Corps (IRGC). On April 22, 1979, they got the official order from Ayatollah Khomeini. The IRGC was now a united group with its own letterhead, offices, stamp, banner, and recruitment centers. It was no accident that the name "Iran" wasn't included in the organization's title. The revolutionary guerrillas had their sights set far beyond the borders of their country. Later on, when the parliament wanted to vote on legalizing the IRGC, many were incensed at this omission. How could Iran have a major military force that didn't even include the name of the country? Yousef Forootan, a founding father of the IRGC, remembers the debate: "Some asked us to use the name 'Iran' in the title. We said no. Ours was an 'Islamic' group and Islam wasn't limited to Iran. Our brothers in the Majlis [parliament] shared our belief that Islam is global. The IRGC belonged to Islam and Islam was global."[7]

If anybody had expected the IRGC to be an ordinary armed force, the name could have offered a clue that their predictions were misguided. The founding statement of the group left no doubt either. "We bow to the thumping blood of the valiant martyrs of the Islamic Revolution!" it thundered. "The revolution of our Muslim people has shocked the world. Its founders tread on the path of prophet Abraham; that of Moses, Jesus, and Mohammad; it has flourished with the blood of Ali, Hossein, Abudhar, and other martyrs."

The IRGC was shaping its own infantile global revolutionary pantheon. Almost in response to the ubiquitous pictures of Marx, Engels, and Lenin, it spoke of the long history of Abrahamic prophetic leadership. These were universalist ambitions for the entirety of humanity, far from the exclusionary fundamentalism that would later characterize Islamism. The force's constitution tasked it with "supporting liberation and right-seeking movements of the oppressed under the supervision of the Revolutionary Council and the permission of the interim government."

But the interim government didn't last long. In November, after a group of pro-Khomeini students ransacked the US embassy and took American diplomats hostage, Bazargan had to resign. Khomeini supported the students and called their actions "the Second Revolution." Young Khomeinist revolutionaries, like those in the IRGC, were quickly inheriting the earth.

The IRGC's constitution tasked it with recruiting "volunteer Muslims" who had to fit four criteria: to believe in "authentic Islamic ideology"; to "believe in the Islamic nature of the revolution and the Islamic Republic"; to harbor "spiritual, physical, and intellectual courage and power"; and to take "a decisive position against imperialism (both that of the West and the East), Zionism, dictatorship, and any form of racism."

The most consequential militia in the history of the Middle East had formed and it started recruiting immediately.

* * *

Once more, developments on the periphery were led from the center. The IRGC had formed in Tehran but it soon dispatched people around the country to find recruits and to engage in armed intervention against the opposition in Turkmen and Kurdish regions. In Kerman province, a 22-year-old guard was in charge of recruitment for those hailing from Rabor county. Gholamreza Karami was a local, born in the city of Kerman. With many people clamoring to get involved by joining the IRGC, Karami had to be careful to not let in just anyone. Years later he

vividly remembered one of his first rejects, a fel\
three years of age. "He very much had the look ot\
said. "He wore short sleeves and a tight shirt, had curl\
belt. I didn't think we should accept this kind of person \

Thus Gholamreza Karami rejected the membership a\
Qassem Soleimani, the young man of tribal origins. Years \
Soleimani rose to global fame, Karami became a MP repres   ng a
constituency that included Soleimani's village of birth. The commander
loved taunting the MP by reminding him of that rejection. "Remember
the guy with the short sleeves?" he would say.

Luckily for the Islamic Republic, Karami's decision wasn't final.
Soleimani could join a local reserve corps connected to the IRGC. "We
were all young and had to work for the revolution somehow and this is
how I joined the IRGC," Soleimani later said. But this cryptic sentence
doesn't tell the real story. Joining a reserve corps didn't mean much in
practice. Soleimani was still but an employee of a provincial water organization, only to be called into action if need be. Despite what many biog-
raphies claimed later, he is unlikely to have been sent to Kurdistan, in
those days the IRGC's most crucial battleground. In 1979 and 1980, the
IRGC would be forged in ferocious fighting with the rival guerrillas who
defended their alternative, non-Islamist vision of the revolution from
the mountaintops and the liberated cities of Kurdistan. Yesterday's
comrades were now each other's enemies. On one battlefront, a leader of
a Kurdish group recognized an old comrade: He had last seen him at a
sit-in in Berkeley, California, where they were both anti-Shah activists.
Now they were shooting at each other.

While destiny was being made in Kurdistan, Qassem was bound to
his modest circumstances in Kerman. He wanted to be part of something bigger. But how? What could a provincial *karateka* offer a revolution filled with distinguished thinkers and fighters? As provincials had
for a long time, did he need to move to Tehran and wait for events?

The events that gave Qassem a new chance at the life he sought came
not from Tehran but from outside the newly formed Islamic Republic.
The revolution was to come under foreign attack and it needed to call up
all its forces to defend and guard itself. This was Qassem's time to shine
and he was not going to squander it.

Chapter 4

"A Gift from the Heavens"

In a cozy room somewhere in Tehran, a group of young Islamist revolutionaries sat down to discuss their movement's prospects. It was early 1978. The idea that the all-powerful monarchical regime could be gone in a year was beyond their wildest dreams. But this was the age of dreamers and they too dared to dream. Who would become a cabinet minister if they overthrew the Shah? What would Islamist policies look like? How would they manage to oppose both the United States and the Soviet Union?

One of the young men raised a question that was on everyone's mind. "What if we formed a revolutionary government and got attacked by one of our neighbors?" he quipped. "Which one of the neighboring countries do you think would attack us first?"

Sat quietly in a corner until that point, Mohsen Kangarloo had an answer: "Iraq's Saddam Hussein. He would attack us first." The 32-year-old activist was known for his bomb-making qualities and not for his diplomatic insight, so few took him seriously. Why would Saddam attack a revolutionary Iran? The more experienced men in the group patiently explained to Kangarloo why this was unlikely.

The Arab regimes of the time were of two general kinds: radical revolutionary republics and conservative pro-Western monarchies. Saddam's

Iraq definitely belonged to the former. As far as the Iranian revolutionaries were concerned, he stood on the right side of history.

The forerunner of all radical Arab regimes was Egypt, where
Colonel Nasser came to power in 1952 through what would become
the standard path for Arab progressives: a "revolutionary coup." This
was a contradiction in terms. Revolutions were meant to be driven by
the people from below, not by army officers. But left-wing officers like
Nasser couldn't wait for the masses to rise up, for the socialists to
build their nascent parties, or for the parliaments dominated by the
landed elites to act. They needed immediate change. Iraq saw its own
revolutionary coup on July 14, 1958, when Colonel Abdelkarim Qasim
came to power, supported by the powerful Communist Party and the
strong Kurdish movement. On the way to the top, he had the entire
royal family murdered, dragging their bodies through the streets of
Baghdad.

Events in Iraq had long reverberated in Iran and vice versa. The two
countries were connected to one another by a thousand threads. Having
gained its independence in 1932, the modern Iraq was new to the
community of nations but its Mesopotamian lands had long been entan-
gled with the Iranian state and its peoples. For generations, the Iranian
Shia flocked to the many shrines of their imams that were dotted across
Iraq. Many had stayed over, operating the shrines and the seminaries
attached to them. Numerous Iranian monarchs had picked the shrine of
Imam Hossein in Karbala as their final resting place. Tens of thousands
of Iraqi citizens were of Persian ancestry. For many of the Iraqi Shia, who
made up a slight majority of the country's population, Iran was a spiritual home, the only significant Shia-majority country in the world.
Furthermore, the mountainous Kurdish lands straddled their shared
border and the Kurdish political parties of both countries saw themselves as part of the same grand movement with a unifying shared goal
of Kurdish self-determination.

Qasim's victory in 1958 and the royal family's brutal murder terrified
the Shah just as it energized his opponents. Less than five years had
passed since the CIA-backed coup in Iran entrenched the monarch's
power and now the old city of Baghdad, barely 120 kilometers from the
Iranian border, became a new Mecca of revolutionary activity in the

region. To the glee of Moscow, the Iraqi Communist Party was the strongest of its kind in the Arab world and it had fully supported the Qasim revolution. Its mass rallies now brought hundreds of thousands to the streets and, for the first time in the region's history, Arab communism seemed like a realistic prospect.

The Shah's worries were not unfounded. Heavily repressed after the 1953 coup, the Iranian communists of the Tudeh Party flocked to revolutionary Baghdad and made it their new base. The opposing regimes in Baghdad and Tehran heralded a new dynamic that has remained in place to this day: They would often give support to each other's domestic opposition forces and use them as cudgels in their rivalries. Unlike Nasser, who ruled Egypt to the day of his death in September 1970, Qasim's rule proved short-lived. In February 1963, the revolutionary president was overthrown in a new "revolutionary coup" led by another group of radicals of the Arab Socialist Baath Party. Qasim was brutally murdered by the new Baathist regime, as were hundreds of his supporters, especially those among the communists. Yet the Tehran-Baghdad dynamic was to remain in place—and it often created strange bedfellows. Even as the Baathists were heavily repressing the Iraqi communists, they were happy to tactically host Iranian communists to use them as leverage against the Shah. The Iranian Shia Islamists overlooked the Baathist repression of their fellow Shia in Iraq so long as Baghdad gave them financial support. The Kurdish movements in both countries betrayed ethnic solidarity by picking up arms against one another to please their respective backers in Tehran and Baghdad.

By 1978, when Mohsen Kangarloo was making his imprudent guess, Saddam Hussein, a Baathist officer who had achieved paramount power in Iraq, had kissed and made up with the Shah, signing the historic Algiers Agreement with him in 1975. Until the very day of the agreement, Saddam's Iraq had been a host to the anti-Shah opposition. From Baghdad, radio stations such as the Voice of the Militant Clergy and the Voice of the Iranian Patriots had articulated the statements of Ayatollah Khomeini and other opponents of the Shah. But, Kangarloo's older comrades explained, Saddam was still on the right side of all the major fault lines of the time. Most importantly, he was ardently anti-Zionist and had helped fight Israel in the 1973 Yom Kippur War. Revolutionary Iran didn't have to fear him.

* * *

Young revolutionaries love to daydream about what they would do after they come to power. For the vast majority of them, this remains an exercise in utopian hypotheticals. But Kangarloo and his youthful comrades belonged to that precious minority of victorious revolutionaries. Less than a year after their innocent conversation holed up in secret, their hated monarch was gone and their hero Ayatollah Khomeini was firmly in power. Their biggest operation had been an explosion they organized in a traditional Persian restaurant in Tehran that was frequented by Americans; this led to one dead and forty injured (only ten of whom were American). Now, together with young men similar to themselves, they needed to build up the defenses of a revolutionary country.

Every revolution, if it doesn't end at the daydreaming stage, is followed by conflicts among the revolutionaries over what the new society should look like. This general maxim couldn't be truer for the Iranian situation. The revolutionaries had been so madly diverse and the leadership so vague that no one really knew what to expect. And in the Cold War world, a question on everyone's mind was about the international orientation of the new state. Had the US "lost" Iran? Would the new revolutionary government be more favorable to its Soviet neighbors? How about the politics of the region, which had had its own Cold War? Had the radical regimes like Saddam's Iraq found an ally in the new revolutionary Iran?

These issues, and in fact almost all others, sharply divided the revolutionary movement. Except one: Israel.

Despite lacking official diplomatic contacts, the Shah's Iran had had extensive ties with the Jewish State. Tel Aviv's "periphery" doctrine meant that it had invested in cultivating relations with non-Arab nations in the region: Ethiopia, Turkey, and Iran. Condemning the Shah's support for Israel had been a talking point shared by almost all revolutionaries, including the leftist Iranian Jews. Long forgotten were the years immediately following the formation of the State of Israel in 1948 when the Iranian communists of the Tudeh Party (many of whom were Persian

Jews) called for diplomatic recognition of the Jewish State by Iran, sang the traditional Israeli folk song "Hava Nagila" at their gatherings, and prided themselves on their extensive ties with both Palestinian and Israeli communists. Nuanced positions of solidarity with the Israeli left were still found in some corners of the Iranian left but stringent anti-Zionism and full support for the Palestinian guerrilla movement was the order of the day. Less than a week after Khomeini came to power, while all airports were still closed, Tehran played host to an unexpected guest: Yasser Arafat, the storied leader of the Palestinian Liberation Organization. In Tehran, Arafat took celebratory pictures with Khomeini, boasted about his new friendship with Iran and was given the keys to a new embassy. He then visited the holy city of Mashhad, host to the country's only tomb of a Shia Imam. But the little-known next stop in Arafat's revolutionary tour of Iran became a serious cause of concern for many in the Iranian government.

Accompanied by Ebrahim Yazdi, the Texas-based chemistry professor who was now Iran's deputy prime minister for revolutionary affairs, Arafat visited the southwestern province of Khuzestan. Visiting Tehran and Mashhad had made sense. But why come to this small oil-rich province? Located on the Iran-Iraq border, Khuzestan was Iran's only Arab-majority province. Its old name had been "Arabistan" and the radical Arab regimes in the region had long included it in their dreams of One Big Arab Homeland that was to encompass all Arabs, from the Atlantic coast of Morocco in the west to the shores of the Persian Gulf (which the Arab nationalists called "the Arabian Gulf," to the great anger of both the Shah and the Iranian revolutionaries) in the east. Joining Yazdi for a mass rally in a stadium in Khuzestan's capital, Ahvaz, Arafat gave a rousing speech in Arabic. But the Palestinian revolutionary, whose Fatah movement had helped train dozens of Iranian revolutionaries, wanted more than a speech. He insisted on opening a PLO office, effectively a Palestinian consulate, in Khorramshahr, a city located right on Iran's border with Iraq and a historical center of ethnic Arab activism.

Arafat's trip to Iran had been such an effective charm offensive that only a few saw its negative side. He had done everything he could to be Khomeini's first foreign guest. "As God is my witness, never in my life have I been as happy as when I saw your victory," he had told the old Ayatollah. He had brought a delegation that made everyone happy: To appeal to the LMI types, there was Hani al-Hassan, the 40-year-old guerrilla leader who was inclined to Islamism and knew Yazdi and his comrades from his days as a Palestinian student leader in Germany; to appeal to the Marxists, he had brought Tayseer Quba, a leader of the Popular Front for the Liberation of Palestine. For emotional appeal, there was a Palestinian mother who had lost several children to the struggle. But the trip to Khuzestan also showed some irreconcilable differences between the Iranian revolutionaries and their old Arab allies. Right after the revolution, Khuzestan, like most border areas of Iran, had become a scene of conflict between the central government and local, ethnically based parties. In this case, the "local" Arab forces in Khuzestan were supported by the radical regimes in the Arab world who saw the province as an Arab land occupied by the Persians. Arafat adhered to the same pan-Arabism and his presence in Khuzestan worried the officials of the fledgling government.

These Persian fears of Arab expansion were a stark reminder that, however powerful a unifying factor anti-Zionism may be, the radicals of the Arab world weren't automatically friends of the Iranian revolution. In the new revolutionary government those with most prudence wanted to pursue good diplomatic and neighborly relations with all sides in the tradition of their political hero, Mossadeq. To them, it was crucial to reassure the US that Iran wouldn't turn communist; to affirm non-hostility to Saudi Arabia and the newly founded Arab sheikhdoms that dotted the Persian Gulf; in short, to make sure Iran could be as neutral as possible in both the global Cold War and the mini Cold War of the Middle East.

Iran's first post-revolutionary foreign minister was Karim Sanjabi, Mossadeq's political successor as head of the National Front. Having rejected the Shah's offer to accept the premiership, Sanjabi had brought himself some revolutionary credit. But it soon became clear to him that his neutralist prudence wasn't welcome in the revolutionary regime. He resigned in less than two months, replaced by Yazdi.

One of Yazdi's first acts as Tehran's new foreign minister was to fly to Havana in September 1979. The Cuban capital was hosting a summit for the leaders of the Non-Aligned Movement (NAM). As he was for much of the global left, Fidel Castro had been a hero to Yazdi for years. Now the hero was to give a warm hug to the Iranian disciple in the halls of the NAM summit in Havana. In Iran and also the United States, much attention was paid to this encounter. Did it portend a communist direction for Iran? But during the same trip, Yazdi had a much more crucial meeting. At the request of the new president of Algeria, Chadli Bendjedid, Yazdi went to see Saddam Hussein, who was staying in a villa in Havana. The old Baathist had recently established himself as the Iraqi president, getting rid of his old rivals and consolidating power in the hands of himself and a small circle, most of whom were his own relatives. There was some irony to a political party claiming to represent the entire Arab world while its leadership largely hailed from one single family. Saddam had recognized the new regime in Iran but the old Iran-Iraq dynamics of treacherous rivalries and interference had re-emerged and intensified. The leaders of the Iraqi Kurdish movement were regrouping in Iran. The Iraqi Shia Islamists, who had borne the brunt of repression under Saddam, now saw a golden opportunity. They wanted to bring Khomeini's revolution to Iraq, where the Shia formed a small majority but had little political power. Saddam was causing his own havoc on the Iranian border, supporting Arab nationalists in Khuzestan (not least through his consulate in Khorramshahr) and the Iranian opposition groups in Kurdistan. Baghdad was also teeming with former generals of the Shah's regime and SAVAK agents concocting wild plans for a comeback.

The Havana meeting was an early experience in statesmanship for Yazdi. Saddam, on the other hand, had been at the helm of his state for years. At the very outset, Yazdi invited Saddam to visit Iran and see the "changes" the revolution had brought. Chomping on his perennial cigar, Saddam welcomed the invitation but then proceeded with a long lecture on the theories and ideologies of the Baath Party, which, he emphasized, represented the true ideals of Islam.

"I am not political and don't know much about diplomacy," Yazdi said. "I have come here to speak frankly and hear frank words." Yazdi was being honest. He had been thrown off balance and didn't know how to discuss the points of contention with the impressive Iraqi leader. Saddam complained about the constant attacks on Iraq made by the press in Iran.

He complained about Kurdish Iraqi leaders given free rein on Iranian television. When Saddam reminded Yazdi that he had recognized the new leadership in Tehran, the Iranian minister told him that this was simply "not enough." Iraqis needed to "praise" the revolution.

"Your revolution was for yourself, not for the Arab countries and not for our people," Saddam thundered. "You had a revolution against your monarchy after 2,500 years, which is a little too late if you ask me! We destroyed our monarchy with a revolution shortly after it came to be and we don't boast about it that much. I am giving you brotherly advice. Your revolution was for yourself. Leave other people to their own affairs."

Yazdi was taken aback by Saddam's blunt retort. He also spoke directly and asked Saddam to stop "sending arms to Khuzestan" and supporting Arab separatists. A skilled manipulator, Saddam changed the topic. He reminded Yazdi that the Shah had occupied three islands in the Persian Gulf which rightfully belonged to the United Arab Emirates. Yazdi protested that this had nothing to do with Iraq.

"Aren't you familiar with the beliefs of the Baath Party?" Saddam responded. "We believe that every Arab issue is an issue for the Baath Party."

Yazdi responded with a threat. When Saddam boasted that the Baath Party went back half a century, the Iranian said: "The Najaf Shia seminary is more than nine hundred years old. If we want to follow this logic, Imam Khomeini can also claim that every Islamic issue is ours. If you want to start doing this, think of the consequences."

The revolutionary foreign minister had threatened a man who didn't like to be threatened. Saddam knew of the links that bound Khomeini and his acolytes to the Shia clerics in Najaf. He knew of the havoc that Tehran could wreak if it chose to activate its Iraqi allies. The Iraqi Shia had founded their own party in 1957. The Islamic Dawa Party had its own Khomeini in the figure of Mohammad Baqir al-Sadr, a 44-year-old cleric whose black turban, just like that of Khomeini, emphasized his descent from the family of the Prophet Mohammad. Khomeini knew Sadr from his Najaf years. Just as the Ayatollah and his acolytes had departed from the conciliatory tone of the Shia clerical establishment to engage in politics, Sadr had long tried to entice the Iraqi Shia away from their main political home, the

Communist Party. His main contribution to this battle was penning two explicitly anti-Marxist pamphlets: *Our Philosophy* (1959) and *Our Economy* (1960–1). The pamphlets aimed to counter the foundations of Marxism—its philosophy of dialectical materialism and its socialist economy—but they had remained marginal and obscure. Different brands of socialism were popular across the board and clerical interventions based on medieval Muslim texts were unlikely to offer much of a serious challenge.

But Khomeini's victory in 1979 had electrified Sadr and the Dawa Party. Here was a Shia cleric sitting at the head of a historical state in the Muslim world. While all the major trends of the Arab nationalist left were in crisis, it was the banner of Islam that had brought victory—and that of the Shia! Sadr declared his most resolute support for the Iranian revolution. On February 12, a day after the revolution, the Iraqi cleric gave a fiery speech in Najaf's Jawahiri mosque. He thanked God for the victory of the revolution in Iran, asked the believers to follow Khomeini, and warned about the conspiracies threatening the nascent revolution. He called for demonstrations in Najaf and in the holy city of Karbala. In a letter written to his supporters, Sadr asked them to "melt yourself in Khomeini, just as Khomeini has melted himself in Islam."

The Iraqi Shia rose in revolt. Starting in May, thousands flocked to Sadr's residence in Najaf to declare their allegiance. The protests were brutally suppressed and Sadr arrested. But one arrest couldn't quell the fire that Iran had helped stoke. The second wave came in June, this time led by Sadr's charismatic sister, Amina, better known as Bint al-Huda. She had long been a comrade-in-arms of her brother, writing in the same Islamist journals as he did. She was the author of many books and an organizer of a previous wave of Shia protests in 1977. Sadr was released but thousands of his supporters were arrested, tortured, and executed. Involved in an exhausting war against the Kurds in the north of the country, Saddam now had to face the restive Shia south. Yazdi's threatening words in Havana therefore rang in his ears. He felt under siege. On the first day of April 1980, the Shia underground made an unsuccessful attempt on the life of Deputy Prime Minister Tariq Aziz. A grenade was launched at him as he was touring the grounds of a Baghdad university. An Assyrian Catholic Christian, Aziz was the highest-ranking non-Muslim in Saddam's government and his closest advisor on foreign issues. By targeting the top, the Shia had gone a step too far.

Saddam's response was immediate and ferocious. The Sadr siblings were summarily arrested on April 5 and executed three days later. The Baathist regime had now given the Shia movement, in both Iran and Iraq, what it had always dreamed of: a high-profile martyr. Baqir al-Sadr was added to a prestigious list of Shia clerical martyrs, dating back to the brutal killing in fourteenth-century Damascus of a jurist who had been adorned with the title of First Martyr. The Iraqi cleric now had the high honor of being known as the Fifth Martyr. Excited by the rise of Khomeini, and to the chagrin of much of the Iraqi Shia establishment, Sadr had abandoned the tradition of careful Shia quietism, a tradition that had helped the community survive generations of Sunni-controlled governments. The politicized cleric wanted Shia in power and spoke with an unmistakable language of blood and martyrdom.

"This might be the last message you get from me," Sadr said in a statement shortly before his execution. "The gates of heaven have opened to welcome the caravans of the martyrs so that God can bring you victory. The Muslim nation, the Ummah, will not get moving unless we sacrifice our blood; the Ummah now needs my blood."

His blood had now been shed; the Shia had their grand martyr. So who would avenge him?

* * *

By executing Sadr, Saddam hadn't just murdered a political ally of Tehran. He had killed a religious authority, a turban-wearing descendant of the Prophet, a member of a class that Khomeini considered to be the rightful source of political power. The Grand Ayatollah of Iran didn't mince his words of condemnation or couch them in a diplomatic language. Nor did he hesitate to target Saddam Hussein himself. Speaking on April 9, a day after Sadr's execution, Khomeini said the Iraqi president was a "traitor," a "parasite," an "un-Islamic and inhumane, disgusting creature" who should be "destroyed." He went on to call directly on the Iraqi people to "rise up" and overthrow Saddam.

At the Havana meeting, Saddam had warned the Iranians about the inflammatory language of the Iranian press and state broadcaster against his Baathist regime, asking them to rein these voices in. Yazdi had responded with the classic diplomatic answer: The government didn't control the newspapers. But there was no denying now. It was the Ayatollah himself who spoke with fire against Saddam. Along with the rest of the Bazargan government, Yazdi had resigned in November 1979 in the aftermath of the US embassy saga. The embassy seizure was used by Khomeini as a political litmus test as he started his rapid purge of all potential rivals. Anyone opposed to the embassy occupation—the Second Revolution, in Khomeini's parlance—stood no chance and had to be purged.

By April 1980, almost all positions of power belonged either to clerical lieutenants of Khomeini or to their close allies in Islamist groups. With their full support, Khomeini continued his relentless diatribes against Saddam. On April 10, he said that it wouldn't be long before the Saddam regime was thrown into the "dustbin of history." A week later, he publicly asked the soldiers of the Iraqi army to organize a "coup" and bring Saddam down. Any support for Saddam was *haram*, sinful and religiously prohibited, and the Iraqis must struggle to form an "Islamic government." On April 22, Khomeini asked the Iraqi soldiers to "either rise up with courage and overthrow the tyranny or abscond and flee their barracks."

Just a few months before, two questions about the new regime in Iran had invited a lively debate: Firstly, would Khomeini remain a spiritual figurehead of the Islamic Republic or would he become an active decision-making leader? Secondly, what would be the international orientation of the new regime in the global Cold War? Would it maintain Iran's ties with the United States, maybe becoming an Islamist pro-US force like Pakistan under President Zia? Would it be a moderate player like others in the NAM, something like a Muslim India?

It didn't take long for the first question to be settled. The restless, stubborn, and firm Khomeini evidently called all the shots himself as a hands-on head of state. The second question was more complicated. But one thing remained clear. Khomeini's Iran intended to be a revolutionary regime and the revolution would not stop at the Iranian borders. Khomeini's daring statements against Saddam and the material support given by Tehran to the Iraqi Shia (whose Dawa Party now had its head-quarters in Iran) left no doubt.

Cooler heads tried to reason with Khomeini. Among them was Mahmoud Doaei, a pro-Khomeini cleric who had spent years in Baghdad before the revolution, helping to spread the messages of the Ayatollah by running a Saddam-funded radio station. Doaei was now Iran's ambassador to Iraq. He urged Khomeini to cool his rhetoric down, lest border skirmishes that had been going on since 1979 turn into a full-on war. Not for the last time, Khomeini ignored all such warnings and turned down Saddam's offer of negotiations mediated by Doaei. The Ayatollah didn't believe in compromise over truth. His Platonic conception of an absolute truth was linked to his mystical Sufi side: The truth was passed down to him through God and the compromises of mere mortal men had no business in dislodging it. His revolution had no intention of respecting a border agreed between the Ottomans and the Persians centuries ago.

* * *

Saddam Hussein was not one to shy away from confrontation. Like Khomeini, his dreams and aspirations went beyond the narrow borders of Iraq. He wanted to be the new Nasser, an Arab leader who could fulfill the grand destiny of his people far beyond the Mesopotamian lands. It helped that a power vacuum had appeared in the international Arab leadership. By recognizing Israel and signing a peace treaty with it on March 26, 1979, the Egyptian president, Anwar Sadat, the man who had been Nasser's deputy and his replacement as head of state, had made himself *persona non grata* in the world of Arab politics. Nasser's pan-Arabism had long been tied to the Palestinian cause. Arabs had now not only ignominiously lost lands to Israel in the 1967 war; they saw their leader speak in the Israeli Knesset, accept the reality of the Zionist project, and make peace with Tel Aviv without the Palestinians. At its November 1978 summit, held in Baghdad, the Arab League condemned the Egyptian-Israeli negotiations, being held at Camp David under the aegis of President Carter, and froze its relationship with Egypt. On March 27, 1979, a day after the Egyptian-Israeli peace treaty was finally signed, the Arab League foreign ministers gathered once more in Baghdad to condemn the treaty in the strongest terms, kick the Egyptians out of the league, and pledge to continue the fight against the Zionist enemy. In addition to ministers from eighteen Arab countries, the Baghdad meeting was also attended by Yasser Arafat as head of the PLO delegation. Saddam was Arafat's strongest ally at the meeting. The Iraqi leader made it clear that any Arab state which wasn't fully committed to the Baghdad resolution "was an ally of Sadat and thus an ally of the Zionist enemy."[1] He warned that the decisions of this meeting should be accompanied by action and not remain "mere ink on paper." But, as always, the Arab leaders were strong on symbolic gestures yet fell short on action. It was resolved to move the league headquarters out of Cairo, where they had been since its foundation in 1945, to Tunis. And as for breaking off relations with Egypt, the heart of the Arab lands? Jordan said it would withdraw its ambassador but not break relations. The Omanis hadn't even attended, effectively endorsing the peace treaty. The rich and powerful Saudis agreed on some "minimum sanctions" but weren't ready to commit more. Arafat was livid. His shouting match with Saud bin Faisal, Riyadh's foreign minister, broke up the conference.

Saddam, on the other hand, saw this as opportunity to stand by Arafat and claim the mantle of Arab leadership. He needed to outmaneuver not only the fence-sitting of the Saudis but also the rival radical states of Syria and Libya. Although he wasn't in fact Iraq's president yet, Saddam pledged to lead. "I am the one who will guarantee this and not you," he said. "We are ready to take on this task."

But taking on the preponderant military power of Israel, backed by the superpower the United States, was easier said than done. Not for the last time, an Arab leader chose another target to prove his credentials for Arab leadership. On this occasion, revolutionary Iran.

Demonization of Iran and its Shia faith carried a long pedigree in Arab lands. The revolution had been welcomed by the likes of Arafat but most major forces of the Arab world soon found reason for worry in the confident march of Khomeini's revolution. The Islamist leaders, such as those of the Muslim Brotherhood—who had initially praised the revolution as a sign of Islam's unique political power—were quickly disillusioned and were back to denouncing the Shia, calling them choice names such as "fire worshippers," alluding to Iran's ancient religion of Zoroastrianism, in which fire has a holy function. Ensconced in their monarchical palaces and palatial presidential offices, Arab leaders were worried about the unpredictable Iranians, about the revolutionary storm coming out of Tehran and Qom. Saddam knew how to tap the sentiments of the moment.

On September 17, 1980, Saddam, by now president of Iraq, called an emergency meeting of the national assembly. He declared that the Iranian provocations had nullified the Algiers Agreement of 1975. He tore the agreement up in front of TV cameras and claimed ownership over the entirety of the Shatt al-Arab River, which partly forms the border between Iran and Iraq. If the Iranians were going to evoke nine centuries of Shia history in the Iraqi heartlands, the Iraqis knew how to play history politics too. Appealing to the Arab world, Saddam awoke the memories of the seventh-century Battle of Qadesiya. In 636, barely four years after the death of the Prophet Mohammad, the nascent Islamic polity had gone to war against the Persian Empire, a major superpower of the late antique world whose capital was located around the suburbs of today's Baghdad. The newly Muslim Arabs defeated the superpower Persians on the western bank of the Euphrates, in the fields south of Najaf known as Qadesiya.

Saddam now promised his own Qadesiya, his own Arab crusade against the Persians. He was going to take back the three islands of the Persian Gulf. He was going to take over the Arab-majority Khuzestan province and rename it Arabistan. He was going to overthrow the Islamic Republic of Iran. The eloquent historical allegories excited the Arab street, demoralized and in despair after its repeated pathetic defeats at the hands of the Israelis. Crude realpolitik stood behind the battle and many Arab leaders were happy to bankroll Saddam on his daring adventure.

On September 22, 1980, around 1:30 P.M., the full-on Iraqi offensive started. Inspired by the devastating Israeli attack on the Egyptian air force in the 1967 war, the hostilities started with 192 of Baghdad's Soviet-supplied planes attempting to destroy the Iranian air force. In the concurrent ground offensive twelve infantry and mechanized divisions and thirty brigades stormed the Iranian border, opening a front as wide as

1,200 kilometers. Parts of Iran's Khuzestan, Ilam, and Kermanshah provinces came under occupation and siege. The longest international war since 1945 had just begun.

By attacking and occupying Iranian territory, Saddam Hussein had triggered forces beyond his imagination. The Iran-Iraq War became not the undoing of the Islamic Republic but a cauldron of fire in which the nascent republic consolidated itself and bolstered its rule. The tales of heroism of the seventh-century Arab warriors against the "fire-worshipping magi" energized the streets of Iraq. But on the opposite side, too, the fierce patriotism of Iranians had been awakened against a foreign invader. From the prescient Kangarloo, whose prediction had come true, and his Islamist comrades to members of small Marxist intellectual circles, countless Iranians would now go to the fronts and defend their beloved homeland. But some political forces would refuse to join what soon became known as the "Holy Defense." Some, including the PMOI, would go so far as moving to Iraq and militarily allying with Saddam against their own country. Still, they were going to have little constituency among Iranians, who, by and large, abhorred the foreign invasion. Wearing the uniforms of the armed forces of the Islamic Republic of Iran, hundreds of thousands of Iranians would fall in the eight years of war with Iraq. Many wore headbands that celebrated the Shia Imams, whose shrines in Iraqi soil they wanted to liberate, but the fallen were to also include Iranian Jews, Christians, Zoroastrians, and even the heavily persecuted Baha'is. Saddam had united the nation like Khomeini never could have.

Not that Khomeini would see this as an opportunity for national unity or for toning down the brutal civil war that his followers were engaged in. Quite to the contrary, he would use the emergencies of wartime to drown his internal opponents in blood. For almost a year after the initial attack, Iran's commander-in-chief was its president, Abolhassan Banisadr. The Sorbonne-educated economist had been a close lieutenant of Khomeini during his stay in Paris and had been elected president in February 1980 due to the Ayatollah's support. But he was a Muslim modernizer in the mold of Bazargan and Yazdi and was to have no place in Khomeini's Iran. Before long, the clerical allies of the Ayatollah brought Banisadr down and hunted down his supporters.

Khomeini didn't go on the record calling the war a "gift from the heavens" for nothing. On the muddy battlefronts, on the mountains and marshlands of the Iranian-Iraqi border, the Islamic Republic mobilized its youth and built a new brand of Islamist warriors. Tapping deep into the reservoirs of Iranian culture and consciousness, Khomeini's regime now portrayed itself as simultaneously destined for global victory *and* oppressed and lonely in the face of evil. It was the regime of the *mazloom*, an Arabic loanword in Persian, untranslatable into English, but which connotes something of a heroic oppression.

Just when Saddam's forces were crossing the frontier, the Ayatollah sent a televised message to the nation. Keeping his fabled calm, he spoke with daring confidence: "Since Saddam Hussein came to power, I have said that he was crazy, that his brain wasn't working and that he would bring about his own destruction." He called on the Iraqi nation and army to rebel against the tyrant and bring him down.

Iran would play up its isolation in the war, faced with the complicated matrix of Cold War and bloc politics. Iraq seemed to have the world behind it. Jordanians fought in its forces; Saudis and Kuwaitis bankrolled it without restriction. The Soviets continued to arm and train its forces. The French military industry continued its solid alliance with Baghdad. And whom did Iran have on its side? If you were to believe Khomeini, none of the powerful and only the righteous of the world.

Meeting with the ambassadors of some Muslim countries on Eid al-Adha, Khomeini boasted: "Some believe that we have become isolated. But we are not isolated. The ones who truly matter are the nations. All the weak nations, even the non-Muslim ones who are part of the oppressed, will stand with us." Meeting with a Libyan envoy, he said: "This war has been imposed on the Muslim nation of Iran by Saddam. Iran will defeat Saddam because we fear neither East nor West, and will resort only to God for help."

The appeal to the "nations, not powers" wasn't just rhetorical. Like the French and Russian revolutions before it, the Iranian revolution started with a particular internationalist ethos: It wanted to unite the righteous against evil everywhere. On October 8, a group of Iraqi youth met with Khomeini in his compound. "May the Almighty give you the power to drive away this dirty man [Saddam] from your homeland," the Ayatollah told them. "God is with you and you will be victorious."

Iran's assertions about its isolation among the world powers held some truth. All in all, Iraq would get more than three times as much foreign assistance as Iran. But the Tehran regime would make many Faustian bargains of its own to survive. It received arms from the United States, China, and smaller powers whose main interest was to balance Iran and Iraq against each other and prevent either side's outright victory. Help came even from Israel. Tehran ceaselessly promised to destroy the Jewish State but the decision makers in Tel Aviv had foresight and patience. They saw Saddam as the greater threat and were to send anti-missile batteries, emblazoned with the Blue Star of David, to Khomeini's Islamic Republic.

Still, Iran's anti-Western internationalism made for special friendships. Among its few allies in the war with Iraq were radical states such as North Korea and Libya. In something of an irony, Iran's war effort was also backed by the only other Baathist state in the world, the Syrian Arab Republic. Damascus became an early and steadfast ally of the Iranian regime, happy to help it fight the Iraqis, whose pan-Arab Baath Party had split with the Syrians' own in 1966. Showing early on its talent for realpolitik, the Islamic Republic of Iran refused to back the Islamist uprisings against the arch-secular Baathist Syrians.

But such realpolitik was not immediately visible to those who now had to guard their revolution against a foreign invader. Iran's Shah-trained army had begun the job of defending the country. Pilots previously imprisoned due to their monarchical past were let out of jail to proudly run sorties against Iraq. Iran's US-made fighters swiftly retaliated and immediately showed Iraq that it did not have an easy fight on its hands. But, like all revolutionaries, Khomeini and his acolytes in the leadership of the nascent regime knew that they couldn't rely on a US-trained professional army to achieve all of their goals. The revolution needed to build its own armies under its own banner. The IRGC now had a far greater purpose than anyone could have imagined. It was to build up its forces and to defend the revolution against all enemies, domestic and foreign.

The IRGC's rivalry with Iran's professional army often hurt the Iranian war effort. Having started as an ad hoc militia, the Revolutionary Guards soon grew to overshadow and dwarf the army. They became a vector of mobilization for millions of Iranians who asked not what the revolution could do for them but what they could do for the revolution. Khomeini relied upon the winning card of revolutionary armies throughout history: zealotry of the newly armed masses.

* * *

Qassem Soleimani had finally been allowed to join the official IRGC on May 22, 1980. He didn't know much about politics, wasn't particularly religious and was unlikely to have had an opinion on the complex regional and international politics of the day. Were it not for Saddam's attack on Iran and the mass mobilization that came with it, the likes of Soleimani might have continued their lives on the margins. But the war changed everything. Soleimani might not have been part of the urban social and intellectual elites but he was exactly who the revolution had championed: the ordinary downtrodden; the sort of man who had been left out of all the circles of influence in modern Iranian life. Besides, he seemed like the kind of man you would want on your side in a war. Years of martial arts meant that he was physically very fit—more than could be said for some of the more experienced revolutionaries. With a shy face and an understated smile, he looked enigmatic and handsome. His calm and quiet demeanor did little to hide his ambition. He planned to make this war his own.

For the first few months after the Iraqi invasion, his job was rather boring. The Iraqis had targeted airports all over Iran with their MiG, Tupolev, and Sukhoi fighters (all made and supplied by the Soviet Union). Iran's effort was focused on protecting key airports like the one in Tehran. Soleimani and the local IRGC unit were tasked with protecting Kerman airport. Deep in the Iranian interior, the airport held neither strategic value nor political importance. It was unlikely that Saddam would even bother attacking it. Soleimani didn't want to spend the war guarding a provincial airport. His drive made his desired destination clear: the front. The battle for liberation of Iranian territory was underway and Soleimani didn't have to wait long to be a part of it. In early 1981, he finally became one of the 300 Kermanis sent to the front to fight the Iraqi enemy. He was a simple soldier then but he wouldn't remain one for long. He did not take off his khakis for the eight long years of the Iran-Iraq War, and indeed Qassem Soleimani was to remain a soldier to the day he died. The shy *karateka* from the tribal margins of Iran had now found his life's calling.

Chapter 5

War Makes Man

Like the rest of Khuzestan, the city of Ahvaz is infamous for its swelter-
ing summers. For foreigners unused to the climate, who have long
flocked to the area for well-paying jobs in oil, the unbearable heat is a
favorite topic of complaint. Like other oil-endowed Persian Gulf areas,
Khuzestan is dotted with settlements aimed at countering the heat. The
British, who excelled equally at seizure of foreign oil and colonial settlement of parching hot lands, came up with a solution: hill stations with
private swimming pools and manicured grass fields constantly sprinkled
with cool water.

On a hill east of the Karun River, Ahvaz has its own heat-escaping
hill station. It was built by the Americans, successors to the British in
running the Iranian oil industry, and it shows. Around a central stone
structure, not only are there the usual facilities like swimming pools
and football fields, but there is also a space for that most American of
pastimes: nine expansive golf courses, giving the station its unofficial
moniker, the Golf Station. The hill station was still under construction
when the revolution broke out. All the Americans fled rapidly, taking
their golf carts with them. The golf club burnt down around the same
time, probably by revolutionary arson which targeted all symbols of

Western decadence. But the balmy climate and solid stone structures remained intact.

On February 14, 1982, a few men in their mid- to late twenties huddled in the so-called Golf Station. They weren't there to pass the time or play a few holes but to plan a major military operation. The post-revolutionary oil ministry had bequeathed the station to the IRGC and a sign outside declared its new name: "The Base for Those Awaiting Martyrdom." Close to Ahvaz airport and secluded behind the mountains, the base was perfect for the IRGC, which used it as the headquarters for the Southern Front Operations in the war with Iraq, now well into its second year.

The Golf Station was where IRGC leaders met daily to plan their war. On that day, one of them, 27-year-old Mohsen Rezayi, spoke with characteristic confidence: "Since we pushed Saddam back from Bostan [a city in Khuzestan], he has ceased to talk about his long list of demands. Now he distributes pictures of himself visiting the Imam Hossein shrine in Karbala. He knows well that this war will destroy him if he continues." Rezayi boasted that the IRGC, not long ago an ad hoc group of volunteers, was now driving the war. It had superseded Iran's official army with all its historic divisions and battalions.

Judging from Rezayi's boastful tone, one couldn't guess that Saddam's Iraq still occupied vast swathes of Iranian territory. The invaders had come up to the Karkhe River in the north of Khuzestan, already controlled important border towns such as Khorramshahr, and seriously threatened key cities including Ahvaz itself. But Rezayi wasn't alone in his elan and faith in coming victories for the "Armies of the Right, Fighting against the Wrong," as the IRGC propaganda declared. At the Golf Station, he was surrounded with young men who had similar outlooks.

These young men couldn't be blamed for their optimism. During their short lifetimes, they had already seen incredibly unlikely victories. They were Davids used to knocking down Goliath. Hailing from a tribal nomadic background, Rezayi had been born in a Khuzestani village a few hours' drive north of Ahvaz. He had grown up in the harsh poverty of the nomadic tent life, unable to enjoy the amenities of the area, which were only open to the employees of the oil industry. The oil workers were the ultimate "labor aristocracy" of their time who often mocked the uncouth ways of the tribal folk. Mohsen had pledged to fight against the discrimination suffered by his people. His enrollment at the National Oil Company's prestigious high school in Ahvaz was followed by anti-Shah activities that landed him a six-month jail sentence in 1973. Since then, he had devoted his life to the revolution, building up one of the many pro-Khomeini guerrilla groups which came to form the IRGC after the revolution. A few months before the meeting, he had been appointed the top commander of the IRGC, a young man tasked with guarding a revolution that had astonished the world.

Most other men in the room boasted similarly distinguished careers, despite their young age. The 26-year-old Ali Shamkhani was a local Ahvaz boy and an ethnic Arab who had met Rezayi in jail and joined his guerrilla group. He was now the IRGC's local commander in Ahvaz.

The man considered to be the true military genius of the room was a quiet, slightly built 28-year-old with a goatee. Hassan Bagheri had the rare distinction of having received military training under the Shah. The young Tehrani had been expelled from his veterinary college program in 1977 and sent off to mandatory military conscription. He had joined the Khomeini movement early on and was among the young soldiers who helped conquer the military barracks for the revolution in February 1979. In the early post-revolutionary days, he had been a correspondent for the newly founded *Jomhouri-e Eslami* ("Islamic Republic"), the newspaper of the Islamic Republican Party. Invited by the Lebanese Shia party, Amal, Bagheri made a fifteen-day trip to Lebanon and Jordan to report on Arab support for Khomeini's revolution. He spoke to Palestinians enthused by the unexpected revolution in Iran, and hung out with the AK-47-wielding Shia militias running the Mediterranean port of Tyre, so close to the fabled "Zionist Enemy." But these young revolutionaries—Rezayi, Shamkhani, and Bagheri—were now beyond the early jubilant days of their revolution. They had to use all they knew to help plan a key operation that was to drive Saddam out of Iranian territory.

During one of their meetings, on February 10, 1982, at around 5 P.M., another young IRGC man, a month short of his twenty-sixth birthday, entered the room. His name was Qassem Soleimani. Though only slightly younger than the others, Soleimani looked up to men such as Rezayi and

Bagheri as legends. Unlike them, he had no revolutionary or political accolades to speak of and had hardly ever left his home province, let alone Iran. He had been a member of the IRGC for less than two years. How had he earned his coveted place in that room of war commanders?

* * *

Soleimani's physical prowess made him stand out. Many of the revolution's supporters were armchair revolutionaries, scrawny young men or clerics who had spent a lifetime preaching. Now that they were building a military force, they would benefit from more athletic men. Initially seconded to a unit that guarded Kerman airport, Soleimani's impressive physique got him noticed by the senior figures. On October 12, 1980, less than a month after the attack by Saddam, he was sent to become a physical education coach at the Quds Training Barracks, set up in a juvenile jail in Kerman. "Quds" is the Arabic name for Jerusalem, a holy city for Muslims and a symbolic rallying cry for Islamists who dream of the day when they can kick out the Israelis and pray in the city that was the Prophet Mohammad's first direction of Muslim prayers before Mecca. As the Islamic Republic built new institutions, it had a limited repertoire of powerful symbolic names, which made for a lot of repetitions. Dozens of schools, streets, squares, art centers, and military barracks were named "Quds" or "Beit-ol-Moqaddas," the customary version of the city's name in modern Persian.[1] This was Soleimani's first appointment to an institution called "Quds" but it certainly would not be the last. Like other Islamists, his dream of conquering Jerusalem remained unfulfilled to the end. But, from the outset, his fate was symbolically tied to the distant lands of Palestine and the Israeli enemy that now governed them. Although he didn't know it yet, Soleimani would come to directly face off the Israelis and fight them; he would come to be known by thousands in historic Palestine, and openly feared by the leadership of the Israeli state. But for now he was simply a coach at a provincial training center.

The IRGC aimed to train its soldiers not just in physical abilities and military aptitude but in revolutionary and ideological outlook. Soleimani's karate moves were impressive but not enough. If he was to coach others, he had to first be coached himself. Soleimani became among the select few Kermanis sent to Tehran for a rapid training period. In the capital city, the IRGC had taken over a luxurious estate in Saadabad and turned it into an elite training unit. The verdant hills of northern Tehran have long been a haven for the richest of Iranians. The Qajars had had their summer residences here but it really came to life under the Pahlavis when each member of the royal family had his or her own expansive estate, filled with forests, natural springs, ancient aqueducts, gardens, and greenhouses. One of these was now turned into the Imam Ali Barracks. The IRGC ran a fifteen-day intense training course with three distinct parts: ideological, political, and military.

The camp's commanders were mostly young men themselves. They had trained in Palestinian camps in Lebanon and now offered an Islamist-friendly version to the Iranians. According to an early trainee, the young soldiers at Imam Ali were taught Iran's political history, were briefed on the latest politics of the day, and were told why most political parties, even many of those pledging loyalty to Khomeini, did not truly support the revolution.[2] They were also taught what all young citizens of the Islamic Republic were soon to learn en masse: the stories of the Prophet Mohammad and the twelve Shia Imams, and the tales of the early years of Islam when the Prophet led his own revolution, built his own state, and raised his own armies. Only then did the recruits proceed to military training, which included everything from combat self-defense to war tactics. The training was intense and the trainees could rest for only three or four hours a day.

Soleimani awed many with his eagerness. The revolution was supposed to have changed everything but those from big cities such as Tehran still made fun of tribals like him. This only made him more eager to stand out. "He was physically strong and had this sense of determination that made him noticeable," a contemporary remembers. "He learnt how to say the right things about Islam and the revolution but his focus was on the military matters. He loved that stuff!"[3]

By the time the Imam Ali–trained Kermanis went back to their city's Quds Barracks, they were considered to be head and shoulders above everyone else. Soleimani's eagerness continued to help his rise, except when it almost had him killed. In one of the early training sessions, he was injured by the friendly fire of a young trainee. This was to be the first of many, many injuries incurred by Qassem Soleimani. In a war effort full of amateurs, such injuries were not rare. But it was Soleimani's response that made the incident memorable. He had been given leave after the injury but he knew his absence would hurt his promotion chances. "We were shocked to see he was back the day after," a fellow Quds Barracks trainee remembers.[4] Instead of the uniform pants and their ammunition belt, Qassem was wearing loose, Kurdish-style pants, which were common in his tribal area. "I remember him firing the AK-47 with one hand," the trainee remembers. "This guy wasn't going to go home so easily."

Home was not where he was headed. Soleimani showed enough promise to be placed at the head of a small platoon of about two dozen soldiers and was sent off to the frontlines. The soldiers had one thing in common. They were all Kermanis, among the 300 people from their home province who headed to the front in the early days of the war, before they had their own brigade. It was still early 1981.

The Kermanis were sent to the flat fields of Meyshan, which had been a point of Iraqi focus since the very first day of the war. The area probably had the highest Arab majority in Iran. For centuries, it had been called Bani Torof after the nomadic Arab tribes whose presence in the area predated Islam. The Persianate policies of the Pahlavis renamed the area with the Persian name of Meyshan, reminiscent of the ancient times when it was a trade entrepot on the routes connecting Mesopotamia to India; when Alexander the Great built one of his many "Alexandrias" on the Persian Gulf, near what is now the Iraqi port of Basra. Over the border, the Iraqi province opposite had also been called Meysaan, an Arabized version of the same name, since 1976.

The main Iranian town in the region, the picturesque Soosangerd, had fallen time and time again to the Baathist army, which was soon to find out that the Shia Arab tribes of the area were no pushovers, and would not be taken in by their grand Arabist slogans. Soosangerd had fallen to the Iraqis on September 28 (a few days after the invasion began) but it was recovered following four days of heavy fighting. The same back and forth happened in November 1980. By January 1981, the city was controlled by the Iranians again but it was now a ghost town, surrounded by the Iraqi forces on all sides.

Starting on January 5, the Iranian ground forces, backed up by the air force, stormed the Iraqi lines around the Karkhe Koor River. Operation Nasr was led by the Iranian army and the IRGC volunteers played only a side role. It failed miserably and the Iraqis were able to maintain their occupation of vast swathes of the Iranian territory. They kept their siege, not only of Soosangerd but also of the main cities of Khuzestan province, Ahvaz and Abadan.

For Qassem Soleimani, however, this didn't count as a failure but as an initiation into battle he remembered fondly. Speaking of the battle in a 1990 interview, he said: "When I first went to the frontlines, I believed the enemy was capable of everything. But in our first attack, we pushed them back and brought casualties upon them. This shattered my wrong perception of the enemy."[5]

These words exaggerate the small role the Kermanis played in this failed battle. But though it was a small step for the Iranian armed forces, it was a giant leap for Soleimani. Much of his life was to be tied, in one way or another, to these lands and to the Iraqis he faced in his first battle. Another persistent theme of his life also took shape here: building a personal rapport and camaraderie with the soldiers of his unit, especially those close to home. Soleimani's closest friend in this battle was Hamid Iranmanesh. He was only about two years older but had much more experience. He had been conscripted under the Shah and joined the IRGC in its early days. He had fought the new regime's battles against the Kurdish left, earning the moniker "Hamid the Guerrilla." The IRGC forces still lacked proper discipline. At night, Iranmanesh and Soleimani would ride motorcycles to the Iraqi positions—careless and daring doings of young men who welcomed the new vistas the war opened up to them.

The regime they served was also finding new vistas. Khomeini's salami tactics were fast removing all obstacles to his total rule. Muslim modernists like Mehdi Bazargan had been so swiftly pushed out of power that one couldn't believe they were among the main founders of the Islamic Republic. A worse fate awaited the outright non-Islamists who were fast filling the jails.

The last non-Khomeinist standing was President Banisadr, the nominal commander-in-chief. Banisadr had owed his election to Khomeini's support but he had stood up to the thuggish Khomeinists and still believed in the ideals of Mossadeq. On March 5, 1981, he commemorated the anniversary of Mossadeq's death with a speech at Tehran University. The speech turned into a scuffle where the pro-Khomeini thugs beat up the supporters of the president. Chief among the latter were the increasingly restive forces of the PMOI who, under Masood Rajavi's charismatic leadership, were now the main opposition party. The failures on the front became the perfect pretext for Khomeinists to push Banisadr from power. The year 1981 became the crucial turning point, the blood-stained birth of total rule by the Khomeinists. By the summer of that year, Banisadr was ousted from power by the Khomeinist-dominated parliament and with the consent of the Supreme Leader himself. The PMOI declared a doomed war against the regime and started assassinating its leaders. Rajavi and Banisadr fled Tehran for Paris and joined the increasing ranks of the opposition abroad. With Banisadr gone and the PMOI followers purged, the war effort, as well as all the levers of the state, were now controlled by the Khomeinists. The IRGC was now the praetorian guard of the Supreme Leader, his first line of defense against all opponents, domestic and foreign.

The IRGC faced the task that Banisadr had failed to accomplish: breaking the siege of Abadan. The port was Iran's jewel on the Persian Gulf and the beating heart of its oil industry. Saddam repeatedly spoke of Abadan as rightfully belonging to the Iraqis. Many thought the regime couldn't survive its fall. The IRGC was to spare no effort in mobilizing resources for this critical operation. This required rapid training of volunteers everywhere—including in Kerman.

Soleimani had incurred another injury, once more to his hand, in Operation Nasr.[6] But it was another man's injury that played a key role in his fate. On July 29, 1981, Ali Mohajeri, the commander of the Quds Training Barracks, was wounded after rebutting an Iraqi attack. Just when the barracks had to train a new set of recruits, Mohajeri lay miles away in a hospital in Isfahan. Suddenly the 25-year-old Soleimani was a relative senior at Quds. He became the effective commander of the camp and helped trained many young Kermanis for the exhaustingly long

Operation Eighth Imam. The sweet victory of the operation came on September 29, 1981. The Iranians finally broke the siege. Abadan was safe and the IRGC had proved that it was more than a melee of excited Khomeini fanatics. The Kermanis had proved their mettle in the battle and the Quds Barracks commander shared a good part of the glory.

* * *

The Iranians had no time to rest on their laurels. Iraq was on the defensive but it still occupied thousands of square kilometers of Iranian territory. With the siege of Abadan broken, the Iranian forces were fast in planning the next operation. It was to be called Tariq-ol-Quds or Path to Jerusalem. The actual goal of the operation was more modest than the name would suggest. The Iranians had to fight once more in the fields of Meyshan to liberate the border town of Bostan, about 30 kilometers to the northwest of Soosangerd, and the strategic Gorge of Chazabe—all areas of Iranian territory that had been occupied by the Iraqis for more than a year. Chazabe was a Persianized version of an old Arabic word that meant "deceiving." The gorge had earned the name due to its treacherously confusing landscape. It was a mix of hills, defiles, and desert-like flatlands, full of mirages that would indeed deceive the most experienced locals, let alone the fighters who were encountering it for the first time.

The victory at Abadan had energized thousands who now rushed to join the war effort. The IRGC, and its auxiliary voluntary force, Basij, were organized to absorb these young men and send them en masse to the front. Such mobilization also helped the regime fight its domestic battles. The radio stations were filled with propagandists asking all and everyone to do their duty by enlisting. At every city, every town, every village, Friday prayer leaders repeated the message. Many remember their own accidental paths to the front. In Kerman, IRGC men went around town on motorcycles and asked acquaintances to enlist. Some needed no encouragement. Mohammad Keshavarz had just returned to Iran in 1981 after seven years of back-breaking labor in the Arab sheikhdoms of the Persian Gulf. He wanted to celebrate his return by treating himself to a pilgrimage to Mashhad, Iran's holiest city. At Kerman bus station, when he saw the crowds preparing to go to war,

Keshavarz changed his mind. He enlisted and was on the frontlines within weeks. Within months, he was killed, one of the many "martyrs" in whose names hundreds of thousands of Iranian streets and alleyways are still named. This was total war; a war of the masses, fought by the masses.

Soleimani's military career was built by channeling this mass energy into an *esprit de corps*. Many of the men he mobilized in those early days of the war would remain with him for decades. Many would fall in this war or the ones to come. In October, he went around and gathered all the Kermanis he could find. Some who had just finished their missions at Abadan and were eligible for leave stayed back to prepare for the next operation. Hossein Negarestani, an Abadan veteran, remembers the day when Soleimani came to recruit him for the next operation. They were at a base in Ahvaz when Soleimani entered in a Toyota Land Cruiser, driven by himself. The Kermanis stood in lines. Soleimani went to the microphone and read out a list of names. These were the people who had to stay. The others could decide for themselves. Negarestani stayed, as did many other Kermanis.[7]

This would be the third operation the Kermanis were fighting in. They were now more than scattered forces and were given increasingly important roles. They were also joined by fighters from the coastal Hormozgan province. Hormozgan had a large Sunni minority and many had assumed it to be an unlikely source of recruits for the IRGC. But the allure of fighting for the nation had attracted many. If you listened well enough in the Kermani training sessions you could pick out the distinctive accent of fighters from the old port of Minab, Hormozgan's second biggest city and a long-time maritime hub for Arabs, Persians, and many others besides.[8]

The Hormozganis were attached to the Kermanis from the outset. In preparation for Operation Path to Jerusalem, they all gathered in Kerman's Imam Hossein Barracks, the IRGC's local recruitment center. The site's beautiful gardens and delicate architecture impressed many. The "barracks" had been a college until a few months prior. Its short history was itself a chronicle of the revolution and its swift turns. It had started life as Arsham College, named after the shadowy Colonel Arsham, the provincial head of the Shah's secret police and a crafty freemason if you believed the revolutionary rumors. After the revolution, it had changed name to Hanifnejad College, after the PMOI's founding father. Then it was one of the many institutions briefly renamed after Mossadeq before the Islamic Republic erased all traces of the popular prime minister. By October 1981, the site was no longer a college. The regime had closed down the universities as part of its cultural revolution and the old Arsham College was turned over to the IRGC in the summer of 1981.[9]

On October 31, 1981, 400 soldiers formed their ranks in the barracks. At least ninety-one of them were from Hormozgan and the rest from Kerman. The IRGC naturally preferred experienced soldiers. Some of the recruits had fought in the previous operations against Iraq or the civil war in Iranian Kurdistan. But most had no such qualifications. Some had never fired a gun before. Many lied to be included. Some were teenagers, barely old enough to fit into uniforms. The commanders overlooked these inconveniences. They would do anything to achieve the stated goal: sending two Kermani battalions into the battle. But who was going to lead them?

There were few obvious candidates. Hamid the Guerrilla had reputation and experience. Another soldier, Abdolhossein Rahimi, had fought in Kurdistan for months. But as the soldiers were forming their ranks in the courtyard of the barracks, one thing became obvious. Those trained and coached by Soleimani were the most disciplined. They seemed to answer to military commands better than the rest. The IRGC bosses were impressed. They decided that Soleimani was ready to lead one battalion while the other would be led by Rahimi. Shortly after the decision was announced, Rahimi went to Soleimani with a proposal: Would he like to lead both of the battalions himself?

This was the moment the ambitious Qassem had been waiting for. He thanked Rahimi and accepted. Ali Akbar Pooriani, the IRGC's provincial commander of operations, who had known Soleimani since their gym days in Kerman, remembers that day very well. "Our brother Qassem Soleimani came to me and asked to lead both battalions. He had an athletic figure and obvious charisma," he remembered years later. The decision was up to the two senior officers who were present. The commanders gave each other a brief look and made a decision that jump-started Soleimani's career. The 25-year-old now became head of two Kermani battalions.[10]

* * *

Late October coincided with the onset of Muharram, the first month of the Islamic calendar and the most solemn time of the year in Shia culture. Muharram is a carnival of mourning central to the Shia faith. The mourning ceremonies start from the first day of the month and crescendo until they reach their height on the tenth, known as Ashura. This was the day in the year 680 when Imam Hossein and his legendary army of only seventy-two men went into battle in the fields of Karbala in one of Islam's first civil wars. According to Shia lore, Hossein knew his men were no match for the powerful armies of the ruling caliph, Yazid. But they had gone into battle because it was the right thing to do. They had welcomed martyrdom so that their righteous brand of Islam could live on. Modern Shia Islamism has turned this central element of traditional Iranian culture into a politicized narrative of a just war. The symbolism of going to battle during Muharram, not far from the lands in which the Prophet's grandson himself had fought and fallen, could hardly be stronger.

As the soldiers gathered their forces in the barracks, Kerman was gearing up for the big day. Streets were filled with banners in black, the color of mourning, and red, the color of struggle, the color of the banner flying high on Hossein's mausoleum in Karbala. Before being dispatched to the battlegrounds, the Kermanis were taken to the holy city of Qom. This would be a religious army. The soldiers had to pray, to be devout, and to commemorate Ashura before being sent off to fight in its name. On November 3 (the sixth day of Muharram) the two battalions left Kerman for Qom by train. After a brief pilgrimage to the mausoleum of Masoomeh, a daughter of the Seventh Shia Imam, in Qom, they went straight to Ahvaz the day after.

One of the Hormozgani fighters remembers a moving scene in Ahvaz on November 4. Muharram commemorations were being held in Conex boxes at the barracks. First developed during the American wars in Korea and Vietnam as transport containers, Conex boxes were now used as standard mobile accommodation for the Iranian war effort. These

Conex mourners were fellow Shia but they were also Iraqi citizens.[11] These Iraqis had fled to Iran in the early months of the revolution and had pledged to fight Saddam by enlisting in the armies of Iran. The Iranians could now see something that they had heard about only in propaganda before. Here were Iraqis ready to join hands with Iranians and fight against the armed forces of their own country. The commonality became clearer when the mourning started. The Kermanis joined the Iraqis as they bared their chests and beat them in the nocturnal mournings for Hossein. The chants and ballads were in a mix of Arabic and Persian:

> Oh, you, Hossein, the banner-bearer! My loyal banner-bearer!
> Oh, Commander! Oh, beloved!

Even though this was an Iranian base in the Iranian territory, the Iraqis were playing host. For dinner, they had prepared a large communal plate of rice and chicken. The Iranian soldiers ate with their hands, just as Iraqi custom had it.

Soleimani had more pressing things to do. For the first time, he went to the Golf Station Barracks to discuss strategy with the legendary young men of the IRGC: Rezayi, Shamkhani, Bagheri. He also went to Soosangerd for operational preparations. Just as his men were mourning a battle in 680, the battalion commander had to prepare for the one that was only days ahead.

* * *

> The one who seeks me will know me;
> And the one who knows me will find me;
> And the one who finds me will love me;
> And the one who loves me, I will love;
> And if I love someone, I will kill them;
> For I myself am blood money.

A contemporary Western audience might find these lines somewhat tacky. But for those well versed in the lyrical traditions of the Middle

East, they were not only familiar but powerfully moving. Their putative author was no other than God Himself. This wasn't part of the holy Quran but a Qudsi Hadith or a so-called Sacred Tradition: words of God, recited by the Prophet. On November 27, 1981, it was Qassem Soleimani who recited them to an audience of hundreds. The Hadith lacks authenticity but it was fit for purpose that night.[12]

Standing on a podium in a base in Soosangerd, Soleimani faced more than 400 soldiers whom he was about to lead into battle. He knew his audience, almost to a man. The vast majority of them were Kermanis, many of them from his tribal areas of the province. His brother Sohrab and his cousin Ahmad were in the crowd, as were the comrades he had made in the previous operations.

In his short time in the force, Soleimani had already shown his physical prowess, his leadership ambition, his military talent, and his capacity for discipline. It was now time to prove that he had the other elements necessary for an IRGC leader: the rhetorical, the religious, the ideological.

The young commander spoke of love and God in his first real speech. He had had little political training but there was something in the Islamism pushed by the IRGC that put him at an advantage. Just like Soleimani, many of the IRGC founders had been no intellectuals, especially when compared to the seasoned Marxists of the opposition or the PMOI cadres with their sophisticated (if warped) version of left-Islamism. As the IRGC gradually developed its ideology, it established one key element: the religious folkloric tradition that every Shia boy or girl would instantly recognize, without any need for formalized education. You didn't need to be educated to know the stories of Imam Hossein; of his brother Abbas, who got his hand cut off on the day of Ashura; or of his sister Zeynab, known for her fiery post-Ashura pursuit of her brother's blood. Using these Shia traditions, the IRGC and its ideologues developed an aura of mysticism that connected to something deep in Shia mythology. The typical IRGC fighter was portrayed as a mystically endowed devout warrior, in love with God and Shia Imams, going to the front while enthusiastically welcoming martyrdom.

These ideas amounted to more than just the vague notions of a few. Backed by the might of state power and finding a ready audience in Iran's mobilized society, they were carried to the millions by prayer leaders and their sermons in every town and village, by round-the-clock TV and radio programs, and by panegyrists whose soliloquy-like performances connected the quotidian events of the war to those of Shia history. TV clerics, war singers, and religious performers became celebrities in the post-revolutionary society.

With his soulful eyes, mystical charisma, and quiet determination, Soleimani fit the profile of the new IRGC man. He didn't have much education but he was smart enough to quickly master the rhetoric that had attracted so many to the front. From then on, to the very end of his life, he excelled at mixing this rhetoric with his military elan and comradely treatment of soldiers to build a brand that was both at home in the IRGC and unique in its own way.

The words of God asking for love and death were central to Soleimani's first speech; they would remain central to his rhetoric to his last day. The speech had started with another string of godly words: verses from a chapter of the Quran entitled "Victory." This was the very last chapter of the Quran revealed to the Prophet, a few months before his death and after his miraculously bloodless conquest of Mecca. The verses promise the Muslims that Allah will help grant them victory and that they will "see people entering Allah's religion in droves."

Thus Soleimani gave hope to the soldiers while also initiating them into the world of martyrdom. "I salute all your faces, full of lights," he said. "God has picked you from among his lovers. The lover and the beloved will reach one another soon. Martyrdom is a wish in all of our hearts. All lovers know that the ultimate path to their beloved is martyrdom. Not just anybody can have such a honor. But I can see the color of martyrdom in your faces."[13]

He continued with stories all tinged with the same themes of love and death but also hope and glory. He spoke of a dream in which Khomeini had promised that this operation would have few martyrs. He spoke of Khomeini once borrowing a gun from his night bodyguard, only to hold it while crying on the rooftop, praying to God and asking for help for the fighters: "Beware, my dears! Our leader has sent you off with his very own prayers!"

And, of course, there was talk of Karbala. It was still the month of Muharram after all and the general name of the Iranian battle plans was

"Karbala." "We will continue our Karbala operations, until we can reach Hossein's Karbala," Soleimani thundered. "We will not leave our Imam alone like they left Imam Hossein alone. You will be victorious not with AK-47s, artillery, tanks, or projectiles, but with the cry of your *Allah-u-Akbar* [God is Great]! You will see the enemy either flee or surrender when faced with your mighty roar."

He ended the speech with another verse from the Quran: "Our Lord! Shower us with patience, and set our feet firm, and grant us victory over this unbelieving people." It is unlikely that Soleimani or many of his crowd knew the provenance of this Quranic verse. In the verse, God was speaking to the Israelites, led by the Prophet David, as they were fighting Goliath, a Philistine giant. Soleimani was leading the Davids against the Goliath.

* * *

Operation Path to Jerusalem started on November 29, at half past midnight. The Kermani battalions had walked kilometers in the dead of night. They had had to pass the dangerously mined fields of Meyshan under the torrential rain that muddied the ground. Their attack was swift, and they were initially able to drive the enemy back from its positions before coming under massive fire from the Iraqi tanks and shells.

Qassem Soleimani was in his Soviet-made BMP infantry fighting vehicle, personally leading the two battalions into action via walkie-talkie commands. He was not the only Soleimani on that front. Sohrab Soleimani, the commander's brother, was there, as was their cousin Ahmad. Ahmad Soleimani sustained a serious injury to his leg in the very first hours of the battle. He asked the others to continue rushing on, as he held on to his injured leg. Many fared much worse. An Ahvazi battalion volunteered for a harrowing course of action that the IRGC had used habitually: deliberately "clearing" the mined fields by sending human waves to walk over them. It was a mass suicide attack in all but name. The Kermanis remember passing the "cleared" fields, now disturbingly splattered with the remains of their Ahvazi comrades.

When the offensive failed to break the Iraqi lines, Soleimani ordered the reluctant BMP driver to advance. A bulldozer was ahead of them, opening the path ahead; but the mud and the dark of the night didn't let the vehicle go beyond a certain point. They had to get out.

Now on foot, Soleimani continued to lead his forces with incessant commands until a massive explosion shut off all voices. One of the soldiers from the BMP was thrown back into the vehicle. The other was found in a ditch, having lost a leg in the explosion. Soleimani was initially nowhere to be found. A projectile had hit him hard in his arm and his stomach but he had got up and continued to walk despite his severe bleeding. When Hamid the Guerrilla came upon him, Soleimani had to turn down his request to join their squad. By dawn, Soleimani had lost consciousness and was taken to a field hospital in a nearby village. He had suffered further injuries to his arms and legs.

"I thought I was dreaming," he remembered years later jokingly. "I was feeling good. I used to be so strong!"

Soleimani was taken to Ahvaz's Naderi Hospital. Brimming with the war wounded, who had filled all the rooms and corridors, and even the courtyard, the hospital was more like a waiting room for death. Having badly damaged lungs and liver, Soleimani would have died if he had stayed there much longer. But some men from his battalions recognized their commander and took him to a better-equipped hospital in the city, run by the oil company. He jumped the queue for an operation. The commander got another lease on life and was sent almost 2,000 kilometers away to Mashhad to recuperate.

Back on the front, the Kermanis pushed on. Hamid the Guerrilla was one of the many who sustained serious injuries. By the time the battle finished, more than 300 of the 400 Kermanis were either seriously injured or dead. But the Iranians were able to achieve their basic goals. They crossed the bridge over the Sabele River which connected Soosangerd to Bostan. They liberated 650 square kilometers of Iranian territory, including Bostan, five border terminals, seventy villages, and the Gorge of Chazabe. The Iraqi Third Corps, consisting of six divisions, had suffered a shattering defeat at the hands of the Iranians. In Tehran, Ayatollah Khomeini praised the victory of Operation Path to Jerusalem.

By the time victory was achieved on December 3, Soleimani was lying on a bed in Mashhad's Qaem Hospital.[14] He had endured life-threatening injuries merely hours after starting out as a battalion commander. His military career had almost finished before it began. Not for the last time, Soleimani survived to fight another day.

In just a few weeks, as soon as he had recuperated, Soleimani headed to the front. He had made up his mind. He chose to lead this life and the battlefront was where he wanted to be. After visiting some of the Kermanis on the fronts near Abadan, he went straight to Ahvaz's Golf Station Barracks to meet Hassan Bagheri. The two men were almost exactly the same age, both about to turn twenty-six (Bagheri was a Pisces, Soleimani on the Pisces-Aries cusp). But he had already awed many with his military genius and his larger-than-life character despite his small physique. The old army hands were impressed by how the young IRGC man had emerged as a serious war tactician. Bagheri surrounded himself with maps of the front, plastered over all the walls at the Golf Station. His time in the IRGC's secretive intelligence department had given him the tools to infiltrate the Iraqi side and boast an impressive knowledge of their movements.

Like many of the Revolutionary Guards, Soleimani looked up to Bagheri. He would subsequently eulogize him as the "Khomeini of the War Effort." Years later, he would remember their meeting in January 1982, a meeting that determined the course of Soleimani's life.

"I told Hassan I wanted to remain at the front and didn't want to go back to Kerman," Soleimani recalled. "'What do you want to do?' he asked. 'It doesn't matter. I will do anything I can,' I said. He sent me to the front at Shush to serve as a deputy commander of forces there."[15]

Bagheri liked this ambitious tribal Kermani. Soleimani's courage and determination impressed him. Others noted this with envy and complained. Wasn't Bagheri trusting this upstart a little too much? As is often the case with relationships in war, Bagheri trusted his own guts more than the words of others.

At Shush, Soleimani didn't disappoint. The city was besieged by Iraqis and Iranians were dying defending it every day. Three previous front commanders had been killed. Like many before him, Bagheri was impressed by Soleimani's discipline. The Iranian forces now methodically repelled the mechanized and air attacks of the Iraqis. Bagheri told a friend: "Your comrade [Soleimani] is a true lion of a man. What we talk about in our training, he actually practices on the ground. Look what he's done in Shush."

The success at Shush led Bagheri to present Soleimani with a bigger demand. He had a good rapport with the Kermanis but they were always dispersed after every operation. Would he like to form an independent IRGC brigade, made up primarily of Kermanis and led by himself? Once more, Soleimani had received an early promotion. He was now the head of a brigade that was to organize not hundreds but a few thousand men.

Although Soleimani hadn't known it before, Bagheri and others were planning a major offensive operation. There was little time to celebrate and Soleimani had to mobilize. He went back to Kerman and called for a meeting in the Quds Barracks on January 25, 1982.[16] Not all Kermanis were in favor of forming the brigade. A good many disagreed. Should they send all IRGC forces to the front? Shouldn't they be busy fighting the Sunni opposition in Balochistan on the Pakistani border? But the opponents were in the minority. Even though it didn't have a name yet, the Kermani brigade was born on that day.

Soleimani got to work immediately. He didn't wait for orders from Tehran. If the Kermanis were going to fight, they needed to find their own resources. A house belonging to Soleimani's father-in-law was turned into a base for gathering donations. A pro-IRGC schoolteacher was asked to find "cars, money, and supply." He took Soleimani to see Kerman's provincial governor. The only cars the governor had at his disposal were two jeeps. He gladly turned both over to the new brigade.

Soleimani left for the front at once. Bagheri wanted to give him instructions for the battle that lay ahead. Joined by two other commanders, Soleimani and Bagheri got into the latter's brown Toyota, which he had confiscated from deserting Iraqis. They drove more than 130 kilometers northeast from Ahvaz on a very difficult minor road, away from the Iraqi forces who controlled the main route. On the top of Dalpari Heights, in Ilam province, Bagheri showed Soleimani the expansive field which he had to take back from the Iraqis. Moving back and forth between Kerman and Ahvaz, Soleimani mobilized his forces and got them ready for battle.

They now needed a name. Due to its high rate of casualties, the Shush front had been called Sarallah, or Blood of Allah, a nickname for Imam

Hossein. Soleimani picked the same name for the brigade. The Kermanis were now organized into the Blood of Allah 41 Brigade. Why the number 41? "They gave it to us, I don't remember why," Soleimani said years later. There wasn't a lot of time to waste on formalities. The operation had to begin soon.

Operation Manifest Victory finally began on March 22, 1982. It was one day after Nowrooz, the Persian New Year, usually a time of celebration and family gatherings for Iranians. The soldiers had spent the previous day marching for twelve hours to get to their positions, and now waited on the final attack order. It finally came from the IRGC's top commander, Mohsen Rezayi: "In the name of God, the compassionate, the merciful." The operation started in the name of Allah and Fatima, the daughter of the Prophet Mohammad and wife of Ali, the holiest woman to the Shia.

In its first test in battle, the Blood of Allah Brigade fought hard and long. Once more, Soleimani was a hands-on commander, moving on the front and supervising as many squads as he could. On March 28, he led a battalion toward the Abu Gharib Gorge on the border. It was going to be a difficult fight. The battalion had had 300 fighters a few days ago. It had now been reduced to about a hundred, with the rest either killed or injured. Soleimani devised a trick. They gathered cars, without any fighters in them, and started a massive caravan toward the Iraqi positions. It worked. The Iraqis fled and the Iranians marched into the border village of Abu Gharib. This looked like Manifest Victory indeed. The Iranians were singing of happiness as they could now see Iraqi territory with the naked eye. But a massive explosion rocked Soleimani's station wagon when it drove over a mine. Another injury for the hands-on commander.

Soleimani was thrown out of his car, his face badly burnt, and shrapnel from shells filled his body. He was luckier than the man next to him who immediately lost half of a leg. When an ambulance came, it also exploded on a mine and all its passengers died at once. Soleimani and his comrades were taken to the nearby Dezful Hospital. But they went back to the front in only a few hours. The injuries faded next to the major news of the day: the absolute success of Operation Manifest Victory. Just a week before, the Iraqis had besieged major Iranian cities in the area: Shush, Andimeshk, Dezful. They had now been driven back to their own borders. Iraq now controlled much smaller pockets of Iranian territory, most importantly the city of Khorramshahr.

In an interview in 1990, after the war had ended, Soleimani called Manifest Victory the best operation of his life. "We had been given our own brigade," he said, "and despite the lack of weapons, we, the militants of Islam, had been able to take 3,000 Iraqis prisoner."[17]

* * *

The news of Kermani valor on the battlefront buoyed the youth of the province. They took pride in their fellow Kermanis who had helped free Iranian territory. Blood of Allah grew to be one of the largest IRGC brigades. The story of those early operations became canonized, as tales of heroism were used to build up the aura around Soleimani. Reminiscing in 2012, he wrote: "Operation Path to Jerusalem was a holy field from which the Blood of Allah Brigade bloomed. Our brigade was a blessed child which became a Mecca of ambitions for all fighters; the Bright Star which had once shined in the form of Hossein, now shined in the form of the holy ranks of the Blood of Allah Brigade. The star of Kerman shined bright in Imam Khomeini's skies."

Soleimani's confidence grew with the size of his brigade and with the successive Iranian victories. The Iraqis seemed to have little defense when faced with the human waves of armies with revolutionary zeal, not least because these armies were fighting in the occupied territories of their own country. In the spring of 1982, Iran's Operation Beit-ol-Moqaddas (once more using a name for Jerusalem) achieved its biggest feat yet: On May 24, it liberated the major city of Khorramshahr. The city had fallen to the Iraqis in early days of the war (October 25, 1980) following thirty-four days of heroic resistance which gave it the nickname City of Blood and made it a symbol of Iranians' defense of their territory. Brutal and tumultuous domestic politics aside, this was a moment of national jubilation for Iranians. In less than two years after Saddam's initial attack, the Iraqis had been almost entirely driven out of Iranian territory.

The victory hadn't come at an easy price. The "human wave" tactic meant that thousands had died. They included some of Soleimani's closest comrades. Hamid the Guerrilla fell on April 30 when leading an audacious grenade-throwing march on Iraqi positions. In his will, he warned against "the superpowers of the West and the East" and "the impending Second Camp David in which some undeserving Arab rulers wish to hand Jerusalem to Mr. Begin [the Israeli prime minister] on a plate." Another Kermani casualty was Naser Fooladi, in charge of the brigade's propaganda department. He was killed on the very day of the liberation, hours after finishing the historic "Salute Khorramshahr" banner which hung on Khorramshahr's grand mosque and became a historical icon of liberation, with its big red block letters handwritten by Fooladi himself.[18]

After all this sacrifice, many Iranians were ready to end the war. Even a strongly anti-imperialist force such as the Tudeh Party advocated an end to the war. On the other side, Saddam had his back against the wall and was also looking for a way to end the costly conflict. But then, less than two weeks after the liberation of Khorramshahr, another factor came into play.

On June 3, an external PLO faction made an unsuccessful attempt on the life of Israel's ambassador to UK, Shlomo Argov. Only three days later, the Israelis responded with an unprecedented, full-on invasion of southern Lebanon. Menachem Begin had won the Nobel Peace Prize less than four years before. He now launched what was arguably Israel's first war of aggression. It later became clear that the attempted assassination of Argov had not been approved by Yasser Arafat and the rest of the PLO's Beirut-based leadership. Instead, it was Saddam Hussein and his embassy in London that had helped organize the attack in the hope of bringing about the precise course of action that followed: an Israeli attack on PLO bases in Lebanon that could divert the attention of all Iraq's major foes: Iran, Syria, and Israel.

Days after the Israeli invasion, Saddam withdrew his forces from Iran and declared a unilateral ceasefire. He gave the Iranians an offer he must have thought they couldn't refuse: Since they were both anti-Zionists, wouldn't it be better if they joined forces to go to the aid of the Palestinians, Lebanon, and Syria? Arafat supported this request. Before decisively taking the Iraqi side in the war with Iran, the PLO leader had repeatedly tried to mediate between the two countries, in his own capacity and as part of a delegation sent by the Organization of Islamic Conference.

The Islamic Republic thus faced a crucial hour of decision. Should they accept the ceasefire and unite with their fellow Muslims against Israel? A High Defense Council meeting on June 17 debated the matter. Khomeini had his doubts but the young men of the IRGC were drunk with temptations of conquest. They were only a few kilometers away from the holiest cities to the Shia faith; they dreamed of conquering Karbala, of praying in Najaf. They told their Imam that now was not the time to retreat. The key Shia port of Basra in southern Iraq is only 35 kilometers away from Khorramshahr as the crow flies. You can stand in Iran and watch the lights of Basra's oil fields blink. Mohsen Rezayi insisted to Khomeini that the IRGC could conquer Basra within weeks. A fellow IRGC man, Yahya Rahim Safavi, claimed that his reading of Islamic tradition proved that all signs pointed to swift Iranian victories and the coming of the Hidden Imam, the messianic figure promised in the Shia faith. "I glean this from the book *The Day of Emancipation*," Safavi said, "which is an antique work, translated by a Sunni named Kamel Soleiman, but based on the sayings of our holy Imams." A thirty-year-old soldier giving messianic lectures to one of the highest religious authorities in the Shia world should have raised an eyebrow or two. However, nobody checked the facts properly to point out that *The Day of Emancipation* was not an old book but a recently written pamphlet authored (not translated) by Soleiman, an obscure Lebanese Shia (not Sunni) writer.

But the young men of the IRGC weren't alone in pushing for war. All the major military and political leaders of the Islamic Republic supported them. The revolutionary Imam was convinced. Iran was not for turning.

Tehran simply said "no" to all peace proposals. Just as the Iraqis had hoped the Arabs of Khorramshahr would come to their aid, Iran now banked on the Shia of Basra as its natural allies. Khomeini called on the "valiant people of Basra": "Welcome your devout brothers and cut off the tyrannical hands of infidel Aflaqites [followers of Michel Aflaq, the founder of the Baath Party] from your land."[19]

The gamble didn't work. Khomeini would later privately admit his message had been a folly.[20] Iran's four previous operations had scored some of the biggest military victories in its history. It would now embark on defeat after defeat. In six more years of war, it would never come close to conquering Basra, let alone Karbala or Baghdad. On July 12, 1982, the UN Security Council unanimously passed a resolution calling for a ceasefire and peace talks. Iraq accepted it but Iran didn't. It launched its failed Operation Ramadan (to take Basra) the very next day.

Iran appeared to have further isolated itself. Days after the decision for war was made, the US *and* the USSR would come to the aid of Baghdad, worried that a revolutionary Iran might become too powerful if it overthrew Saddam. Washington removed Baghdad from its list of state sponsors of terrorism and Moscow increased its arms sales to Iraq. Later in the year, Soviet leader Leonid Brezhnev died and was succeeded by Yuri Andropov, who took a much more straightforward pro-Iraq position. Furthermore, Saddam and Arafat now seemed ready to welcome Egypt, under President Hosni Mubarak, back into the fold of the Arab League. All seemed to be going against Iran.

To justify the fact that it was waging war on a fellow Muslim non-aligned country and not the Zionist enemy, Tehran came up with an ingenious slogan: "The path to Jerusalem passes through Karbala." The armies of Iran were to liberate the Shia shrine of Imam Hossein before heading west to face off Israel. The radical-sounding slogan notwithstanding, Tehran's decision was a relief for Tel Aviv, which continued to be a de facto partner of the Islamic Republic in its anti-Saddam war. It was the Israelis, after all, who had attacked Saddam's Osirak nuclear reactor on June 1981, dashing Baghdad's nuclear dreams. Before the end of the war, Israel would increase its military help to the militantly anti-Zionist Islamic Republic of Iran.

Meanwhile, in southern Lebanon, the Israeli invasion was welcomed by many of the local Shia. The PLO and its allies in the Lebanese civil war had tormented the Shia of the south for years. Hassan Nasrallah, who was a 21-year-old cleric then, remembers how "some of the Shia believed that only the Zionist regime could save them from the Palestinian tyranny. In some regions, the Shia went to welcome the Zionist tanks and throw flowers and rice at them."[21]

Could Israel hope that the Iranian and Lebanese Shia, oppressed and marginalized as they were in the broader Arab world, would become its de facto allies? Some Israeli strategists had such too-clever-by-half schemes; they could hardly have been more wrong. Iran had different ideas. It would soon reveal how serious it was about its anti-Zionist commitments. In an action initially not approved by Khomeini, Rezayi and a group of IRGC leaders went to Syria and Lebanon to plan for the long haul of their anti-Zionist dreams.

Soleimani was too small a player to have a role in the two crucial decisions taken in Tehran in June 1982: to continue the war against Iraq; and to establish a serious IRGC presence in the Levant, right on the Israeli border. But both of these decisions would come to shape his life.

Chapter 6

No Islamism in One Country

As the Israeli tanks rolled into southern Lebanon, Mohammad Hussein Fadlallah was attending a conference in Tehran,[1] far from his home in Beirut. The 46-year-old Shia cleric was young and inexperienced by the standards of the Shia clergy but he led the Lebanese delegation. Next to him sat four fellow Lebanese clerics who were soon to help give birth to an unpredictable new force in Middle Eastern politics.

The Tehran conference was organized by the IRGC's shadowy Liberation Movements Unit (LMU), headed by the energetic, chain-smoking Iranian cleric Mehdi Hashemi.[2] The summit meant to commemorate the newly created Day of the Global Dispossessed, which, Hashemi had decided, was to be held on the birthday of the Twelfth Imam, a descendant of the Prophet Mohammad who, according to the Shia doctrine, had gone into occultation in 941, only to return at the end of times when, arms locked with Jesus Christ, he'd raise a global messianic army and defeat the forces of evil once and for all. Belief in a messianic end of times is mainstream to the Shia, as it is to many other faiths, inside and outside Islam. But for most of their history, believers in the Messiah were content to passively wait for Him to arrive. The exceptions mostly lay outside Shia Islam: Muhammad Ahmad, the Sunni Nubian leader who raised a Mahdist army in the mid-1880s to drive the British out of Sudan; or the Zionists who had decided to not wait around for the Messiah but take back their Promised Land by force. The swift victory of the Iranian revolution gave hope to many who wanted to defeat evil in honor of the Hidden Imam, even if he hadn't shown his face yet. The global army of the revolution had to be raised right here and now.

As in all revolutions, the Iranians needed to debate the delicate issue of whether and how to export their movement beyond their borders. The Islamist-dominated assembly that wrote the new regime's constitution saw many heated debates about the exact wording of its global promises. If Iran was to be a beacon of global revolution, would it help only the Muslims or also non-believers? How would it reconcile the ideals of national independence with promotion of the revolution? How would it distinguish itself from the communists in the midst of the Cold War?

In the end, the text of the new constitution managed both to promise a global effort and to do so in a newly minted language sharply distinct from that of the secular left. The Iranian revolution, it said, had been the victory of "all the Dispossessed [*Mostazafin*] against the Arrogant [*Mostakberin*]," using Arabic neologisms that would have meant little to most people. The constitution was thus tasked with "preparing the conditions to continue the revolution inside and outside the country" and "help free the deprived and oppressed nations of the world." The armed forces were specifically asked not to remain limited to "safeguarding the borders" but to "do their duty which is Jihad in the path of God and struggle to expand the rule of God around the world." The constitution was being written as the fifteenth century in the Islamic calendar was set to begin, marking 1,400 years since the day the Prophet Mohammad moved from Mecca to Medina to found a new community. The new century, the constitution hoped, was to be "the century for the global government of the Dispossessed and the defeat of all the Arrogant."

Words on paper didn't settle the internationalism question in the real world. Mehdi Bazargan and his fellow Muslim modernizers wanted the very opposite of exporting the revolution. If their unstable republic was to have any chance of survival, they argued, it had to reassure powers of the region such as Saudi Arabia that it wanted to be a good neighbor and had no intention of provoking their Shia minorities. "The revolution isn't a bag of beans or chickpeas you can export," Bazargan quipped. He also was adamant that Iran should keep peace with the Americans, whose non-intervention had helped secure the downfall of the Shah. The struggle that ensued over the occupation of the US embassy in November 1979 had settled the latter question. Bazargan's government resigned and, before long, his LMI would be completely purged from the political scene.

At the opposite end of the spectrum stood Hashemi and his brother-in-law Mohammad Montazeri. As the copious SAVAK files on him show, the 35-year-old Montazeri had spent all of his life on ceaseless promotion of a global Islamic revolution. Moving far and wide across the Middle East and south Asia, he wanted to wage struggle not only in the countries of the region but in places as far-flung as the Philippines, where he backed an Islamist insurgency. With the revolution now victorious, Montazeri and Hashemi were intent on making sure the promises of the constitution would not remain mere words on paper.

What divided the Iranians wasn't just the question of whether to export the revolution. In the long years of oppositional activity abroad, and with the tumultuous world of Arab radical politics in the background, the Iranian Islamists had been divided among themselves. Many of these divisions harked back to Lebanon, itself marred in a multi-sided civil war since 1975. In the revolt-filled decades of the 1960s and 1970s, Beirut had been a hotspot. Just a year before his death in 1970, Egypt's President Nasser had worked out a pact between the PLO and the Lebanese government which allowed the former to have more or less free rein over its training camps on Lebanese territory. Yasser Arafat and comrades were in charge not only of the 300,000 Palestinians in Lebanon but of throngs of activists from around the world who went there to get armed training and, if they were lucky, see active combat, supported by Arafat's state-within-a-state.

Dozens of Iranians from all ranges of politics came to the PLO camps but this wasn't the only axis of connection between Tehran and Beirut. The gorgeous port on the Mediterranean had long attracted Iranians of all hues. Those in search of modern secular education went to the excellent American University, best in the region. But Beirut fever wasn't limited to them. As a young newlywed in the 1930s, Ayatollah Khomeini himself had visited Beirut on his way to Mecca, writing of its beauties to his beloved wife at home: "I am now in the beautiful city of Beirut. I truly miss you. How lovely it is to see this city and to look at the sea. Alas, my dear beloved is not with me so that we can enjoy it together."

Another Iranian cleric was to have a more lasting journey to Lebanon. Just as Khomeini and others were shaking up the quietist clergy in the Iran of the 1950s and 1960s, Musa Sadr, a pioneering cleric-intellectual, was collaborating with his first cousin Mohammad Baqir al-Sadr in Najaf. The cosmopolitan world of Shia clergy meant that the clerics moved easily across national borders. The Shia of southern Lebanon, in the Jabal Amil area, prided themselves on being the first Shia community in history, supposedly founded in the early days of Islam by Abudhar, a companion of the Prophet Mohammad who had backed Ali and was thus seen as a proto-Shia. When Iran adopted the Shia faith in the early sixteenth century, it imported clerics from Jabal Amil. In 1959, the Lebanese Shia wanted the favor returned. As they struggled to find their place in the sectarian order of the Lebanese state, they asked Musa Sadr to be sent to Lebanon to lead them.[3] Thus took place one of the most successful transnational transplantations of a political figure in modern history. Sadr, who spoke Arabic with a thick Persian accent to the end of his days, went to Lebanon, received Lebanese citizenship, and helped found Amal—Arabic for "hope" and also an acronym for "Lebanese Resistance Regiments"—a political party for the Lebanese Shia. The Iranian cleric emerged not only as a key leader in Lebanese politics but as an international interfaith figure whose many world trips included a 1967 meeting with the Pope in the Vatican in the aftermath of the Six Day War.

Although he was now known to the world as Lebanese, Sadr carried much Iranian baggage to his new home. He kept his links with the Iranian opposition, even while asking the Shah to do his duty as the world's only Shia head of state by helping to fund social projects for the Lebanese Shia. It didn't hurt that Iran's ambassador to Lebanon was related to Sadr's wife. But the two-way relationship was not to be tolerated by either side. That Sadr's loyalties lay strongly with the opposition became clear in June 1977.

When Ali Shariati passed away in Southampton, his comrades pressured the British authorities to have his body sent to Damascus. The

Shah had tried to coopt Shariati as an Islamist who could neutralize the communist threat, like Anwar Sadat was doing with the Muslim Brotherhood in Egypt. He now wanted him buried in Iran in a state ceremony. Sadr, using his extensive international connections, helped foil the plans of Tehran.[4] The insurgent intellectual could now be buried next to one of his top historical heroes: Zeynab bint Ali, sister of Imam Hossein, immortalized by her powerful oration at the court of the caliph Yazid in the aftermath of Karbala. Sadr officiated at the burial in Zeynab's Damascene shrine and held a rowdy memorial for him in Beirut shortly after.

The first row at the memorial was occupied by Shariati's wife and children and a close comrade of his, Mostafa Chamran. Chamran was a non-clerical counterpart of Sadr, another seamless Iran-to-Lebanon transplantation. After he got his PhD in electrical engineering and plasma physics from Berkeley in 1963, Chamran secured a teaching position and could have lived a comfortable life in the US. Instead, together with his friend and fellow US-based professor Ebrahim Yazdi, Chamran eschewed that life and spent much of his years between the revolutionary camps of the Middle East. They first went to Egypt, where they got funding and arms from Nasser before clashing with the pan-Arab leader over his anti-Persian tendencies. They then ended up in Lebanon, the land of itinerant revolutionaries. But Lebanon wasn't simply a stop for Chamran. He planted roots there, seriously developed his military skills, and became a key comrade of Sadr and a leading light in his political party, Amal. Chamran's American wife couldn't bear the tough life between California and Jabal Amil and left him. Soon after, the Iranian physicist married Ghada, a Lebanese Shia introduced to him by Sadr. He became further anchored in his new home.

If Chamran had sat next to Sadr at the historic June 1977 memorial in Beirut, Mohammad Montazeri had to sit a few rows back. More importantly, Montazeri had failed to give a prominent place to Khomeini in the memorial. He had wanted to place a massive picture of the Ayatollah above the podium but Sadr intervened and only a small image was allowed.[5] Like most political exiles, the Iranians in Lebanon were a rowdy bunch, as the incident suggests. The heady clashes between the PLO and Amal had also divided the Iranians. Chamran passionately hated the PLO and Arafat[6]—so much so that when the Palestinian leader came to Iran in 1979, the now powerful Chamran, soon to become defense minister, couldn't hide his anger. Montazeri and some other Iranians were on the other side. They resolutely backed the PLO and attacked Amal for not giving enough support to the Palestinian cause.

Sadr's Rolodex of international contacts and his global profile provided a cause for envy. But Montazeri and his comrades had a patron with deeper pockets than anyone on the other side: Muammar Gaddafi, the young colonel who had come to power in oil-rich Libya in 1969 to add exciting new dynamics to the turbulence of the Arab revolution. The flamboyant Brotherly Leader and Guide of the Revolution of Libya used his petro-dollars to give support to forces as diverse as the Iranian Montazeri, Maltese socialists, Filipino Muslim separatists, the infamous British Trotskyist Gerry Healy, the Black Panther Party in the US, Japanese communists, and Armenian radicals.

The bad blood between the two sides of Iranian Islamist internationalists reached a most dramatic high point in 1978. Excited with the rise of the anti-Shah movement in Iran, Sadr had reconciled with Khomeini and even helped organize a key interview for him with *Le Monde* that helped put the Ayatollah on the map. In August 1978, Sadr went to Libya by invitation from Gaddafi himself. He was never to be seen again. The Libyans claimed he had left the country for Italy. But all of Sadr's relatives and comrades were adamant that Tripoli was responsible for the imam's life.

Had Sadr lived, he would have been a serious counterweight to Khomeini, both in Iran and in the broader Shia and Muslim world.[7] The style and content of his politics could have hardly been more different than those of the Iranian Ayatollah. Khomeini wanted an Islamic government ruled by the clerical elite. Sadr believed in Lebanon's democratic character. Khomeini's success lay in his adamant intransigence against the Shah. Sadr had been able to maintain ties with both the Shah and his opponents for years. Sadr's acolytes were intellectuals and progressives of the LMI type. Khomeini's lieutenants were thuggish pro-Gaddafi clerics such as Montazeri. What would the future of the region have looked like had Sadr lived past the 1979 revolution? What would the regional civil war have looked like had Sadr butted heads with Khomeini and his brand of Shia Islamism?

That fateful trip in August 1978 is why we will never know the answer. Of the two Iranian clerics, one became the Supreme Leader and the Imam of Iran; the other became the Vanished Imam, one more romantic hero, lost in the annals of Middle Eastern history.

* * *

Following the 1979 revolution, Chamran and other Iranian comrades of Sadr clashed with Montazeri and other pro-PLO and pro-Gaddafi Iranians. They adamantly wanted Khomeini to distance himself from Gaddafi and call for an investigation into Sadr's whereabouts. Khomeini didn't have to go far to hear the complaints by Sadr's relatives: His own son, Ahmad, had married a niece of Sadr, Fateme Tabatabai. Fateme's brother, Sadeq, was among the closest non-clerical advisors to Khomeini in the early days of the revolution.

But Montazeri didn't want anything to delay his Islamic global revolution. He had hated Sadr and his bourgeois politics anyway. Not for nothing did some call him the "Trotsky of the Iranian revolution."[8] In contradistinction to Joseph Stalin, who wanted to build "socialism in one country," his rival, Leon Trotsky, had believed that the Russian revolution wouldn't survive unless it spread to other countries. Trotsky loved quoting Lenin, who had said that Moscow was only the temporary headquarters of the world revolution; the revolution had to take Berlin.

For Montazeri, too, taking Tehran was the beginning not the end. Days after the victory of the revolution, he organized a "Revolutionary Organization of Islamic Jamahiri Masses," the obscure term *jamahiri* being a Gaddafi neologism. Montazeri wasn't satisfied with helping this or that Iraqi Shia. He looked far beyond. Taking after his Libyan mentor, Montazeri wanted Iran to give arms and aid not only to Islamists but to Irish armed movements and Latin American leftists. He also wanted Gaddafi to visit Iran and for the countries to join hands in supporting his "Islamic internationalism."

The likes of Chamran and Sadr's relatives had enough power to block Montazeri in the early days of the revolution. Gaddafi never came to Iran and his prime minister, Abdessalam Jalloud, had to wait weeks before receiving an audience with Khomeini, when the Supreme Leader publicly asked him to help find Sadr. Montazeri was denounced by his own father as suffering from mental problems, and the authorities, worried about the consequences of his adventurist exploits, constantly blocked him. In June 1981, he was killed in a PMOI attack on the headquarters of the Islamic Republican Party. Just a week later, Chamran, Mohammad's bête noire of Lebanon days, also lost this life. He was killed fighting the Iraqi forces on the front.

The twin fathers of Iranian Islamist internationalism had very different approaches and very different allies. They were to be both lionized as martyrs by the Islamic Republic but the internationalism actually adopted by the nascent regime was neither Chamran's nor Montazeri's.

The LMU continued its work under Mehdi Hashemi. It was a perennial headache for the foreign ministry, whose conduct was stabilized under Ali Akbar Velayati, a patrician medical doctor with a degree from Johns Hopkins who became foreign minister in December 1981 and stayed in the position until 1997. The LMU's amateurish adventures included smuggling arms to Saudi Arabia by using pilgrims as carriers and an easily foiled attempt at organizing a coup in Bahrain, the small island nation of the Persian Gulf which has a Shia majority but a Sunni monarchy. Not only was the LMU kicked out of the IRGC but, before long, Hashemi would be tried and executed and his memory maligned in the official histories of the Islamic Republic. The regime's internationalism would not be in the mold of Sadr's progressive Islamic modernism; but nor would it be that of Montazeri's Gaddafi-like radicalism. It would be its own creature, the likes of which the world hadn't seen before.

* * *

Not all the Lebanese Shia cheered on the Israeli invasion of June 1982. A courageous few took up arms and fought against the invading army under the banner of Khomeini. The pro-Khomeini sentiment was no surprise to anyone who had been paying attention. A few months prior, in April 1982, the fourth congress of Amal had payed homage to Khomeini and one of its fiery leaders, cleric Husayn al-Musawi, promised that the Shia would march to Jerusalem if the Ayatollah ordered them to. But the Khomeinists still didn't control Amal. The party founded by Chamran and Imam Sadr was being torn apart by an internal conflict. Since April 1980, its leader had been Nabih Berri, a suit-wearing lawyer, born in Sierra Leone, who liked to work within the system and was a far cry from fiery clerics like Musawi.

Iran's immediate response to the Israeli invasion was to dispatch a number of experienced soldiers to Damascus. They arrived less than a week after the invasion but were humiliated when the Syrians sent them to a decrepit camp on the Lebanese border. Rifat Assad, the influential brother of the Syrian president, visited them and pointed out the cease-fire signed by Israel on the very day of the Iranians' arrival.[9] After more than two decades of turmoil and revolutions in the Arab world, the Syrian Baathists were now cynical rulers. They knew well the disruptive potential of an insurgency fueled by excited Iranians in their very back-yard and didn't wish to ruin Damascus's excellent ties with Amal. In turn, the Iranians were grateful for Assad's help in their war against Saddam and didn't want to rock the boat. The soldiers went back home in a few weeks. Iran instead sent hundreds of "cultural workers," mostly clerics, probably seen as harmless by all parties involved.

The strategists in Tel Aviv were jubilant. The new revolutionary Iran had refused Saddam's offer of teaming up against Israel; now Syria hadn't allowed it to use its territory to attack the Jewish State either. "We smiled and thought, oh well, one more revolutionary contender is out," an Israeli general remembers. "Their fervent fire will subside."[10]

The Israelis rejoiced too soon. The Islamic Republic was playing the long game. As outlined in the previous chapter, in its official slogans, the "path to Jerusalem" passed through the Iraqi battlegrounds; in other words the fight against Israel had to be delayed so that Saddam could be defeated first. In reality, Iran's long anti-Israel game passed through the internal quibbling of the Lebanese Shia, a demographic that the Jewish State had seldom worried about.

In June 1982, Mohammad Fadlallah wasn't alone in Tehran. He had with him a few young clerics who were to help him engineer a split in Amal and change Lebanese politics forever. There was Ragheb Harb, a thirty-year-old cleric from the small, pleasant village of Jibchit in southern Lebanon, which had also been the birthplace of Musawi. There was the Najaf-born Mehdi Shamseddine, who had worked with Musa Sadr. There was Subhi Tufayli, an enterprising 34-year-old cleric with a past in the Iraqi Dawa Party. They had their differences but they all agreed that Israel must be fought and Nabih Berri's conciliation wasn't the way forward.

Back in Lebanon, they discovered that the mood among the rank and file of Amal was turning in their favor. The brutal Israeli occupation was aided by the Maronite-dominated South Lebanon Army (SLA). The ugliest symbol of this collaboration shocked the world in September 1982: Under their defense minister, Ariel Sharon, the Israelis watched as the SLA militia massacred hundreds of Palestinians in the Sabra and Shatila refugee camps outside Beirut. This was a revenge attack on the Palestinians following the killing of the Maronite president-elect Bachir Gemayel a few days prior. What most of the reports then, and historical accounts since, have ignored are the many Shia who died in Sabra and Shatila as they had taken refuge there. With such actions, it didn't take long for the Shia to turn against Tel Aviv. As Ehud Barak was to later admit, the Israeli occupation managed to turn one of the least anti-Israeli communities in Lebanon into one of its most fervently anti-Zionist.

The Americans were anxious to lower Levantine tensions. Ronald Reagan sent an American diplomat of Lebanese origin, the legendary Philip Habib, as his personal envoy to Lebanon's President Elias Sarkis. Attempts were made to form a Committee of National Salvation, representing all communities of the country, to negotiate with the Israelis. Nabih Berri was delighted to represent his people, the Shia, on the committee. But the Iranians had different ideas. Iran's ambassador to Lebanon openly asked Berri to resign from the "American-Zionist Committee." Many of Amal's leaders, including its representative in Tehran, openly sided with the Iranians against Berri. The split in Amal was taking shape.

Ali Akbar Mohtashamipour, Iran's ambassador to Damascus, saw a golden opportunity. Prior to the revolution, Mohtashamipour had spent years in the Beqaa valley, a fertile area in eastern Lebanon, about 30 kilometers outside of Beirut. Located between Mount Lebanon and Anti-Lebanon mountains, the valley had been the site of many a PLO training camp. Mohtashamipour used to live in a beautiful little village called Yammoune, admired for its excellent cannabis and its associations with Phoenician mythology. The guerrilla-turned-diplomat now gathered the internal opposition of Amal in the same valley. There were three general groups: the self-declared "Islamic" faction of Amal led by Musawi; the Dawa Party people, led by Tufayli; and a group of Shia clerics, leaning toward Khomeini. The Iranians remembered that the IRGC had been put together by merging different armed groups. They wanted to do the same for the rowdy Lebanese Shia. There was an easy solution for arbitrating differences, agreed on by everybody: Tehran would decide on everything important. Three representatives from each group, a total of nine, were sent to Tehran. They met with their idol, Khomeini, and with other Iranian leaders.

Before the end of the year, a secret five-person committee, the Council of Lebanon, was formed to lead an organization which was usually called the "Islamic Movement" but was soon to be known as Hezbollah, the Party of God. The council consisted of Mohtashamipour; Ahmad Kanani, the IRGC's commander in Lebanon; Mosa Fakhr Rouhani, a cleric and Iran's ambassador to Lebanon; Musawi; and another Lebanese named Mohammad Raad. Debates over the degree of Iranian sponsorship of Hezbollah sometimes fail, shockingly, to mention this fact: A majority of the party's body of leadership consisted of Iranian officials and its composition had been decided upon in Tehran, not Beirut. There was no question about who was calling the shots. According to Hassan Nasrallah, then a young founding member of Hezbollah and now its secretary-general, "all the management work was done by the IRGC." Hossein Dehqan, the IRGC's man in Lebanon, later boasted about having written every line of the by-laws of Hezbollah. The "cultural workers" sent by Iran turned out to be effective political organizers who soon built up the new organization into a formidable force.

Hezbollah transformed the social, political, and cultural face of Lebanon, starting with the Beqaa valley. Women donned Iraqi- and Iranian-style long black chadors, previously unseen in the region. Bars were forced to go non-alcoholic or close. More consequentially, a campaign of terror raged against the main political home of the Shia at the time, the Lebanese Communist Party. Anti-communists of the world had long known the communist-killing talents of Islamists. The Islamists had long had an inferiority complex toward Marxists and a chip on their shoulder against them. Hezbollah didn't disappoint. It killed dozens, if not hundreds of Communist Party members.

It didn't take long for the world to notice the new Shia force. The conditions of Lebanon offered a perfect setting: the lack of a central state amid a civil war, and the presence of the Israeli occupying enemy and international forces sent there by the UN to observe a ceasefire. Hezbollah took on the use of suicide bombings, soon to be employed by forces as diverse as the Tamil Tigers in Sri Lanka and pro-Damascus militias in Lebanon. In April 1983, a Hezbollah suicide bomber hit the US embassy in Beirut, killing sixty-three. This paled compared to the next attack: On October 23, two truck bombs organized by Hezbollah struck the Beirut barracks hosting American and French soldiers of the Multinational Force in Lebanon (MFL), an ad hoc peacekeeping force also including Italy and the UK. With the loss of only two suicide bombers, the Shia force that still didn't even have a public profile inflicted 305 casualties on the enemy: 241 American soldiers, 58 French, and a Lebanese janitor together with his wife and four children. Syria's defense minister, Mustafa Tlass, said that he made sure no Italian forces would be attacked—not due to usual diplomatic sensibilities but because he did not want "a single teardrop to fall from the eyes of [Italian actress] Gina Lollobrigida, whom I've loved ever since my youth."[11]

Sparing the tears of the dreamy Lollo didn't impress the Lebanese state, which broke off diplomatic relations with Tehran in November. This mattered little to the Iranians. Who wanted diplomatic relations with a quasi-state when you had a firm alliance with the Syrians (who still occupied much of Lebanon) and command of a force like Hezbollah? Not only were the Hezbollah attacks chilling and spectacular, they were politically effective. The MFL left Lebanon and the Israelis were ultimately driven back from Beirut in January 1985. They now occupied only 10 percent of the country's territory in the south.

Hezbollah's engagement in the signature action of Lebanon's civil war, the taking of Western hostages, also hugely benefited Iran. Tehran had isolated itself by trying to fight "both the West and the East" but it now had a powerful asymmetric, if ethically fraught, weapon against the

Americans. The government of Ronald Reagan would come to the negotiating table and sell the Iranians hundreds of millions of dollars' worth of weaponry, with the primary intention of having Hezbollah release American hostages. This process only came to an end when Mehdi Hashemi leaked it to a Lebanese newspaper, heavily embarrassing both sides about what became known as the Iran-Contra scandal. Hashemi paid for the leak with his life, as he was sent to the gallows in 1987 on an unrelated charge.

The Lebanese party also came to do Tehran's dirty work. It helped assassinate numerous foes of the Islamic Republic, from Qolamreza Oveysi (Tehran's last military governor under the Shah's regime) to two successive leaders of the Socialist International–affiliated Kurdish Democratic Party, Sadeq Sharafkandi and Abdulrahman Qassemlo. In these endeavors, Hezbollah utilized the impressive global reach of the Lebanese Shia, who, after all, hailed from the most diaspora-producing country in the world. From Dakar, Senegal, to Ciudad del Este, Paraguay, Iran now had an active Arab ally.

The Iranian cleric-diplomat who had done most to establish Hezbollah paid a heavy personal price. A letter bomb sent to Mohtashamipour in 1984 left him with many injuries and cost him a couple of fingers, but he had helped form a powerful fist for the Islamic Republic: The Party of God was here to stay.

* * *

The creation of Hezbollah, Iran's first serious experience in Islamist internationalism, was an unabashed success. It had helped create a powerful new ally in the Arab world—on Israel's doorstep, no less—which declared allegiance to the ideological foundations of the Tehran regime.

Is Hezbollah an independent Lebanese force or a proxy of the Islamic Republic of Iran? The question presents us with a false dichotomy. The party is clearly both. The leaders of Hezbollah, and much of its cadre, genuinely believe in the vanguard role of Iran and the doctrine of *Welayat al-Faqih*, according to which the Iranian Supreme Leader is not just the leader of Iran but the guardian of the devout. It was for the same reason that members of communist parties around the world saw the Soviet Union as a "Big Brother" they were prepared to support, whether or not they got the fabled "Moscow gold," whether or not they agreed with all its decisions. This is not to deny the importance of the massive material support that Iran has given Hezbollah, providing the vast majority of its funding. But it is to stress the symbiotic relationship between ideology and state sponsorship.

As with the Soviet support for communist parties, the Tehran-Hezbollah relationship can also come into conflict with Tehran's diplomatic state-to-state ties. In 1987, Syria killed dozens of Hezbollah operatives when it clashed with them in Beirut. Once more keen not to lose its only major Arab state ally, Tehran ordered Hezbollah to look the other way. In the very same year, when Syria refused to allow Iran to use its territory to aid Hezbollah (which was now locked into a ferocious battle with the Damascus-supported Amal), Iran used a backdoor: Through its links with Gaddafi, it sent its dispatches, aimed for Hezbollah, to the port of Khalde, which was then controlled by the Libyan ally Walid Jumblatt, the Druze leader of the Progressive Socialist Party. These two events, happening so close to each other in time, show that the strategists of the Islamic Republic attempt to balance the goals of their state with those of the global movement they support.

* * *

As the IRGC helped build the apparatus of Islamist internationalism for Tehran, Qassem Soleimani was mired in the battlegrounds of Iraq. Hopes for quick victories after the liberation of Khorramshahr were quickly dashed but Soleimani's star rose as his brigade played an increasingly large role. In the summer of 1983, Soleimani's Blood of Allah Brigade was turned into a division and in the next major operation, Operation Kheybar in February 1984, Soleimani teamed up with the legendary Ebrahim Hemmat, head of the Prophet Mohammad Division, to help achieve a strategic Iranian victory in the Battle of the Marshes by capturing Iraq's oil-rich Majnun Island. Hemmat was killed in battle as was Soleimani's main deputy, Seyyed Hamid Mirafzali. Soleimani's men also played a role in the next major Iranian victory, in February 1986, when Iraq's al-Faw peninsula finally fell to the Iranians in Operation Dawn VIII.

Islamist internationalism was also being deployed in the war in Iraq. Buoyed with the success of the Hezbollah experiment, the IRGC heads were quick to attempt to repeat it. Under an order from President Ali Khamenei, Mohsen Rezayi established the Ramadan Base in May 1983, a unit which was explicitly tasked with doing international and "irregular" work. Iraqi Shia revolutionaries, mostly members of Dawa, were organized into the newly formed Badr Division. They fought the armies of their own country under the banner of Iran, just as the PMOI had joined Saddam in Baghdad on the other side. An "Abudhar Brigade" was formed out of Afghan volunteers, headed by IRGC's Mohammadreza Hakim Javadi, an Iranian who had been training the pro-Khomeini Afghans from the early days of the revolution, in close collaboration with Abdolali Mazari, a Shia cleric of Afghanistan's Hazara minority and part of the country's anti-Soviet Islamist fight.

Soleimani was nowhere near any of these international operations. His war diaries show he was laser-focused on the affairs of the division he commanded, where he developed close ties with his soldiers. As the war dragged on, over many years, the soldiers developed a world of their own sensibilities on the muddy barricades: proud of their fallen comrades, bitter because the war had been prolonged, suspicious of politicians who might sell them out. But, like all wars, the Iran-Iraq War came to an end and the men of war now had to find a role for themselves in peacetime. The manner of the war's ending, and the character of the peace that followed, didn't make the transition easy for these proud, bitter, and suspicious veterans.

Mostafa Chamran poses with Ahmad Khomeini, son of Ayatollah Khomeini, the leader of the 1979 revolution and founder of the Islamic Republic. The photo was taken before 1979 when the two spent time in southern Lebanon. Many of the regime founders underwent armed training in the camps of the Palestine Liberation Organization or with Shia groups of southern Lebanon.

Mostafa Chamran eating with frontline troops in the Iran-Iraq War, during which he served first as defense minister and then as commander of guerrilla operations. The Islamic Revolutionary Guards Corps (IRGC) initially promoted an egalitarian ethos on the battlefront where everyone would eat together. Chamran was killed in June 1981, not far from the Iraqi border.

An IRGC document from 1981 confirms that Soleimani is allowed to operate in the area. Despite entering the war with Iraq as a soldier with no experience, he soon rose to become a division commander.

Qassem Soleimani in the years of the Iran-Iraq War (1980–8).

Soleimani with Supreme Leader Ayatollah Khamenei (right), who appointed him head of the Quds Force in 1998. Soleimani believed in unreserved devotion to Khamenei, and repeatedly asked people to support the Supreme Leader in his will.

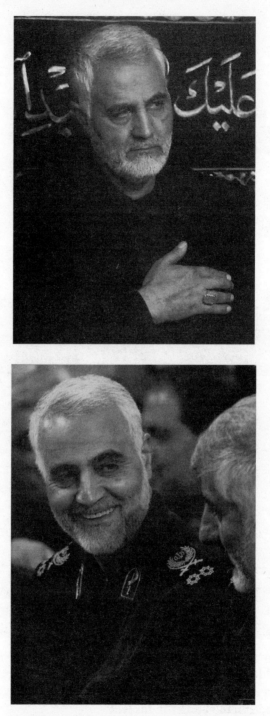

In the last years of his life, Soleimani emerged as one of Iran's most powerful men, popular even outside the ranks of the regime supporters.

Chapter 7

A Chalice Full of Poison

July 20, 1988, was perhaps the worst day in the life of Ayatollah Khomeini. He had to do the last thing he had wanted: compromise by accepting a UN-mandated ceasefire, effectively putting an end to the Iran-Iraq War. Throughout his career, much of Khomeini's success had come from his draconian opposition to compromise. It had been his unapologetic "no" to the Shah that had made him the leader of the revolution. It had been his single-minded defense of a divinely inspired government that had allowed him to purge all the non-Islamists from the republic he founded. He had adopted the same tone for the Iran-Iraq War. For almost eight years, Khomeini had made it clear that Iran would not cease the fight against Saddam; not only would the Iranians overthrow Saddam, they would fight until they brought "the end of sedition in the world."

Karbala, after all, was going to be only a stop on the way to Jerusalem. Mecca and Medina were to be freed from the Saudis, the Prophet Abraham's tomb in Hebron was to revert back to Muslims, God's sovereignty was to spread around the world. By that hot summer day, it had become clear that none of these goals would be attainable. The war was at a stalemate: Iran had failed to capture any major Iraqi city after years of trying, and now it found itself mired in a hair-raising conflict with

Americans in the Persian Gulf. The United Nations Security Council had adopted a unanimous resolution, UNSCR 598, on July 20, 1987, calling for a ceasefire, repatriation of prisoners of war, and withdrawal of both sides to the international borders. The UN was to then dispatch a group of observers to monitor the ceasefire but also determine the aggressor and impose reparations and war damages. The Iranians were furious. The Security Council had adopted the resolution without even consulting them, and it had clearly been Saddam who had started the war by his massive invasion of Iranian territory in September 1980. Why couldn't the UN have determined that before calling for a ceasefire? The Iranians had very little trust in the Peruvian diplomat Javier Pérez de Cuéllar, who, as UN secretary-general, was in charge of implementing the deal. They said a firm "no" to the resolution.

Iran's official slogan had called for "War, War, until Victory." Throughout the 1980s, Khomeini had tolerated no compromise on this account, just as he allowed the execution of tens of thousands of dissidents. The Islamic Republic was establishing itself by ceaseless shedding of blood, in prisons and on the battlefronts. At the same time, Khomeini was no messianic irrational figure. He had proved to be a shrewd strategist. He helped rein in the brutality against citizens with an order in December 1982 (now that the major domestic foes had been defeated) protecting the privacy of citizens against illegal search and seizure. He allowed the dissolution of the Islamic Republican Party in 1987 and formation of rival political parties so long as they were all loyal to him and to the regime.

But on the issue of the war, he long opposed all voices clamoring for peace. On June 11, 1983, he said in a speech: "The war is at the top of our issues. Some deviants and hypocrites might infiltrate the people and ask for an end to the war. If you accept it, you should know that Islam is threatened by apostasy. If we take one step back, if our nation shows any weakness, they'll take its honor [women], its property, the lives of its youth. All of it!"

"Those who ask us to compromise are either ignorant or mercenaries," he said on July 1, 1984. "To compromise with the oppressor is to allow him to go on oppressing. This goes against what all prophets stood for." He always claimed to have the full support of the people. On March

9, 1985, he said: "Have you not seen that the brave mothers and fathers of Iran pull their beloved offspring from under the debris, all the while shouting 'War, War, Until Victory'? God salutes this courageous and believing nation who will not accept compromise and submission."

The annals of Islamic history display many examples of peace-making. There was the Treaty of Hudaybiyyah, signed in 628, between the Prophet Mohammad, representing the nascent Muslim state of Medina, and the Quraysh tribe of Mecca, opening a period of peace that allowed the world's first Muslim state to survive. In the Shia tradition, there was the peace made in 660 between Hassan, the Second Shia Imam, and the Damascus-based caliph Muawiyah. Hassan's father, Ali, had considered Muawiyah an illegitimate usurper of the caliphate seat and had fought him to a stalemate leading to arbitration, in which the throne was given to Muawiyah. Hassan, based in Kufa, Iraq, had picked peace over war. These examples gave Khomeini an easy way out. Decades later, his successor, Ayatollah Khamenei, would cite the example of Imam Hassan's "heroic flexibility" to justify nuclear talks with the United States. But Khomeini didn't take that easy way. On August 24, 1986, he celebrated a Shia occasion by attacking all those who wanted peace with Iraq as "deceitful traitors." "Even when it comes to Imam Hassan, peace was imposed on him," Khomeini thundered. "Hassan's friends, those traitors who had gathered around him, left him no other choice. Deceitful people were behind the imposed peace in Imam Hassan's time, just as they were behind the imposed arbitration during Imam Ali's time. We should accept neither." The Islamic Republic had described the conflict as Saddam's "imposed war" that had necessitated a "holy defense." Now the term "imposed peace" also started to circulate.

From his house in the small, pleasant village of Jamaran, north of Tehran, the ever more embittered Khomeini issued increasingly unrealistic orders that the country's political and military leaders had to pursue. Iran was ever more internationally isolated. In the twilight years of the Cold War, it seemed that the only topic on which the Americans, Soviets, and Chinese could agree was the need to restrain Iran. Despite the fact that the diplomats of the Islamic Republic now had a degree of sophistication and maturity, these three powers unanimously supported UNSCR 598, which had been adopted without even consulting the Iranians.

The resolution came during the season of Haj, the annual pilgrimage of Muslims to Mecca and Medina. In his message to the pilgrims on July 28, 1987, Khomeini once more denounced compromise. "Now that we approach absolute victory and are taking our last steps, have the oppressors and warmongers suddenly become pacifists?" Khomeini asked. "They now defend freedom and security for humanity. They now eulogize the blood of the youth of Iran and Iraq. Why is it that the world arrogance [Khomeini's term for global imperialism], led by the United States, is now such a fan of the world's nations? Have they resigned from the insatiable thirst for blood that is in the nature of capitalism and communism?"

Khomeini was adamant that the war must continue despite such pretensions of peace from the world powers. "I decisively declare to the world," he continued: "If the oppressors of the world want to stand up against our religion, we will stand up to their world and will not stop until we have destroyed them. There is no doubt today that the fate of all Islamic nations and countries is tied to our fate in the war. The Islamic Republic of Iran is at a stage in which its victory will be that of all Muslims and, God forbid, its defeat will lead to failure, defeat, and humiliation for all the devout. To leave a nation, a country, a great cause halfway to victory is to betray the cause of humanity and the Prophet Mohammad."

Buoyed by such messages, the Iranian pilgrims staged a demonstration in Mecca that led to a bloody skirmish. When the dust settled 275 Iranian pilgrims; 85 Saudi citizens, including police officers; and 45 pilgrims from other countries had been killed. The Saudis broke diplomatic relations with Iran.[1]

But war couldn't be fought with letters to pilgrims or Haj skirmishes. The commanders, even those of the IRGC, increasingly spoke of the need to finish it off. The war effort was officially led by Akbar Hashemi Rafsanjani, the parliament's speaker, Khomeini's neighbor in Jamaran, and the deputy commander-in-chief. In June 1988, he went to see Khomeini, with a group of other leaders, to argue for accepting the UN-mandated ceasefire. Crucially, he had the support of the IRGC's top commander, Mohsen Rezayi. They were especially shaken by Saddam's increasing use of chemical weapons. In early 1987, Iran had put Basra under siege in Operation Karbala V but had failed, for the sixth time, to capture the elusive port, despite losing more than 50,000 of its troops. The Karbala V failure was followed, on March 16, by one of the single most harrowing events of the war. To the north of Basra, the Iranians successfully took the Kurdish border town of Halabja with the aid of both major Iraqi Kurdish parties, Masoud Barzani's Kurdistan Democratic Party and Jalal Talabani's Patriotic Union of Kurdistan. Forty-eight hours later, Iraq attacked by unleashing mustard gas and a range of other nerve agents.

Up to 5,000 civilians died on the spot, thousands more were injured, and the area has seen an increased rate of cancer and birth defects to the present day. To the shock of the Iranians, the US and the UN, despite having good intelligence about Iraqi use of these internationally banned weapons of mass destruction, refused to take action or to condemn Baghdad in any way. Iran was truly alone. Many commanders felt despondent and had no plan to advance. Qassem Soleimani was no exception. Speaking on December 31, 1987, he told his fellow commanders: "We don't have a plan for the war. After Karbala V, I really don't know what the goal is and what we want in the future. We don't even have a plan for the next six months. Like wandering and lost people, we keep moving from this place to that."[2]

Rafsanjani pleaded with Khomeini to accept UNSCR 598. But the Imam would not have any of it. When Rafsanjani said the country didn't have any money, Khomeini said taxes should be raised. When he said they lacked hard currency, Khomeini told him to "do something about it." When he said the youth were no longer volunteering to serve in their droves, the Ayatollah threatened to call for a universal Jihad which would compel all men to serve.

But even the iron will of Ayatollah finally broke. The game-changing event might have been the one that took place on July 3, 1988. An Iranian airliner, Iran Air Flight 655, scheduled to fly from Tehran to Dubai, via a stop in the Persian Gulf port of Bandar Abbas, was shot down by a surface-to-air cruise missile of the United States Navy. All the 290 occupants were killed. The US said it was a mistake and compensated the victims, but Ronald Reagan said he would never "apologize for America."

A few weeks later, on July 20, once more in his annual message to pilgrims, Ayatollah Khomeini accepted the ceasefire, using a dramatic phrase now etched onto the history of the revolution. "For me, to accept the ceasefire was to drink a chalice of poison," Khomeini wrote. "I am ashamed before the greatness and sacrifice of this great nation. To accept this is more lethal than poison. But I did it for God. You know that I had promised you that I would fight to the last drop of blood and to my last breath; but today's decision was for expediency. If I had any respect, I traded it for a deal with God."

But even at the moment of defeat, Khomeini found words to allege that the "true clergy" never compromises, "even if they break every bone in our body, if they hang us, if they burn us alive in the flames of fire, if they dangle our wives, children, and property in front of our eyes," his thunderous message read. Likewise, it advised the pilgrims to "stand up to capitalism and communism," to fight against "Zionists, the US, and the Soviets" and to liberate Mecca from its Saudi usurpers.[3]

These were not the words of a man at peace with himself or his world. In accepting peace with Iraq, Khomeini had ignited a fire within himself. His Islamic Republic had meant to bring about the unapologetic rule of the divine. But it had been mired in compromise and expediency. The Imam would remain furious to the end of his days.

* * *

At the front, Qassem Soleimani wept at the unbelievable news. Together with a group of commanders he wanted to leave for Tehran to meet Khomeini and declare allegiance to him. They were told to stay back. The Imam wasn't ready to meet anyone. He would never again hold another of his well-known receptions in Jamaran. The "chalice of poison" did its work quickly. An embittered Khomeini died on June 3, 1989, at the age of eighty-six.

In the last year of his life, the Ayatollah did all that he could to keep alive the zeal of the revolution, threatened by his historic compromise. A week after Iran accepted UNSCR 598, Khomeini asked for special courts to try soldiers on the front for violations and to execute anyone "who has done anything to defeat Islam." The usual procedures were to be set aside in favor of speed. Among those arrested and under threat of execution were leading IRGC commanders such as Ahmad Vahidi, who had helped train Hezbollah. An intervention from Rafsanjani stopped this effort. But another decree was taken very seriously.

In the last days of July, the PMOI, now an ally of Saddam Hussein, launched an invasion of Iranian territory. Its leader, Masood Rajavi, promised to be in Tehran within a week. The PMOI were roundly defeated after four days, lost around 2,000 of their forces, and were driven back to Iraq. But Khomeini wanted to take revenge. He now turned to the thousands of political prisoners in Iran, whether they were past members of the PMOI or of Marxist groupings such as the pro-Moscow Tudeh Party. They all had to be executed, even though most of them had been tried years before and were serving their prison sentences. Around 3,000 political prisoners were killed before the summer ended. Ayatollah Montazeri, Khomeini's second-in-command and his anointed successor as Supreme Leader, was furious at this action. He attacked those who perpetrated it as "criminals." Khomeini would accept no dissent. Montazeri now lost his job and was marginalized politically, months before Khomeini's death.

Khomeini's next two actions demonstrated just exactly how unbalanced he had become. In January 1989, as Iran was getting ready for the tenth anniversary of the revolution, the national radio ran a show on Women's Day, which the new regime celebrated on the birthday of Fatima, the Prophet Mohammad's daughter. In vox pop interviews, women were asked to name their role models. Almost everyone noted Fatima herself but one brave young woman had a different idea: Her true role model was not a woman from 1,400 years ago, she said, but Oshin, protagonist of an eponymous Japanese TV series which portrayed the trials and tribulations of a Japanese woman during the turbulent twentieth century. Like many people around the world, Iranians had connected with the Japanese show, especially since Oshin's hard times during the Second World War were not unlike their own wartime troubles.

Khomeini heard the interview and was furious. This was an unforgivable insult to Fatima, he decided. The day after, on January 29, 1989, he wrote an open letter to the head of the national broadcaster, Mohammad Hashemi Rafsanjani, Akbar's younger brother. He said if the intent to insult was established on the part of any of those who had aired the interview, they had to be executed. Many high-ranking radio officials were immediately arrested by the judiciary. It was only the intervention of the elder Rafsanjani that, once more, saved them from the crazed Ayatollah.

But he was not done. A mere fortnight later, on Valentine's Day, 1989, Khomeini gave a much more determined order. This was a fatwa, a religiously enshrined edict, against Salman Rushdie, an Indian-British author whose last novel, *The Satanic Verses*, had become the subject of demonstrations by some Muslims in Britain and south Asia who believed the book to be insulting to the Prophet Mohammad.

Khomeini brought back his "no quarters" approach. Rushdie, and all his publishers, had to be killed. "I ask valiant Muslims to immediately execute them, so that no one would ever dare insult what is sacred to the Muslims," the fatwa read. "Anyone killed on this path will be considered a martyr, Inshallah."[4]

The brutal fatwa wasn't an exercise in rhetoric. The Iranian government declared its full support for the edict and a foundation declared a $3 million bounty for anyone who could kill Rushdie. The British Muslim author had to go underground and change his place of residence more than fifty times. Even after he published an essay of apology, upon Khomeini's death, the Iranian government didn't retract the fatwa. His signing a declaration of his faith in Islam and calling upon his publisher, Penguin, to not issue the book in paperback or allow its translation didn't help either. In the end, Rushdie survived to become Sir Salman and a world-renowned icon for freedom of speech. But not all of those associated with the book were so lucky. In 1991, the Japanese translator was killed and the Italian translator seriously wounded. In July 1993, a literary festival in Sivas, Turkey, was attacked by a group of Islamists, demanding that Aziz Nesin, the book's Turkish translator, be handed over. When he wasn't, the whole place was burnt down. Months later, the book's Norwegian publisher was shot and seriously injured.

Through this shockingly brutal campaign against a novelist, the Islamic Republic wanted the world to know that the fires of its revolution hadn't died down. It would do anything to keep the flames alive.

* * *

Khomeini's death nevertheless ushered Iran into a new period, known as the Second Republic. The key question of the economy was the first to be settled. Islamism had long held shifting and ambivalent positions on the economy. The coalition that built the Islamic Republic included socialists who wanted a state-run economy and mercantile capitalists who loathed the former. Khomeini had adjudicated between them, stressing a third way between capitalism and communism, although no one quite knew what this meant in practice. The revolution had immediately confiscated much of the property of the former elite, who had fled the country or been executed. The war economy had been run on a left-leaning basis, not least because the prime minister, Mirhossein Mousavi, was an open socialist in his economic thought and his cabinet harbored those of a similar mindset, like the industries minister, Behzad Nabavi.

There would be a quick but fundamental shift following Khomeini's death. The eminent Iranian historian Ervand Abrahamian calls this turn the "Thermidor of the Iranian revolution." Rafsanjani helped secure the succession of Ayatollah Ali Khamenei as the new Supreme Leader. Despite what the constitution stipulated, Khamenei was not a high-ranking Shia cleric; but the constitution was changed for that condition to be lifted. Rafsanjani himself replaced Khamenei as president. With the position of prime minister eliminated in the new constitution, the president now became the sole head of the executive branch. If Mousavi, with his austere ethics and devotion to revolutionary ideals, had represented the left wing of the revolution, Rafsanjani represented its capitalist tendencies. Mousavi's demise and the rise of Rafsanjani and Khamenei represented a capitalist turn. Privatization of state assets started in earnest. The war had finished and with it had gone the ethos that had developed on the battlefront: that of the oppressed being the true leaders of Iran; of devout men and women fighting, respectively at the battlefronts and the home front, not just for military victories but for the realization of the causes of 1979. It didn't hurt that the greatest cause of the previous generation, socialism, had also experienced a world-historical defeat, evident with the fall of the Berlin Wall in 1989, and ever more glaring with the collapse of the Soviet Union in 1991.

As president, Rafsanjani became known as the "commander of reconstruction." Exhausted after a bloody decade of war, turmoil, and revolution, Iran would now witness peace, calm, and even consumerism. While the poor and the marginalized rioted and protested Rafsanjani's neoliberal policies, a new middle class rose in the reconstruction years. Ever the shrewd diplomat, who had, after all, handled direct talks with Americans at the height of the war, Rafsanjani re-established ties with Saudi Arabia and the West and bought himself a reputation as Iran's true leader (despite Khamenei having the top position) and being someone you could do business with. He openly spoke of admiring the Chinese reforms. If Mikhail Gorbachev's political *glasnost* had ultimately brought down the Soviet Union, Deng Xiaoping had managed to make China capitalist without loosening up the authoritarianism of the one-party state. He had famously said that he didn't care whether a cat was white or black; just that it could catch mice. The cleric-president wanted to be Iran's Deng. His co-thinkers came to be known as anti-ideological "technocrats," a radical shift from the ideology-heavy language of the revolution.

But if the Islamic Republic was jettisoning its revolutionary and wartime ethos, what was going to happen to the IRGC and to the hundreds of thousands of men who had fought at the fronts and lost their dearest comrades? What would be their role in the new age of reconstruction, consumerism, and technocracy?

Time and time again, history has shown the perils of demobilizing soldiers. Men taught to fight often struggle to find their place in society, not least when the war was a failure, thought to be a wasteful adventure by much of the population. Many of the Vietnam War veterans in the United States became a base of right-wing politics in reaction to a society that had sent them to die in tropical jungles far from home in the cause of anti-communism but which seemed to now consider the whole thing a vain tragedy.

The end of the war and the changes in Iran around the end of the 1980s left the IRGC veterans of the war in a similar situation; and they gave birth to a similar brand of reactionary politics. The painful way in which Khomeini had accepted the end of the war allowed him to remain a martyr while the men of the IRGC now looked for traitors who had made it happen. Rafsanjani came to be blamed for having lured Khomeini to the path of compromise. Iranian diplomats at the country's permanent representation to the United Nations were denounced as having conspired with the powers that be against the interests of the revolution. Iran's ambassador there, Mohammad Jafar Mahallati, was so vilified that he found no way out but to defect to the West. He held a MA from the University of Oregon, where his thesis had been an Islamist critique of the Marxist theory of imperialism. Resuming the academic path, he got a PhD from the renowned Department of Islamic Studies at McGill University, writing a dissertation on the "ethics of war in Muslim cultures."[5] A younger diplomat at the Iranian mission, Mohammad Javad Zarif, survived the purges to later emerge as Iran's most celebrated UN ambassador and finally its foreign minister. Back in the 1990s, many newspaper editorials attacked the "New York Boys" as having been agents of betrayal. Although they seemed to be out of fashion, the men of the IRGC bided their time, built their institutions, and planned their comeback.

* * *

When the war with Iraq broke, Qassem Soleimani had been a 23-year-old man whose most exciting experience in life was working at the water department and practicing karate in gyms. When it ended eight years later, he was a high-ranking division commander who had proved his mettle in battle. What was next for him?

Many of his IRGC comrades attempted to enter politics in the post-war era. Some others made a transition to economic activity and made millions in the new age of reconstruction. Many embarked on graduate studies, often at the newly built cadre-training institutions of the Islamic Republic, and pursued lives as soldiers-cum-academics, not unlike a path common in the United States.

But for commanders like Qassem, the IRGC was a home they were not prepared to leave. It had grown from an ad hoc militia to rivalling and soon surpassing the country's official army. Khomeini had appreciated the benefits of an ideologically committed armed force. In 1985, he ordered its expansion and its launch of ground, air, and marine forces. The IRGC, which also had its own ministry, was now the main driver of the war on all fronts. This worried an emerging group of regime states-men who questioned the wisdom of giving the reins of the war effort to the typically young and brash men who led the IRGC. Chief among these statesmen was Hassan Rouhani, a protégé of Rafsanjani and a MP since 1980, who headed the parliament's influential defense committee during the war years (1980–8) and led the country's air defense (1985– 91). Rouhani repeatedly clashed with the IRGC minister, Mohsen Rafiqdoost, and complained to his mentor Rafsanjani of the "IRGC's expansionism."[6] Together with a few other politicians who fancied themselves as wise elders of the revolution he had formed an informal "Assembly of the Wise" in which they discussed ways of cutting the IRGC out. When Khomeini got wind of it, he asked them to quickly disband.

The efforts of the elders had all failed given Khomeini's unshakable support for the IRGC. A genuine revolutionary, the old Ayatollah preferred zealous young revolutionary men in fatigues to the self-styled "Wise" statesmen any day of the week. With the dawn of the Second Republic, men like Rouhani hoped that Rafsanjani would rein in the IRGC. After all, he was closer in outlook to the "Wise," although he also had a good relationship with Mohsen Rezayi, the IRGC's top commander.

Young IRGC men like Soleimani found purposes for themselves in the peacetime IRGC. Supported by President Rafsanjani, Rezayi kept his position at the head of the force. He would become both the recognizable face of the IRGC's cult of victimhood and an agent of its expansion. He repeatedly claimed that had the government given the necessary support to the IRGC, it would have marched to Baghdad. He also built new institutions that helped carry the IRGC into the peacetime era. Already, in 1986, he had helped turn a barracks in Tehran into a military college named after Imam Hossein. By 1987, Imam Hossein University had become a fully fledged institution of higher education, offering degrees in liberal arts, engineering, and the humanities in addition to military studies. In 1995, its medical science department turned into its own separate university, named after none other than the Hidden Imam himself. Rezayi thus helped found prestigious universities, tightly controlled by the IRGC and no longer reliant on the traditional academic caste of the country. The militia now turned out not only its own officers, pilots, and soldiers but also its own doctors, technicians, and philosophers.

Rezayi's most consequential brainchild, however, was no university. In 1989, ordered by the new Supreme Leader, Khamenei, he helped launch a military-run engineering behemoth, the Khatam-ol-Anbia Construction Base. The goal of this new entity was simple: The country needed reconstruction and rather than relying on the private sector, it was the IRGC that had to get the job done. In the early years of the revolution, much of the rural development was led by the Jihad of Construction (JoC), a revolutionary body formed in 1979 and upgraded to a full ministry in 1983. The IRGC commanders had long made fun of JoC folks as left-leaning idealistic intellectuals who wanted to practice their socialist creed with projects such as electrifying the countryside, which had once been a favorite of Lenin. The JoC efforts helped improve the quality of life in the countryside, even as the war raged on, and its forces helped realize many of the engineering marvels of the war effort, such as the impressive pontoon bridges that allowed Iranians to take over Iraqi islands and marshlands.

Khatam-ol-Anbia (literally meaning "Last of the Prophets," one of the many titles for the Prophet Mohammad, who Muslims believe is the final prophet sent by God) was to be a very different organization. Run by military men and receiving massive contracts from the government, Khatam-ol-Anbia offered a way to occupy the tens of thousands of IRGC men mobilized for the war effort. It built water pipelines, it helped export oil and gas, and it put up dams, power plants, and endless miles of roads. Most importantly, it became an octopus through whose tentacles the IRGC spread all over the Iranian economy. Not surprisingly, it also became an infamous den of corruption. The JoC was meanwhile sidelined and limited to agricultural projects before ultimately being merged into the agriculture ministry in 2000.

Rezayi's comrades each found their place in his new peacetime IRGC. During the war years, the commanders who had distinguished themselves most had a regional base and a talent for organizing the men of their provinces for the national war effort. Three such men became close comrades and helped build a web of influence that strengthened their respective positions: Mohammad Baqer Qalibaf, Ahmad Kazemi, and Qassem Soleimani. When the war ended, they were respectively 27, 29, and 32 years old. They had respectively led IRGC divisions in Khorasan,

Isfahan, and Kerman provinces, three of the biggest territorial units in the country which together accounted for much of the country's population.

After the war, Qalibaf became deputy commander of Basij, the IRGC's massive voluntary force with branches all over the country whose members were to become the foot soldiers of ultra-conservative politics. In 1994, he was appointed the head of Khatam-ol-Anbia, a base for his ever-widening corruption and political ambition.

The other two followed more straightforward military paths. Kazemi had more experience than Soleimani or Qalibaf. Hailing from Najafabad, the hometown of the Montazeris, he had been arrested before the revolution. After 1979, he had joined the other acolytes of Mohammad Montazeri in a trip to Lebanon and Syria where he was trained by the PLO. He had helped fight the Kurdish rebels before joining the war effort. Already a division commander, he had played a key role in the liberation of Khorramshahr. Following the war, Kazemi led the IRGC's fight against the Iranian Kurdish rebels. After the Gulf War of 1991 and the setting up of a de facto independent Iraqi Kurdish statelet, the Iranian Kurds found a new base from which to attack the Islamic Republic. Kazemi took up the fight against them, ultimately leading to the little-known yet historically important Koy Sanjaq Agreement of 1995: The Kurdish forces, led by the Kurdish Democratic Party (two of whose key leaders had been assassinated in Europe in foreign operations by the Islamic Republic) effectively gave up the little territories they still held on Iranian soil and pledged to cease military skirmishes with Iran.

For Qassem Soleimani, there was little doubt as to where he would be most useful: his home province of Kerman and its adjacent Hormozgan and Sistan and Balochistan provinces, that is exactly the areas that his Blood of Allah Division covered. Vast swathes of these provinces were mired with outlaws, road bandits, and drug lords who benefited from one of the most profitable drugs routes of the world, coming from neighboring Afghanistan and Pakistan. Soleimani was to pacify these areas by using the same men he had mobilized to fight Iraq. Unlike commanders coming from urban areas or, worse, far-flung metropolises like Tehran or Isfahan, Soleimani was a local, a tribal who understood the ways of the land and its people better.

Had Soleimani, the tribal boy, been given a lower position than his fellow wartime commanders? After all, Qalibaf was leading the nation-wide reconstruction efforts and Kazemi was battling the most serious domestic armed insurrection, whereas Soleimani was sent battling drug lords and road bandits. As things turned out, however, Soleimani once more used an opportunity he was given to impress, shine, and rise through the ranks. He would be a crime fighter like no other.

* * *

For Iranians of the main urban centers, the country's southeast is seen as something akin to the American Wild West. The sprawling hills, fields, and deserts covering much of the eastern Iranian territory, and forming its borderlands with Afghanistan and Pakistan, are caricatured by Tehranis and Isfahanis as unruly tribal lands infested with smugglers and drug dealers. Like all unfair caricatures, this one also has some basis in reality: The long arm of the central Iranian state has struggled to control these areas and lucrative smuggling routes have connected them with neighboring states to the east. The Balochis, a mostly Sunni ethnic minority straddling the border of Iran and Pakistan, have a long history of marginalization. Many experienced systematic enslavements on the shipping routes of the Persian Gulf. Today they form the majority of the population in Pakistan's Balochistan province and Iran's Sistan and Balochistan province, and have a history of joining insurgent armed movements on both sides of the border.

For Soleimani, the tribal Iran of the south and the southeast wasn't a caricature of urban lore; it was home. Growing up, he was told to be care-ful not to get into a fight with boys of the wrong tribe. "Even in the urban Kerman, one simple boys' fight could lead into a tribal feud," a close family friend remembers.[7] The locals knew the no-go areas. Just over an hour's drive east of the city of Kerman is the town of Shahdad, one of the hottest points on the planet and gateway to the massive salt desert Dasht-e Lut. There were roads that connected Shahdad to Khorasan, Iran's biggest province and home to its second biggest city, Mashhad. But in practice they saw so much banditry and so many armed gangs that ordinary people feared ever traversing them. Such areas abounded in the region. Drive a few hours west of Kerman and you reach the mountain-ous passes around Darab in the Fars province, a route for drugs to make their way west. Smugglers didn't just sell drugs. They sold weaponry, alcohol, contraband, gasoline, and oil products. The criminal cartels were too powerful to take on. Their victims included a Chinese mining engineer kidnapped in Kahnooj. Many of the roads in the three prov-inces of Kerman, Hormozgan, and Sistan and Balochistan had regular curfews after 4 or 5 P.M. As it happens, these were the very provinces whose soldiers had been organized in Soleimani's Blood of Allah brigade-cum-division.

The biggest no-go area of them all was the Avertin Triangle, a difficult mountainous area straddling the borders of these three provinces. It barely had any paved roads, and no central government had been known to truly control it for decades. The last major military campaign there had been around the 1930s, in the time of Reza Shah, and even his forces had given up next to the organized power of the Avertin masters.

Avertin was the stuff of the legends, even for local boys like Qassem. There was the tribe of Salar, which now called itself Kamrani after Kamran the Great, a local criminal notable who had been captured and executed under the Shah. There was the Balochi nomadic tribe of the Bameri, which claimed to have been in the area since before Alexander the Great invaded Iran in in 334 BC. Some of the Bameris had joined the Blood of Allah Division but their main leadership had spent the 1980s running a lucrative drug trade from their mountain strongholds in Avertin. In 1987, the local police forces killed Gholamhossein Bameri, the main drug lord of the region. The mantle then passed to his teenage son Eyd Mohammad, diminutively called Eydook Bameri. Eydook had gone to primary school in Delgan in Sistan and Balochistan, near the border with Kerman. He had been known to be anointed as heir appar-ent since age twelve. The teenager now took his place in Avertin and awed many by his successful operations against the police forces. For his second marriage, he wed a daughter of Jalal Kamrani, from the other major crime family. He helped bring together the two families and to take revenge on the men who had killed his father. The upgraded local lords were no amateur road bandits. Using the immense wealth made through smuggling, the Bameri-Kamrani confederacy boasted Toyota pick-up trucks that would have been the envy of the Iranian war effort and a seemingly endless supply of AK-47s.

The Bameris and the Kamranis were just two families. This region abounded in criminal clans. Around Balochistan, the Narooyis were another such family. In the 1980s, just when the IRGC was involved in the heat of its battles in Iraq, some of its forces were dying fighting the Narooyis. In one battle alone in November 1987, thirty-six IRGC fighters were killed not far from the regional capital of Zahedan. Sixteen soldiers of the gendarmerie were killed in another skirmish. Living in urban centers didn't provide immunity from becoming collateral damage. In 1991, two of the Narooyis attacked a bank in Kerman, took the staff hostage, and demanded a ransom and the freedom of one of their gang members, Jamil Narooyi.

With the end of the war, and Iran's crusade for reconstruction, there was some hope that law and order could now be applied in these areas. The early 1990s saw some crucial local, national, and international changes that affected the scene. In 1991, Iran formed a national police force by merging the city police forces, the gendarmerie, and the revolutionary committees. The ever-growing IRGC had a key role in the new police force and all its major commanders were to be IRGC members. The new police force wanted to systematically bring order to all parts of Iran, especially those areas neglected during the war years.

In 1992, the government of Mohammad Najibullah, the last communist president of Afghanistan, finally fell to the Islamist coalition that had fought it for more than a decade, supported by the CIA and the Iranian and Pakistani governments. The Soviets had withdrawn from Afghanistan in 1989 and Najibullah's heroic efforts to build an inclusive coalition government failed. Kabul's new government was made up of various Islamist forces, based on a pact signed in Peshawar, Pakistan, where these forces had headquartered themselves, buoyed by American, Saudi, and Pakistani financial support which they used to mobilize thousands of Afghan refugees. The Islamic Republic's anti-communist stance meant that Tehran had always resolutely backed the Islamists and opposed the Afghan government and its Soviet partners. The new government, led by Persian-speaking Islamist Burhanuddin Rabbani and his charismatic defense minister Ahmad Shah Masood, was to be friendly to Tehran. There was hope that it would cooperate in cutting down the drug routes that filled the coffers of the local gangs. But one major Islamist group refused to join the new coalition and continued the war against Kabul: This was the Islamic Party, led by Gulbuddin Hekmatyar. Hekmatyar's refusal to join the Peshawar accords prolonged the civil war and had a direct effect on Iran's war on drugs. The Afghan warlord allied with the Narooyis and became an irritation to the Iranian authorities. With the help of Iran's criminal gangs, Hekmatyar's forces slipped back and forth across the Iranian-Afghan border.

This was the landscape into which Soleimani stepped when, in 1992, he was tasked with using an IRGC ground force base in Kerman to pacify the area.

* * *

Soleimani proved to be anything but a desk commander. His offices were in Kerman but he was rarely to be found there. He was frequently in the provincial capital, Zahedan, unlike many IRGC heads who were afraid of the Sunni-majority Balochi city.

"What became very clear, very quickly, both to our own forces and to the enemy, was Qassem's fearlessness," an IRGC mid-level soldier of those days remembers. "There was a skirmish in Saravan near the Pakistani border? Soleimani would go in person. Jalq, where the Balochi forces were known to rule the roost? No problem, Hajji Qassem was there. When his helicopter landed on the ground, he'd come running out and talk to as many people as he could. You felt like he'd fight with you and die with you if need be."

"In Balochistan, I feel like I am back in the war," many remember Soleimani saying. Iran-Iraq War veterans often had trouble adjusting to peacetime. Soleimani simply avoided making such an adjustment by engaging in a war in the eastern borderlands that was sometimes as ferocious as the one he had fought in the west of the country.

He started his energetic campaign by closing the eastern borders with Afghanistan and Pakistan as much as he could. He knew that shutting off the revenue streams of the gangs was key to winning this war. In a trip to the border city of Mirjave, right opposite the Pakistani city of Taftan,

President Rafsanjani was impressed by a wall of cement and concrete put up by Soleimani. The president caused some amusement by comparing Soleimani to Alexander the Great, who had built up his famous gates to deter the Gog and Magog, mythical tribes mentioned in both the Hebrew Bible and the Quran.[8] Rafsanjani would pay regular visits to his fellow Kermani and make sure he had the support he needed.

Soleimani also used the engineering capabilities of the IRGC to dig hundreds of kilometers of canals, embankments, and roads to help move heavy weaponry around. He tried to rely on the local population instead of vilifying them. The tribal boy from Qanat Molk understood the locals better.

The new approach quickly paid dividends. In April 1992, his forces helped capture Abas Narooyi, killing three of his main associates, including his elder son, in the process. Major drug lords were hunted down and killed one after the other. In the same year, he helped free 100 captive soldiers whom the gangs had taken to Afghan territory, probably with Hekmatyar's help. Here he showed one of his first diplomatic initiatives. He crossed over the border to see the local Afghan village elders, showing humility not expected of a major military commander. He asked the elders to force the gangs to hand over the hostages lest an attack kill innocent people in the village. "He told them, 'We don't want to hurt your women and children,'" an IRGC soldier remembers. The initiative seemed to work and all the hostages were freed.

Such successes never resulted in a total uprooting of all the drug and smuggling gangs. The war was for the long haul. In early 1993, Rahman Narooyi helped kill twenty-one police officers in an operation. The same man killed seventeen villagers around Darab. Shortly thereafter, eighty-two police officers were taken hostage by another gang north of Zahedan. A local police commander was killed 20 kilometers south of Kerman. But the overall improvement brought by Soleimani remained unquestionable. The mountains around Zahedan were now often safe again. The southern areas of Khorasan opened to trade. More impressively, Soleimani helped promote agriculture and got the IRGC to dig wells. Thousands of gang members received amnesty and, heeding the lessons of his childhood, Soleimani often made deals with tribal leaders to make sure revenge actions wouldn't be taken.

This was possible because most of the IRGC men who fought under Soleimani were the locals who had worked with him for years during the war. They didn't come from distant lands and were more understanding of the local customs. Some even stayed afterwards. Years later, when Soleimani became a global celebrity, Mohammad Ali Pardel still remembered him as a commander who had changed his life. Pardel had fought in the war with Iraq and had been taken prisoner while leading a company in Operation Kheybar of 1984. Upon his release in 1990, he didn't hesitate to rejoin the forces of his old commander. After three years of fighting in Soleimani's war on drugs, he took his recommendation and settled in Baranjgan, a village 8 kilometers away from the Afghan border. "Do what Kermanis do and grow some pistachios," Soleimani told him. He heeded the advice and continues to live there with his family, cultivating his pistachio fields and his ostriches.

But if Soleimani's name was established across the country, it wasn't because of small stories like this but a massive operation that did what no government had dared to do for decades: take on Avertin.

* * *

On the morning of November 5, 1994, a band of five helicopters left their base in Kerman. The American-made Boeing Chinooks and Bell Cobras flew more than 400 kilometers, refueled in a base, took on some new forces and descended upon Avertin, which was being simultaneously stormed by ground forces of the Salman Brigade.[9] The goal was the killing or capture of Eydook Bameri, who, according to the intelligence work done by Soleimani, was staying in a village outside his mountain base.

The Bameris had never seen anything like this. They were faced with a ferocious assault from air and ground, supported by many from the region who knew their way around the forbidding gorges of Avertin. Eydook tried to flee to his mountain base. His forces fought back, hid behind the palm trees, and fired RPG-7 anti-tank grenades at the helicopters. Some of Eydook's brothers died in the fight and his uncle was injured, but the warlord got away, hiding behind some rocks. Hundreds of Bameris and Kamranis were arrested on the second day of the operation but Eydook still got away, walking his injured uncle around for days. Given the terrain, it was difficult for the helicopters to coordinate with the ground forces and Eydook had a way of disappearing. On the fourth day, November 8, as many were losing hope, another helicopter brought a new man to the field: Soleimani arrived at around 3:30 P.M., just before dark. The hands-on commander didn't like to stand back. He ordered an assault before sunset. The IRGC forces got close to the rocks behind which Eydook was hiding but faced massive fire. A heated battle took place and two of the main commanders of the Salman Brigade fell. Of the hundreds of forces that the gang had brought only three got away, including Eydook himself.

Eydook's subsequent fate is the stuff of many tales. Some report he was arrested, tortured, and killed without the details being leaked, to avoid disturbing local sentiments. Some claim he continues to survive, decades after, concealed behind a rock, planning a comeback. In later years, insurgent organizations would claim him as a symbol, a Balochi Robin Hood. Some, however, claimed that Eydook had surrendered to Soleimani, so impressed by his magnanimity that he was now an adopted son to the general, secretly helping him and even fighting for him in Syria.

Opening of the archives might one day tell us the truth about Eydook but, in 1994, what mattered more than facts was the emerging myth of the shadow commander; the man who came out of nowhere in a helicopter; the man who knew no fear and would go where no commander had dared to go. The myth of Qassem Soleimani was, for now, mostly a local one, but it would not stay that way for long.

* * *

By the time Soleimani took on the Avertin Triangle he boasted a new sobriquet. He was now *Hajj* Qassem Soleimani. In 1992, as Rafsanjani was building better ties with Saudi Arabia, Soleimani went on the pilgrimage that is obligatory for all Muslims at least once during their lifetime: a trip to the holy cities of Mecca and Medina, known as the Haj, which gives the right to the participant to attach the prefix "Hajji" or "Hajj" to their name. On the trip, Soleimani was accompanied by a

Kermani cleric, Mahmood Khaleqi, who would remain close to the commander to the end of his days. They had met during the war with Iraq, in Operations Dawn VIII and Karbala IV. "Right in the courtyard of the Great Mosque of Mecca, we pledged a pact of brotherhood," Khaleqi remembered years later. When Soleimani wrote his will, he appointed Khaleqi to undertake his religious burial rites.

Hajj Qassem Soleimani was now a name to be reckoned with, albeit at an intermediate tier. He could have expected to follow the path of many of his commanders: rise in the ranks, become a local magnate or a politician in Tehran. He could have used his connections with his fellow Kermani Rafsanjani or the province's powerful governor, Hossein Marashi, to enrich himself. But the particular experience he had gained, in dealing with tribes and armed militias, was noticed by a man who was quietly using the IRGC to build up his base: the Supreme Leader, Ayatollah Khamenei.

Khamenei's grip on power had been weakened by a political earthquake that hit Iran in 1997. Ever since the dismissal of Iran's first president, Abolhassan Banisadr, in 1981, all presidential elections had been lackluster affairs with the result previously determined via jockeying in the halls of power. Khamenei's two terms had been followed by two by Rafsanjani, who was now expected to pass the baton to a conservative, pro-capitalist cleric, Ali Akbar Nateq Nuri. The much-diminished forces of the Islamist left, who now toned down their anti-imperialism and were starting to emphasize the need for a political opening, were allowed to run their candidate, the mild-mannered 53-year-old cleric Mohammad Khatami, a previous culture minister and head of the national library. Not for the last time, the people of Iran surprised everyone by flooding the voting booths. Almost 80 percent voted in the elections and more than 69 percent of the voters chose Khatami. The shy cleric-librarian with uncharacteristic chocolate-colored robes was now the president of Iran, expected to carry out a program of reforms, and pushed on by a constituency dominated by youth and women, who were determined to be the new agents of Iranian history.

How would Khamenei rise to this significant challenge to his rule? For Iranians of the present generation, used to Khamenei's omnipresent authority, it is perhaps hard to imagine the days when student activists loudly criticized the Supreme Leader in mass meetings, to the cheers of crowds. The movement that started in May 1997 seriously embattled Khamenei, along with the rest of the ruling caste of the Islamic Republic. Appearing increasingly anachronistic in the age of liberal democracy and the fall of ideologically committed systems like the Soviet Union, Tehran's regime seemed set for imminent downfall in the eyes of many.

While the drama of the domestic political scene captured most of the headlines, Khamenei's quiet plan for entrenching his leadership was based on the IRGC—the militia which, after all, had been founded for precisely this purpose. The most worrying poll numbers for Khamenei were those that showed significant backing for Khatami among the IRGC ranks.

On May 7, just a few weeks before the elections, Soleimani went to see President Rafsanjani to express worries about the "divisions in the IRGC." After the elections, on June 3, Soleimani and other IRGC commanders would again go to see Rafsanjani, widely perceived to be a more powerful figure than Khamenei. They were worried about the political future of their top commander, Mohsen Rezayi. It was widely rumored that his time was up in the IRGC, but after years of fighting for the regime, and backing the reconstruction efforts, they expected him to become either a powerful vice-president or an interior minister in the new Khatami government.[10]

As these meetings show, the postwar anxieties of veterans about their place in a changing Iran increased after 1997. If many of the most ardent anti-imperialist leaders of yesteryear were now clamoring for ties with the US and the need for a "kinder Islam," as Khatami loved to say, where would that leave the men raised to become "the militants of Islam"?

Khamenei had an answer to this question. The Guards were at the center of his long-term plans. A militia now more powerful than the country's official armed forces became a shadow opposition party to President Khatami's government, while gradually increasing its power inside and outside the borders of Iran. In the crucial year of 1997, the Supreme Leader shuffled the IRGC leadership to help it transition to the new era. After serving as the top commander for sixteen years, Rezayi was replaced by Yahya Rahim Safavi, the man who, fifteen years before, had gone out of his way to convince Khomeini of the need to continue the war against Saddam's Iraq. The three old comrades of the war (Soleimani, Qalibaf, and Kazemi) were to do very well under Rahim Safavi. They received new appointments once more. Qalibaf was put in charge of the powerful air force of the IRGC; Kazemi was made the commander of Isfahan's Imam Hossein Division (in 2005, he would be promoted to head the IRGC's ground forces).

Soleimani's official appointment didn't come until January 1998. He was assigned as the commander of a force little known to anyone outside IRGC circles: the Quds Force, one more body named after Jerusalem. "On the recommendation of the top commander of the IRGC, I hereby appoint you as the commander of the IRGC's Quds Force," Khamenei's order on January 25, 1998, read. "With the important tasks assigned to it, the force can bring many blessings to the Islamic world."

These cryptic words did little to reveal the nature of the Quds Force, whose very existence had been shrouded in secrecy since its foundation in 1988. Soleimani would retain his position as the Quds Force's commander for just short of twenty-two years, right to the very last second of his life. In these two decades, he would turn the nondescript force into the most ambitious expeditionary army in the history of the modern Middle East, in the process elevating the global ambitions of his boss, Ayatollah Khamenei. The Supreme Leader had just made the most consequential appointment of his life.

Chapter 8

An "Unwritten Pact"

On January 1, 2000, as the world ushered in a new millennium and the much-feared global internet collapse didn't come to pass, many pundits offered reflections on the shape of the new century. The previous decade had been rife with such predictions. The abrupt end to the Cold War had confused many. The global battle between capitalism and socialism had defined so many lives for so long; what would replace it? The state of confusion is perhaps best captured in the words of Yitzhak, a fictional Jewish drag queen from Zagreb in the musical *Hedwig and the Angry Inch*. As he found himself in Berlin just when the wall collapsed, Yitzhak mused: "We thought the wall would stand forever, and now that it's gone, we don't know who we are anymore."

The last decade of the twentieth century saw dreams rise and fall: Genocides in Rwanda and the former Yugoslavia tarred utopian hopes for the emergence of an idyllic state of global liberal democracy. The global left suffered the most serious blow in its history but it was gradually rising up again, flexing its muscles in 1999 with massive anti-capitalist demonstrations to greet the WTO's ministerial summit in Seattle. Two years later, in July 2001, the movement showed its power in the streets of Genoa. Carlo Giuliani, a 23-year-old Italian student, fell to the bullets of the riot police. The new movement had its first martyr. The old struggle between capitalism and socialism seemed to be back. Then a few months later, one Tuesday morning, an event of a wholly different character changed the calculus and made the world forget the Battle of Seattle and the young Roman martyr of Genoa.

The first major global event of the millennium did not come from the established political left or right. It did not come from factory workers or student demonstrators. It was not the work of political parties or national armies. On September 11, 2001, nineteen men affiliated with a little-known Islamist organization, Al-Qaeda, hijacked four airplanes and changed the course of world history. Of the nineteen, fifteen were from Saudi Arabia, two from the United Arab Emirates, one from Egypt, and one from Lebanon. They were all Arabs, they were all Muslims, and they had attacked the world's sole superpower in its capital, the first foreign power to do so since armies of the Canadian provinces of the British Empire burnt down the White House in 1814. Among the many soothsaying pundits of the 1990s, most attention had been paid to two political scientists: Francis Fukuyama with his Hegelian vision of the world leading to the triumph of liberal democracy and the "End of History"; and Samuel Huntington, a mentor of Fukuyama at Harvard, who rebutted his former student by offering his own framework on the coming "Clash of Civilizations." The 9/11 attacks would give prominence to another academic whose predictions for the post-Cold War world, and his use of the "Clash of Civilizations" framework, predated the other two: Bernard Lewis, an aging British-American scholar and a giant in the field of Middle Eastern studies. In 1990, Lewis wrote a cover story for the *Atlantic* warning about the "Muslim Rage" that was going to trouble the West in the years to come. The attacks on New York seemed to vindicate the old man. Lewis had been at this game for a long time. As early as 1954, he had compared Islam and communism due to their supposedly shared anti-Western animus. The long-influential Princeton man now became a favorite at the White House of newly elected President George W. Bush.

If the 1990s had seen the US side with the Islamists in Afghanistan against the godless Soviet empire, the new decade was going to be defined by a "War on Terror," a battle against the Islamist terrorists, starting from their haven in Afghanistan. Bush was quick to point out that he was against terrorists and not Islam as a whole. A few days after the attack, he rushed to a mosque in Washington, DC, to declare that "Muslims all across the world" had been "appalled and outraged" at the attacks. He quoted the holy Quran, declared that "Islam is Peace" and condemned the attacks on hijab-wearing women in America.

But the voices of those like Huntington and Lewis, doomsayers about a civilizational battle between the West and Islam, comprised a dominant and powerful discourse in world affairs. Generations of young Westerners would go on to fight in wars in the Muslim lands on an unprecedented scale. The first war started less than a month after the attacks. On October 7, the US and allies launched an invasion of Afghanistan to dislodge the government of the Taliban, a tribal Islamist movement in power since 1996, though only recognized by Saudi Arabia, the UAE, and Pakistan. The Taliban had harbored the masterminds of 9/11, Al-Qaeda and its leader, Osama Bin Laden.

According to the logic of Bush's new war, everybody had to take sides. In a speech to a joint session of Congress on September 20, he said: "Every nation, in every region, now has a decision to make. Either you are with us, or you are with the terrorists." Where would the Islamic Republic of Iran stand in this new global battle? What would be its attitude to the US-led war on terror?

Iran in 2001 was in the throes of a political civil war. Backed by millions of Iranians clamoring for change and reform, President Khatami had been comfortably re-elected in 2001 and continued to battle conservatives in his quest for the democratization of Iran. In the international arena, Khatami offered a narrative of peace and coexistence that couldn't have been more different rhetorically from the stern Khomeini and his open call for the murder of an innocent writer. In 1998, President Khatami went to New York with much fanfare to attend the United Nations General Assembly, only the second Iranian head of government ever to make the trip (the first had been the erstwhile President Khamenei in 1987). "Clinton, Khatami likely to take center stage," CNN headlined. Rumors about a possible handshake between the two men swirled around the world. According to one version, Khatami had at some point hidden in a bathroom to avoid encountering Clinton in the halls of the UN and cause the ire of conservatives in Tehran. The handshake would not come but Khatami's Iran proposed a resolution roundly passed by the assembly. With the support of the UN secretary-general, Kofi Annan, it was decided that UN would name 2001 as a year of "Dialogue among Civilizations," explicitly to counter Huntington's narrative of clash.

Much of Khatami's narrative of dialogue was crafted by Mohammad Javad Zarif, now a forty-year-old diplomat at the Iranian mission to the UN and perhaps the chief figure among the "New York Boys," so reviled by the anti-Americans of Tehran. But when the UN's year of "Dialogue" was marred by the deadly 9/11 attacks, Iran couldn't rely on words alone. It had to take a side—and it did so resolutely. Khatami had condemned the 9/11 attacks and sent messages of commiseration to the US. In the invasion of Afghanistan that followed, Iran squarely backed the United States. As the "Great Satan" started its long military adventure in the Muslim lands, it found on its side the Islamic Republic of Iran, the world's leading Islamist state, still heavily sanctioned by the US and one of the very few countries on its list of state sponsors of terrorism.

Zarif had spent most of his adult life in the US and had several degrees from American universities. His career had been dedicated to building an Islamist diplomacy for Iran that could improve its relations with the West. He had mastered the halls of the UN. In late 2001, when the US gathered a group of Afghan leaders in Bonn's Hotel Petersberg to help set up a new interim government, Zarif played a crucial role in bringing the meeting to fruition. In shock, Americans watched as the representative of the Islamic Republic worked hard for America's choice, Pashtun leader Hamid Karzai, to get the consent of the Shia parties and become the new Afghan president.

Iran's help to the US efforts in Afghanistan would not remain limited to Zarif-style diplomacy. With thousands of US and Western boots now on the ground in its eastern vicinity, the Islamic Republic needed a different sort of diplomat to lead its efforts there: someone who could be comfortable far from the serene surroundings of the German former capital or the UN headquarters on New York's East River; a man who understood the world of war now engulfing the region. Luckily for Iran, it had just the man.

* * *

When Qassem Soleimani was tasked with fighting the drug lords of eastern Iran, he hardly knew anything about diplomacy. He was the farthest thing one could imagine from a diplomat. Diplomats were known to be crafty, educated, wordy, and worldly, usually with an ability to speak foreign languages and one or more degrees from foreign universities. Soleimani had hardly ever left Iran, had no postsecondary education and spoke no foreign languages. He was a straight-talking man, obsessed with military affairs and not necessarily tuned in with the latest world events. Furthermore, military veterans like Soleimani often viewed the diplomats, even those of the Islamic Republic, suspiciously. Zarif and his associates had helped build a corps of Islamist diplomats who were, at least in appearance, sharply different from those of pre-revolutionary Iran. They almost never wore a tie or shook hands with women.[1] Nevertheless, the revolutionary zealots in Tehran often distrusted the wheeling and dealing that was the bread and butter of all diplomacy. Years later, when running for president in 2013, Mohammad Baqer Qalibaf would speak for many IRGC veterans when scolding the conservative candidate Ali Akbar Velayati, Iran's wartime foreign minister, for "having coffee with [French president François] Mitterrand in Paris, when we were being hit by his Dassault Mirage missiles on the battlefronts."[2]

Yet Soleimani's postwar job had always included diplomacy by another name. Even if he didn't use that word, he had had to be "diplomatic" in his dealings with the complex tribal lands of eastern Iran. Not only were these lands home to a variety of tribes who spoke different languages and had various loyalties, they seamlessly blended into the neighboring countries of Afghanistan and Pakistan. Soleimani had impressed by showing diplomatic initiative and, even before being appointed as the Quds Force commander, he had become one of Iran's Afghanistan specialists, repeatedly traveling to the country in the 1990s. It was this experience that led Khamenei to appoint him as the commander of the Quds Force, in charge of all of the IRGC's operations abroad. Soleimani had become a top diplomat in spite of himself.

In the two decades that followed, Zarif and Soleimani, two very different diplomats of the Islamic Republic, worked from their respective positions to further the goals of Tehran. In the process, they both achieved global fame. Their apparent differences baffled many. Zarif often sounded like a law professor and was known for his perennial smile and showing off about his long years in the US. Soleimani's stern face on magazine covers reminded the readers that he had personally masterminded the killing of hundreds of American forces. Which was the true face of Iran? Smiling Javad or Frowning Qassem? In attempts to answer this question, so many heads were scratched, so much ink spilled, so many hackneyed clichés employed.

They often forgot two facts: First, both men were trusted acolytes of Ayatollah Khamenei, a man who prized loyalty; second, Soleimani's first experience of dealing with Americans had been not enmity but close military cooperation and assistance.

* * *

The Taliban had been a thorn in the side of Qassem Soleimani years before he allied with the Americans against them.

In 1992, the left-wing Afghan government finally fell and it was replaced by an Islamist coalition with the support of both Washington and Tehran. The supposedly united government immediately faced armed challenges from tribal-based Islamists who did not consent to its rule. Concentrated in the Pashtun-dominated east and south of the country, the Taliban emerged from among these Islamist groups as the strongest contender to challenge the government. In the summer of 1996, just as the Taliban were close to winning the Battle of Kabul and overthrowing what little remained of the central government, Qassem Soleimani arrived in the capital.

Whatever changes Soleimani's military career went through, one crucial element remained constant across the years: He liked to be in the heart of the action. His driver would often complain that nothing seemed to deter the commander from wanting to be right at the center of things.[3] He seemed to know no fear. "He was there in person, right in the middle of Kabul, sitting on the ground with us, warming our hearts with hope," an Afghan cabinet minister of the fledgling 1992–6 government recalls.

The 39-year-old Iranian commander was thus "giving hope" to old hands of Afghanistan's Islamist movement who had helped bring down a superpower. By 1996, Burhanuddin Rabbani was a respected elder politician, a father figure for mainstream Islamism in Afghanistan. In the 1960s, he had got his PhD in Islamic philosophy from Cairo's Al-Azhar, the Sunni world's most renowned institution of learning. He had built links with the Muslim Brotherhood in Egypt, impressed by the fight they put up against the rule of Nasser. In the 1970s, as Afghanistan slid toward secular socialism, Rabbani, now a professor at Kabul University, founded his political party, Jamiate Islami. Among his acolytes was a young, fellow Persian-speaking Afghan, Ahmad Shah Masood, who became the party's brightest military figure. The close pact between the Islamist professor and his guerrilla lieutenant, who looked like Che Guevara, proved key in the 1980s as they battled the Soviets.

Now, in 1996, Rabbani and Masood, the leading lights of Afghan Islamism, were being reassured by an Iranian commander with no official status. "Soleimani was calm but stern," the cabinet minister remembers. "Rabbani and Masood were legends in their own right. But this man spoke to them with such charisma that they were taken by him. He also reassured them of Tehran's support."[4]

Soleimani sat down with Masood and his men and spoke with an almost mystical tone: "Have some hope, boys. I will support you. You have my word. Iran will support you. Look into my eyes and listen: We won't leave you on your own. You might have to leave now but you will come back victorious."

Soleimani's message was simple: They had to leave Kabul if they wanted to survive. They had to wait to fight another day. Rabbani and Masood took the advice. It turned out to be prescient. The brutal Taliban murdered anybody they didn't like. Mohammad Najibullah, the communist statesman who had tried hard to bring Afghanistan together after the Soviets left, was taking refuge in the UN compound, together with his brother Shapur. Immediately after the fall of Kabul, the Taliban attacked the compound and arrested the two men. They were castrated and brutally tortured, their bodies left hanging from a lamppost right outside the Arg presidential palace, Najibullah's office as president from 1987 to 1992.

Rabbani and Masood fled to the north and found a new base in the Panjshir valley, near the Hindu Kush mountains. There they set up the

United Islamic Front for the Salvation of Afghanistan, internationally known as the Northern Alliance. The alliance controlled less than 10 percent of Afghan territory but while the Taliban was backed by neighboring Pakistan, the Rabbani-led alliance had the backing of Iran and the US, plus that of Russia and post-Soviet states of central Asia such as Tajikistan and Uzbekistan.

Masood was the unquestionable star of the Northern Alliance. In 1975, even before the communists came to power, Masood had led a failed uprising against the government there. But in the 1980s, when the civil war broke out and the Soviets invaded, Masood put up a legendary defense of the valley. He would now defend it from the Taliban, which earned him the nickname Lion of Panjshir and made him the most celebrated military figure of modern Afghanistan in the process.

Years later, in January 2020, after Soleimani was killed, one of the many Afghans who commemorated him was Masood's son, Ahmad. Now aged thirty, he was seven years old when his father was consoled by Soleimani in Kabul. He completed his high school years in Iran and his military studies at the Royal Military Academy, Sandhurst, and King's College London. On his Instagram page, Ahmad posted a picture of his father with the slain Iranian general, commemorated Soleimani as "a superman of history," and shared a poem: "When men who are lions die, one has to mourn | When will we have another such lion again?"

* * *

The Taliban government shocked the world with its brutality. Before the rise of ISIS two decades later, it was the most gruesome form of government anyone in the region could remember. Communists and political opponents were summarily executed. Music, TV, cinema, the internet, painting, photography, and most sports, including soccer and chess, were banned. You couldn't fly kites or keep pigeons (a popular Afghan pastime). Women were barred from education, work, or going outside the house without a full body covering. Men had to shave their beards or they'd be arrested on the spot. Thieves had their hands and feet amputated. Although Iran previously constituted one of the strictest Islamist regimes in the world, Ayatollah Khamenei would come to call the Taliban "a zealot and wild group, alien from the enlightened teaching of Islam and ignorant of the general rules of the world."

In promising support to Rabbani and Masood, Qassem hadn't been bluffing. In 1998, based on his success in liaising with the Afghans, he was appointed head of the IRGC's Quds Force. Founded in 1988, the force had overseen the maintenance of Iran's links with like-minded movements abroad (the other form of foreign operation, assassinating opponents abroad, was entrusted to the intelligence ministry). Before Soleimani took over, their most notable operation had been a mostly failed attempt to intervene in the Bosnian War in the early 1990s. In the battlegrounds of Afghanistan, Soleimani would transform the Quds Force into one of the most successful units of its kind anywhere in the world.

The Taliban didn't take easily to Iran's open support for the Northern Alliance. In August 1998, when the northern city of Mazar-i-Sharif fell to the Taliban, the Iranian consulate was attacked. Eight Iranian diplomats plus a reporter from Iran's state news agency were killed. Many of them were relatively local men whose hometowns were a few hundred kilometers to the west, over the Iranian border. Soleimani had had a role in promoting such appointments to help ease the relationship with Tehran's Afghan partners. Among the nine "martyrs" of Mazar was the 31-year-old Naser Rigi, Iran's head consul in the city, who hailed from a major Balochi Sunni tribe, as his last name suggested. Like Soleimani, he did karate, and unlike Soleimani, he actually had a black belt. Mazar had been his first foreign posting. Then there was Mohammad Nasseri from the little village of Sistanak in Khorasan, not far from the border with Afghanistan. When the Islamist insurgency was battling the Soviets in 1980s, Nasseri had been among the young IRGC hands sent to help.[5] After their deaths, Soleimani made a point of visiting the families of the "martyrs." He had often done this for men of his unit killed in the war with Iraq. But this was now harder. The war against the foreign enemy had finished. Now Soleimani had to console families who had lost their loved ones in foreign lands, even though Iran was not supposedly at war anymore. The newly appointed commander of the Quds Force would get very good at this. Visits to families of the fallen, where he would hug and kiss the children and gift the relatives his signature rings, became a constant part of Soleimani's life.

The 1998 attacks gave Iran a *casus belli*. Almost 200,000 Iranian forces gathered on the Afghan border, ready to attack and overthrow the Taliban. As Iran's main liaison with the Afghan forces of the Northern Alliance, Soleimani was consulted. The strategic decision made by Ayatollah Khamenei in that fateful moment determined the course of Iran's operations. Less than a decade after the war with Iraq had ended, Iran would not start another international war. It did not have the resources, human or military, nor the support of a population that had seen two tumultuous decades already. Instead, Iran would rely on a stealthier path: It would bide its time, continue to build its relationship with its Afghan partners, and try to instill in them deep-seated support for the Islamist government in Tehran. Building another Hezbollah wasn't prudent since the Afghan Shia were a small minority and Iran had an excellent relationship with Sunni Islamists. They followed a different sect of Islam but their mother tongue was Persian and their Islamism was historically influenced by Khomeini. The Quds Force made itself indispensable, this time not by religious-political affinity, but by the seriousness it showed in offering advanced military help. The Iranian advisors were not those revolutionary clerics and students who had helped build Hezbollah in the 1980s. They were now battle-hardened commanders like Soleimani with years of conventional warfare under their belt. Working closely with Soleimani on this front was another battle-hardened commander, Esmayil Qaani. The Mashhad-born man was a few months younger than Soleimani and had succeeded Mohammad Baqer Qalibaf as commander of the Khorasani division in the war with Iraq. Like Soleimani, he became an "eastern hand," helping develop the IRGC's work with Afghanistan and Pakistan.

To the north of Afghanistan, another area of opportunity opened for Iran. Some of the elites in the Muslim central Asian republics that had gained independence following the collapse of the Soviet Union looked positively to Iran as a land of a historically enlightened Islam and home of a Persianate civilization that had long influenced their lands. This was especially true in Tajikistan, which, together with Iran and Afghanistan, was one of the world's three Persian-speaking countries. Soleimani attempted to build on those ties. On January 18, 1999, the Iranian commander made his first trip to the mountainous, doubly landlocked country.

The visit barely made any media headlines. Soleimani was there at the head of a military delegation that met with the Tajik minister of defense, Sherali Khairullaev, to discuss a memorandum of understanding in security ties and a joint defense commission. It was the sort of official news usually buried at the bottom of inside pages of newspapers.

But the really important meetings in this visit were not those in the brutalist Stalinist defense ministry building on Dushanbe's Bokhtar Street but a few hundred meters south on the same road, in a modest rural-looking building that housed the Iranian embassy, across the road from the massive Rudaki Park, named after a canonical Persian poet of the ninth and tenth centuries. There Soleimani met his old comrade Ahmad Shah Masood and also many other leaders of the Northern Alliance, all of whom continue to be major figures in Afghan politics today. There was Mohammad Mohaqeq from Balkh, a rowdy warlord from the Shia Hazara minority and a frequent cabinet minister in the years to come. There was another Hazara, the quiet Karim Khalili, who had lived in Iran for many years, representing the Shia Afghan Islamists in Tehran. He would later head President Ashraf Ghani's High Peace Council in talks with the Taliban. Also present in the room was Abdul Rashid Dostum, an ethnic Uzbek whose National Islamic Movement of Afghanistan (usually known as Junbish or "Movement") claimed to represent the Turkic speakers of the country.

Soleimani once more had a simple message for the Afghans: Iran would back them but they had to unite and quit the bickering that had doomed the earlier 1992–6 government. The commander also had a message for Dushanbe. He reassured the Tajik officials that Tehran wanted to cause no disturbance in their country, which had just finished five years of civil war in June 1997. Tajik Islamists who had battled the pro-Moscow government of Dushanbe had hoped for support from their fellow Islamists in Iran. Soleimani promised Dushanbe that Iran would not betray its strategic interests by helping the Islamist opposition, which, after all, had been backed by the Taliban and Al-Qaeda. A participant in the meeting later spoke of his surprise at Soleimani's "pronounced modesty and courtesy" as he "spoke in a quiet, calm tone, without drawing attention to himself, which is not typical for post-Soviet military commanders."[6] Similar words would be repeated dozens of times, by interlocutors around the world, about the quiet visits of the Iranian shadow commander who made his down-to-earth charisma into an art.

* * *

Iran's official history might be opaque on many points but it has never hidden the Islamic Republic's support for the Americans in Afghanistan after 9/11. Writing in 2020, Mostafa Zandiyeh, a top Iranian diplomat, put the matter pithily: "Following 9/11, the interests of the United States and the Islamic Republic of Iran were aligned in Afghanistan. There was ground for a series of collaborations. We had an unwritten pact."[7]

Iran's support for the American offensive against the Taliban was unambiguous. Shortly after the attacks on the World Trade Center in New York, Soleimani made a secret repeat trip to Dushanbe. Speaking to representatives of Northern Alliance groups, he pledged Iran's collaboration with the United States in bringing down the Taliban. He also went on a regional tour, visiting various central Asian countries and reassuring them of Iran's support for an independent, post-Taliban Afghanistan. It was Mohammad Javad Zarif's theatrical role in the Bonn conference that made media headlines (and the history books) but it was Soleimani who had helped gain the trust of Afghan militias, not in a meeting room in a European hotel in 2001 but in a Kabul surrounded by Taliban in 1996, and in battlefield valleys and gorges of the north in the five years following.

As Iran started talking to America, once more, it was Soleimani, not the foreign ministry, who was in control. Iran undertook direct negotiations with the Americans in New York, Geneva, and Paris. The diplomat leading many of these talks was Iran's ambassador to Tajikistan, Mohammad Ebrahim Taherian-Fard. But Taherian-Fard was clear to the Americans that these talks were being run not by Khatami's foreign ministry, even though they had his support, but by a man most Americans had barely heard of: Qassem Soleimani. The IRGC had long supplanted the country's main military. It had taken over much of the country's civil infrastructure. It now took over some of the most important diplomatic functions of the foreign ministry.

On the American side, the talks were run by the veteran diplomat Ryan Crocker. Crocker was a star Middle East operator, known as an exemplary on-the-ground diplomat who had learnt the intricacies of the region not from books but by spending decades serving there. Speaking both Persian and Arabic, he had started his career at the US consulate in Khorramshahr in 1972 and had since served in some of the most difficult postings in the region. He was the US's man in Lebanon in the years after the civil war in the early 1990s. He was its envoy in Syria when Hafez al-Assad died in 2000 and was replaced by his son. Crocker was now asked to prepare to head the US's embassy in the new Afghanistan. He knew well that the path to a successful Afghan policy went through working with a country that had done more to fight the Taliban than any other: the Islamic Republic of Iran. Crocker's biographer would later claim that his "most important contribution was enlisting the help of Iran."[8]

To keep the talks confidential, Crocker flew from DC into Geneva on weekends, when no one was around the UN compound there. Swirling as it did with foreign envoys of all sorts, the Swiss city had long been the best place to hide in plain sight. The Iranians aimed to charm their American partners by showing off their US degrees and local knowledge of the US sports scene. But much more attractive than casual diplomacy was the wide front of cooperation offered to the US.

Few men knew the area around Afghanistan and its borders with Iran better than Soleimani. He had spent more than a decade of his career focused on this area. His men came to the meeting with Crocker not with platitudes or lectures about Islam, as some Iranian diplomats were known to do. They came with maps and operational plans. The soldier-diplomat meant business. The maps indicated the exact bases and likely movements of the Taliban forces. The Iranians also explained their plans in Herat and Farah, the Afghan cities close to the border with Iran, and how they could collaborate with the US to ensure maximum efficacy. In an arrangement that was to be repeated in the future in other countries, Iranian ground forces would fight Sunni Islamists with American air support.

This military cooperation wasn't the first attempt at rethinking Tehran-Washington ties. There had been many false starts during the Clinton years, although important milestones had also been reached. Clinton's secretary of state, Madeleine Albright, had done the unthinkable in March 2000 by accepting American responsibility for the 1953 coup in Iran which crushed Iran's left-leaning and democratically elected prime minister, Mohammad Mossadeq, and solidified the Shah's power. Speaking to the American-Iranian Council in Washington, Albright admitted to the US's "significant role" in the coup and acknowledged that it had been "clearly a setback for Iran's political development."[9]

The stumbles of Khatami's project for change in Iran, as he faced off the conservative establishment, and the victory of the Republicans in the 2000 US elections had dimmed the hopes for rapprochement. But, following 9/11, Iranian-American de facto cooperation was at its highest level since 1979. As Iranian and American diplomats worked together in quiet hotel rooms in Geneva, their military figures were allies in the Afghan battleground. There was significant cooperation in intelligence too. Iran thus cooperated with the American "Great Satan" against a leading Islamist organization.

Al-Qaeda's Islamism, of course, included hatred of the Shia, although not yet the murderous kind that would soon become mainstream among Salafi-Jihadists. However, this anti-Shia attitude had not precluded pragmatic cooperation between Iran and Sunni Islamists, Al-Qaeda included. In the battlegrounds of Bosnia in the early 1990s, Quds Force advisors had sometimes led units that included Al-Qaeda figures. The Iranians had even offered a chance for these figures to go to training camps run in Lebanon's Beqaa valley by Hezbollah, the party that was denounced in the extremist Sunni literature as "*Hezb-ul-Shaytan*," the Party of the Devil.

On December 19, 2001, just as the Iranians were planning military cooperation with the Americans, a leading Al-Qaeda figure managed to get himself to Iran. Mahfouz Ould al-Walid was a scholar and poet hailing from Mauritania, a little-known Muslim country in northwestern Africa. In Al-Qaeda circles, he was simply known as "al-Mauritani" (the Mauritanian) and had made his name with his beautiful Arabic poetry, which was a favorite of Bin Laden himself. Traveling under a counterfeit identity, al-Mauritani boarded a bus from Quetta in Pakistani Balochistan to the Iranian border crossing at Taftan. He managed to get an audience with Soleimani. Al-Mauritani tried to charm the Iranian commander by praising his military skills. He also made it clear that he had opposed the 9/11 attacks and didn't agree with the anti-Iran bent of some of the Al-Qaeda leaders.

"He came to us with an offer: Let's build a united Islamist front against the Americans," recalls an Afghan member of the Quds Force who was privy to Soleimani's meeting with al-Mauritani. "Hajj Qassem didn't agree. He believed the general interests of our revolution, as set down by Ayatollah Khamenei, went against this. Bringing down the Taliban took priority."[10]

Al-Mauritani wasn't alone. Much of the Bin Laden family and many Al-Qaeda fighters would find their way to Iran in the next few months. Many of the women and children stayed in the four-star Howeyze Hotel, owned by the parastatal Martyr Foundation, while the fighters stayed across the road in the Amir Hotel.[11] This was later used by the Trump administration as an example of Iran "supporting Al-Qaeda." Nothing could be further from the truth. When Al-Qaeda figures fled to Iran, they were put under the charge of Soleimani's forces. He kept them under tight control, in a situation of virtual house arrest, and repeatedly offered them as tokens in negotiations with the US. Iran's hosting of Al-Qaeda leaders was to strengthen its hand in negotiations with the US, not to support their crusade against the Americans.

Soleimani's clear "no" to al-Mauritani and the close cooperation he offered to the Americans marked the moment. For a brief period in December 2001 and January 2002, you would be forgiven for believing that it was only a matter of time before an Iranian-American rapprochement came to be. But on January 29, 2002, an event unforeseen by either Crocker or Soleimani changed everything.

In his first State of the Union address, President Bush said Iran "aggressively pursues these weapons [of mass destruction] and exports terror, while an unelected few repress the Iranian people's hope for freedom." He also mentioned North Korea and Iraq and put these three countries in a new category: "States like these and their terrorist allies constitute an axis of evil, aiming to threaten the peace of the world."

Iranians were not the only ones who first heard about this new "Axis of Evil" in the address. Numerous accounts from Crocker and other American diplomats show that they were as shocked as non-Americans. In Bush's White House, the State Department and its experienced staff were so marginalized that they had hardly been consulted about this major pivot. The men and women running things were now either linked directly to the White House staff, Vice President Dick Cheney, or the powerful secretary of defense, Donald Rumsfeld.

This particular speech had been mostly the work of David Frum, a 41-year-old speechwriter who hailed from an influential Jewish family in Toronto. His mother, the New York–born Barbara Frum, had been among the most acclaimed journalists in Canadian history. David Frum had started political life as a volunteer for the left-leaning New Democratic Party in his teens before turning sharply to the right and pursuing a future in the United States by getting degrees from Yale and Harvard.

Frum's task was to justify a patently unjustifiable goal. The United States was going after Saddam Hussein's Iraq, even though Saddam had no known links to those who had perpetrated 9/11. Like Iran, Saddam had been approached by Al-Qaeda, via none other than al-Mauritani, and, like Iran, he had turned them down. Why was the US bringing him down then?

Frum took inspiration from the 1941 speech by President Roosevelt that had committed the US to the Second World War in the aftermath of Pearl Harbor. As he told the story years later, Frum saw striking similarities between the Axis powers of 1941 and the anti-Western group and regimes in the Middle East of 2002. For him, it didn't matter that Iran and Iraq had fought a major war, that Al-Qaeda openly hated the Shia, and, most crucially, that Iran was closely collaborating with the US in the fight against Al-Qaeda. All that mattered was what Saddam Hussein's regime and Iran's Islamic Republic shared with Al-Qaeda: They "all resented the power of the West and Israel, and they all despised the humane values of democracy." They formed an "Axis of Hatred." The phrasing was changed to "Axis of Evil," better to remind the public of "the Evil Empire," the term used by Ronald Reagan about the Soviet Union.[12]

The speech has lived on as a traumatic moment for many American diplomats and those who saw use in continuing the US's collaboration with Iran. Crocker couldn't have put it more dramatically: "One word in one speech changed history."[13] This was, to him, "the point where the Iranians made the decision 'Can't work with those sons of bitches. Told you all along, can't do it.'"[14] Bill Burns, a respected elder diplomat and then assistant secretary for Near Eastern affairs, wrote that the speech "killed the diplomatic channel that Ryan Crocker had so skillfully developed with the Iranians."[15]

The shock of having watched their most treasured program destroyed on live television explains why the likes of Crocker and Burns treated the speech as a catastrophe that changed history. But this wasn't just one speech. It wasn't just a turn of phrase by Frum that ended the Iranian-American collaboration and ushered in a new era of US policy on the Middle East. The top of the Bush administration took a conscious decision that the United States would now adopt a breathtakingly daring course. It would run a crusade-like battle to challenge and ultimately bring down the two major illiberal revolutionary regimes of the Middle East, Iran and Iraq. The confident Bush administration was replete with people who believed as zealously in spreading their ideas as the Iranian revolutionaries. Only they had the backing of the resources of a superpower. Some of them believed they were doing God's work. Some had a Marxist past and had not kicked the habit of having grandiose visions of history. The Bush crusade could thus benefit from the oratory of Christopher Hitchens, a star wordsmith on the Marxist left, who became a passionate supporter of Bush's next big project: the invasion of Iraq in 2003.

Men like Crocker, who had spent decades working on the Middle East, repeatedly tried to raise alarms and give warning. They tried to explain that now was the time for the patient work of international diplomacy, not a rush to arms. But the heady scent of power blurs the mind. Just a few decades ago, the Kennedy administration had been filled with bright young men, the so-called "whiz kids" of the high Cold War era, whose folly was immortalized by David Halberstam in his 1972 account, *The Best and the Brightest*. The Bush people seemed to not have read that best-selling book. As Burns put it bitterly, years later in 2019, "It was not the season for nuance, caution, and compromise. It was the season for the risk-tolerant and the ideologically ambitious, bent on inserting ourselves aggressively into the regional contest of ideas, militarizing our policy and unbuckling our rhetoric."[16]

The "unwritten pact" between Iran and the United States was torn up by George W. Bush in that live speech in January 2002. The Bush administration went head-on to its next adventure. In just over a year, its forces were on the Tigris, overthrowing Saddam Hussein and occupying Iraq. Iran knew that it could be next. "Anyone can go to Baghdad, real men go to Tehran," was reported to be the scary echo in the halls of power in DC. Fears were confirmed later when the PMOI, now primarily based in Baghdad, declared in August 2002 that Iran had an active nuclear program, giving out the addresses and detailed descriptions of places that would soon become familiar names to those who watched the evening news: a facility to enrich uranium in Natanz; a plant to produce heavy water in Arak. It was clear that the US, or the Israelis, had provided the PMOI with the necessary intelligence.

The Iranians were certainly angry that the US had turned on them just when they were working together in Afghanistan. But they were also terrified at the very real prospect of a US attack. The Islamic Republic did not shut down its negotiations with the US over Afghanistan; it opened new ones about Iraq. Unlike Saddam's regime, it quickly allowed the inspectors of the International Atomic Energy Agency to visit Natanz, Arak, and other cites, and by 2003, they could confirm that Iran had ceased enrichment. Around the same time, Tim Guldimann, who as Swiss ambassador to Iran was also charged with looking after US interests there, took a one-page letter to the Americans that purported to offer a grand bargain coming from Tehran. If the US committed to non-aggression against the Islamic Republic, Tehran would work with it. The letter had been primarily the work of Sadeq Kharazi, Iran's tie-wearing, cigar-chomping ambassador to Paris, close friend of Soleimani, son of a leading ayatollah, nephew of the foreign minister, and a relative of Ayatollah Khamenei (Sadeq's sister had married the Supreme Leader's son).

Washington wasn't interested. "Real men" didn't sit down with the regime they despised. They not only rejected Tehran's offer, they humiliated the man who had brought it. Advocates of a hawkish attitude to

Tehran would later dissect the Guldimann memo. They would claim it wasn't serious and had not been approved from on high. Iranian-American columnist Sohrab Ahmari referred to the document as "one of the central myths of Iran apologetics," and went on to concoct wild stories about Guldimann's supposedly bad intentions and high ambitions in this case and others.

But no game of smoke and mirrors can hide the basic facts: As the world entered a new era following 9/11, an "unwritten pact" had come to exist between Iran and the United States. Geopolitical realities had put Tehran and Washington on the same side. It was the United States that broke the pact.

* * *

What course would history have taken if the Frum speech had never been made, if Bush hadn't listened to the neocons? What if he had done what another Republican, President Richard Nixon, did when he made peace, and a close alliance, with another ideological enemy, the Chinese communist regime? Counterfactual history is not a credible exercise. We can't seriously answer these questions. We can, however, enumerate the direct consequences of the course of action followed by the United States.

With its overtures broadly rejected, the Islamic Republic now sought to ensure its survival and security by disrupting the US plans for the region. It had worked with the Americans in Afghanistan; it would come to fight them in Iraq. The dimming of hopes for rapprochement didn't do Khatami's reform movement any good either, although the movement had plenty of problems of its own, including the unwillingness of the president to stand up to the Khamenei loyalists who vetoed his legislative plans and banned his supporters from running in the 2004 parliamentary elections. The masses had lost their faith in Khatami. Even when the main reformist candidate was allowed to run in the 2005 presidential elections, he was humiliated by garnering less than 14 percent of the vote and coming in fifth place.

Ayatollah Khamenei was no longer the scrawny and insecure Supreme Leader of 1989. He had been bolstered by gathering the conservative opposition that had successfully defeated the reform movement. He would now formulate a new strategy for the Iranians by employing slow-burn tactics of irregular warfare, conducted by Hezbollah and other forces that the Quds Force would train in the region. Although he was still mostly unknown, Qassem Soleimani would take center stage in these plans.

In later years, when he emerged as a national military hero, Soleimani was careful to stress that he was above the conservative-reformist division of Iranian politics. But the strict loyalty he always offered to Khamenei made it very clear which side he stood on. This had always been clear to those who paid attention. In July 1999, when students in Tehran launched the largest protests in decades, Soleimani joined his old IRGC pals, including Mohammad Baqer Qalibaf, Ahmad Kazemi, Esmayil Qaani, and Mohammad Ali Jafari, in writing an open letter to Khatami with a simple message: Either control the situation or we will bring you down.

"Dear Mr. Khatami, How long do we have to keep shedding our tears, having our hearts tarnished, and keep watching as the 'practice of democracy' brings chaos and insults?" the letter read. "Should we keep our revolutionary patience to the point of losing our regime?" In closing, it said: "Our patience has come to an end. Unless something is done, we can't bear this anymore."

As it turned out, Khatami had no interest in seriously transforming the Islamic Republic. He meekly retreated in face of an emboldened Khamenei and his foot soldiers in the IRGC. In the 2005 elections, Soleimani backed his comrade Qalibaf, who was running on a technocratic ticket that emphasized not his wartime service but his skills as a trained pilot who had flown Airbus airliners. His posters showed him not in the IRGC khaki or greens but in a Western-style pilot uniform. He compared himself not to Khomeini but to Reza Shah, the popular autocratic monarch and founder of the Pahlavi dynasty. But this was not the sort of man Khamenei wanted for the post-reform future. Ideology-light technocracy would threaten the foundations of the regime, he thought, and give power to Rafsanjani, who, while no reformist, wanted to strike a balance between the different wings of the regime. The old fox Rafsanjani, without whom Khamenei could have never dreamed of becoming leader, had also thrown his hat into the ring of the 2005 presidential elections.

Khamenei withdrew support from Qalibaf and gave it to an unknown upstart: Mahmoud Ahmadinejad, the 48-year-old mayor of Tehran who, with his austere look, characteristic beard and populist oratory, looked like a caricature of a pro-regime Islamist that would have made sense in the 1980s but was alien to many in 2005. Yet his message of economic equality resonated with millions upset at the growing inequalities. Conservatives who wanted a total rejection of the reform years loved him. In the first round, Ahmadinejad came second with 19.43 percent to Rafsanjani's 21.13 percent. The two men now went to a second round. Many believed organized rigging by Basij had pushed Ahmadinejad over the line. In the second round, despite a wide coalition, including secular nationalists and leftists, calling for a vote for Rafsanjani to "stop fascism," and no doubt helped by Basij's organized irregularities, Ahmadinejad won the presidency hands down with 61.69 percent of the vote.

Iran was now to have a very different face and a very different course. Khatami had quoted de Tocqueville and Hegel and loved buzzwords like "civil society." Ahmadinejad would deny the Holocaust and claim 9/11 was an inside job. More consequentially for Khamenei's project, and for Soleimani's men, Ahmadinejad purged not just the men of Khatami but much of the establishment bureaucracy of the Islamic Republic and its institutional memory. He filled the regime with men like himself: young, ambitious, revolutionary, and daring. While Mohammad Javad Zarif was forced into early retirement, Quds Force men would take over embassies in the region and the IRGC youth became influential all over the government. At least half of Ahmadinejad's cabinet were IRGC members.

Ahmadinejad was also, perhaps ironically, the most globally oriented leader of Iran. He became a celebrity worldwide, reviled by his opponents and courted by his many fans. For the first time in the Iranian history, he made the annual trip to attend the United Nations General Assembly an unmissable occasion. He took entourages of dozens of people to New York and spoke not only in the chamber but inside events that were a ceaseless source of controversy and outrage. He sped up Iran's nuclear program and tarnished its relations not only with the US but with the Europeans. Instead, he became friendly with President Hugo Chávez of Venezuela and other left-wing leaders around the world who liked his daring anti-Americanism. In Havana, the ailing Fidel Castro got out of bed to greet the young Iranian president.

Soleimani's Quds Force was now given free rein by both the Supreme Leader and the president to do all it could to disrupt the Americans' plans. The Americans only understood the language of force, Khamenei's thinking went. They had to be hit. Iraq provided the perfect theater. As the US found itself in a quagmire in Mesopotamia, Soleimani made sure his was a name to be reckoned with in DC. This time, not as a pragmatic commander who brings maps to meetings but as the man who would come out of nowhere to ruin even the best-designed plans; as the shadow commander of Iran.

Chapter 9

We Protect the Shrines

Tears ran down Ahmad's face; his eyes were red with crying and his hands were shaking. This was a moment he had waited for all his life. He was standing in the courtyard of the shrine built for the greatest man who had ever lived: the Lord of Martyrs, the Master of Tears, the Blood of Allah, the Third Shia Imam, Hossein, son of Ali, grandson of the Prophet Mohammad. This was Karbala, the city near the Euphrates around which, in 680, Hossein and his comrades had lost their lives fighting the forces of the caliph Yazid, playing their parts in the most monumental event of Shia history.

Like any typical Shia, Ahmad had grown up on the stories of Hossein and his cruel death in Karbala. But he had a more personal connection. For eight long years, he had fought the Iraqi soldiers led by Saddam Hussein, a man who appeared as the Yazid of his age: a Sunni tyrant, out to drench a rightful movement, this time led by Imam Khomeini, in blood. Ahmad had been stuck in the mud of the Iraqi battlefields, he had been injured, he had come close to death. Now the Yazid was gone and he could enter Iraq as a proud Shia pilgrim. When he saw the golden dome and double minarets of Imam Hossein's shrine, when he saw the red flag shaking in the wind, he couldn't help his tears of joy and honor.

Ahmad was no ordinary pilgrim. He was among the first party of Iranians sent to staff the diplomatic missions of the Islamic Republic in the new Iraq. Officially, he would be an employee of the Iranian embassy in Baghdad, headed by an ambassador who had to answer to the foreign ministry. In reality, he was a soldier-diplomat and his ambassador answered to a man who had never been in the ministry: Qassem Soleimani, the head of the Quds Force.

In March 2003, a few months before Ahmad's arrival, the Americans, joined by troops from the UK, Australia, and Poland, invaded Iraq and overthrew forty years of rule by the Baath Party. Faced with the preponderant might of American firepower, the Baathist state quickly collapsed. By May 1, after about five weeks of combat, the Americans controlled most of the country. A transitional government named the Coalition Provisional Authority (CPA) was set up. Plans for a government led by Iraqi dissidents had quickly come to naught. The men (and they were mostly men) of Iraqi exile politics had run their mini political parties from Tehran, Birmingham, England, or Dearborn, Michigan, often along with their grocery stores or dental practices. Like all political exiles, especially those away from home for decades, they were a squabbling bunch who knew how to shout each other down in a meeting but not how to govern. The CPA was instead a straightforward foreign occupying power, whose top executives were US military officials, even though it was adjoined by an Iraqi Governing Council, formed of Iraqi politicians, that it theoretically had to answer to. After the initial combat was over, forces from dozens of countries—those who had joined Bush in his Coalition of the Willing, defying the rules of the UN by overthrowing a sovereign government—now had to help run Iraq. It was a truly colorful scene: Britons were policing Basra in the south, South Koreans were learning their way around Iraqi Kurdistan, Hondurans and Spaniards were roaming the streets of the holy Najaf.

Cheerleaders of the invasion had promised quick victories. The Iraqis would come to greet their foreign liberators and build a model democracy on the ashes of the old regime. The fall of Saddam did indeed involve street celebrations. For years, the Baathists had claimed to run the country in the interests of the entire Arab world but actually did so in the interests of an ever narrower clique. Not only were they all from the

Sunni minority, they were mostly Saddam's family members or denizens of his hometown, Tikrit. Now the downtrodden, especially those from the Shia majority, cheered as they took down the statues of the tyrant and dreamed of a new Iraq.

But there would be no quick victory, no happy-ending story, no "mission accomplished." The invasion had instead led to exactly the nightmare warned about by those who had opposed the rushed march to war: the rise of sectarian militias, civil unrest, the collapse of infrastructure. Iraq was now a canvas upon which different groups of men with guns competed for control. Some were foreign armies, mostly formed of young men in search of adventure abroad who knew very little about the ancient lands they were now roaming in. Some were militias, organized around political leaders with ethno-sectarian bases. The Shia politicians soon found out that forming a militia was the quickest way to gain political muscle. On the other side, the disastrous decision to dissolve the Sunni-dominated Baath Party meant that tens of thousands of young men were now potential foot soldiers for anybody willing to organize them. Iraq of 2003 was a Hobbesian dystopia, not so much stateless as a place full of mini-states.

Ahmad didn't mind any of this just yet. As his convoy passed the American-manned checkpoints on the way to Karbala, his whole heart and mind were focused on his rendezvous with Imam Hossein. He had entered the country through the Mehran border crossing and had to travel a few hundred kilometers to the city. It would have made more sense to get settled in Baghdad first or visit Najaf, an arguably holier city, host to the shrine of Ali, the First Shia Imam.

"You don't go to see Imam Hossein because he is holy," Ahmad says. "You go because you love him."[1]

This was personal.

Ahmad wept as he thought of the infant son of Imam Hossein, Ali Asqar, who is supposed to be buried on his father's chest. Like many Iranian children, Ahmad had been dressed up as Ali Asqar in the Ashura ceremonies of his childhood. The infant martyr of Karbala is one of only three people known to the Shia as "Gates of Prayers." God is understood to grant any wishes if any of these three intercede on the supplicant's behalf. The other two were also buried nearby. From the courtyard, Ahmad could see the shrine of Abulfazl Abbas, Hossein's half-brother and his field commander in Karbala, who ferried water back and forth from the Euphrates, taking the bucket with his teeth after they cut off his hands. His birthday is now celebrated as the national day of war disabled in Iran. The third "gate" was al-Kazim, the Seventh Shia Imam who was buried in his namesake, Kadhimiya, a neighborhood by the Tigris in northern Baghdad.

"As I prayed in the shrines of Karbala, I promised my beloved Imam that I would bring back honor to the shrines of the family of the Prophet," Ahmad remembers.[2] He was offended by the disrepair that the shrines had fallen into. Gone were the days when the Iranian kings and tycoons financed the upkeep of the shrines to keep them in excellent shape for pilgrims. The hotel Ahmad stayed in Karbala offered no food, no television, no telephone, and only a few hours of electricity per day. The water was not drinkable. In Najaf, he was furious to see the shrine of Imam Ali controlled by American forces who restricted access. A foul smell surrounded the whole place.[3]

Shrines to the family of the Prophet Mohammad dot the landscape of Iraq. In the civil wars that broke out in the early centuries of Islam, Iraq, home to the capital of the Persian Empire before it was destroyed by the rising Muslim polity, had been the political base of Ali and his sons, the proto-Shia. Of the twelve Shia Imams, six were buried in Iraq: in Najaf, Karbala, Kadhimiya, and Samarra. There were also smaller shrines, such as the twin-domed beauty in Musayyeb, near Baghdad, for Ibrahim and Mohammad, two teenage boys who had fled Karbala only to be arrested and ultimately beheaded. Their father, Moselm, who was reputed to be half-Iranian, had been among the most loyal comrades of Hossein before he was killed in Kofa. In Balad, near Samarra, there was a shrine to Seyyed Mohammad, brother of the Eleventh Shia Imam and an uncle to the Twelfth Imam, the man who had gone into occultation in 941, only to come back at the end of times. Collectively the shrines were known as Atabat Aaliyat, the Sublime Gates.

The Shia were used to being in opposition. Ali had lost the caliphate to his Damascus-based rival, Muawiyah, who started a traditional Arab dynasty, the Umayyad. The Second Imam, Hassan, son of Ali, had accepted the rule of Muawiyah's son, Yazid. The Third Imam, Hossein, had lost to Yazid in Karbala. All the subsequent Imams had lived between being persecuted and barely tolerated, even when, following a revolution in 750, the Abbasid dynasty came to power and moved the capital to Baghdad. Every single Shia Imam was murdered by the powers that be, according to the Shia narrative of history. The caliphs who killed the Imams couldn't be expected to build shrines to them. The first shrine to Hossein had been built of brick and plaster by Mukhtar, a revolutionary from Arabia who led a revolt shortly following Karbala and even headed a government for eighteen months in the Iraqi city of Kufa, before being killed by a rival. But the Abbasid caliphs repeatedly destroyed the shrine, most notably in 847, when Mutawakkil dispatched a group of local Jews to do the job.

In the tenth century the time of the Shia arrived. This era has gone down in history as the Shia Century. Shia dynasties came to power across the Muslim world and led an age of cultural effervescence: The magnificent Fatimids ruled a gilded empire from Cairo, the Hamdanids reigned from Aleppo, and the Persian-origin Buyids revived a Muslim polity that considered itself heir to the Persian Empire. The Buyids had come to power just as the Twelfth Imam started his Major Occultation. They reached their peak under Adud al-Dawla, who ruled from 949 to 983 and whose empire stretched west to the Mediterranean shores of the Levant, east to the deserts that today straddle Iran's borders with Afghanistan and Pakistan, north to the Caspian Sea, and south to the Persian Gulf. This remarkable king resurrected the use of the Persian title *shahanshah* and revived the imperial traditions of the Persians. He built observatories, dams, and ports (not least, the port of Khorramshahr) and restored glory to the Shia shrines. For Imam Hossein, he built porticos on all sides and a grille made of teak, covered by lavish textiles. He built walls around Karbala and launched irrigation projects that turned Hossein's resting place into a major city.

The years of Shia power didn't last. The empires fell one after the other and the shrine of Imam Hossein, and those of the other Shia Imams, saw regular desecration throughout the ages. In 1801, the Wahhabi movement, born in the Arabian Peninsula, stormed Karbala and destroyed the shrine, since it believed all such places to be idolatrous. And in 1991, as the Shia rose in revolt against Saddam, the Baathist forces, led by the president's own son-in-law, attacked the shrine with airstrikes and heavy weaponry, a wound still remembered bitterly by the Shia in Iraq and elsewhere; a wound that had to be treated.

With Saddam gone, and the Bush administration rejecting all initial Iranian pleas for compromise, Soleimani and his men started a long game. In something of an orientalist fantasy, the Shia shrines were put squarely at the center of this game. Iran was going to rebuild each and every one of them and defend them against all aggression.

Ahmad was one of the hundreds of Iranians who rushed to the post-Saddam Iraq in an official capacity. They would be led by Hassan Kazemi Qomi, a 44-year-old diplomat who got his instructions not from the lame duck Khatami government, but directly from Soleimani. Previously head of the Iranian consulate in Herat, Afghanistan, Kazemi Qomi had been Soleimani's man for years.

As the Americans were hard at work in controlling the deluge of unrest that had been unleashed in Iraq, they barely noticed the formation of an Iranian cultural body with a seemingly modest goal: The Center for Restoration of the Sublime Gates (CRSG) wanted to take care of the Shia shrines just like the kings of Qajar, some of whom are buried in Karbala, had done in the nineteenth century. The CRSG employed preservationists and artistic experts who paid careful attention to every aspect of the shrines. They would help to find the right tiles, the right texture, and the right historical design. They would soon enable marches of tens of millions, chiefly from Iraq and Iran, who once more flocked to Karbala on the holy day of Arbaeen, marking the fortieth day of Hossein's passing. In February 2003, around three million had gathered in Rome to oppose the US attack on Iraq, marking the largest anti-war rally in history. By 2009, when the initial conflicts had subsided and the CRSG's work was rebuilding tourism capacities, up to fourteen million gathered in Karbala for Arbaeen, marking the second largest recorded gathering in entire human history, second only to the 2001 Hindu festival of Kumbh Mela in India's Allahabad. The crowds would only grow in the years to come, topping at up to thirty million in 2016, hundreds of thousands of whom had marched, at least for some of the way, all the way from Iran. The leftie anti-war crowd in Rome hadn't stopped the American guns; but the ten times larger crowd of Shia pilgrims was symbolic of the forces that would disrupt the American plans.

What made the CRSG different from your usual group of preservationists was that it was essentially a unit of the Quds Force. All its major officials were Quds Force people, soon earning the nickname "Soleimanis in suits." They did much more than shrine restoration. They lobbied local politicians, they helped run guns to the Shia militias that mushroomed after 2003, and they went the extra mile where official diplomats couldn't go. Anchored in the population centers of the Shia heartlands of southern Iraq, the shrines became symbolic and actual axes around which Iran would construct its policy. Whether diplomats, soldiers, or even civilians, Tehran's men in Iraq now had one function: to be *Modafeyine Haram*, Defenders of the Shrine.[4]

* * *

Iran's Islamist internationalism had initially been rooted in the cosmopolitan culture of the Global Sixties. Men like Mohammad Montazeri and Mostafa Chamran differed widely from one another (and hated each other) but they wanted to rebuild the entire world in the interest of global justice. Both men died too soon—and their political successors were purged out of power shortly after—to see the rise of the first major experiment in Tehran's internationalism, Lebanon's Hezbollah. Hezbollah departed from the internationalist visions of either man but it became an unabashed success. Building on the previous work of Shia mobilization, Hezbollah constructed a militant party loved by millions. Its tentacles spread from Argentina to Europe to west Africa to Thailand and it was ready to do Tehran's dirty work, whether in Vienna or in Buenos Aires. Despite its obvious sectarian basis, Hezbollah had respect among wider crowds because it had resisted Israel and helped expel its occupation army from Lebanon, a task finally achieved in 2000.

In the previous generations, many Shia of the Arab world had picked the same political path as Jews and other excluded minorities: They joined communist parties. With the crisis of communism, and the final collapse of the Soviet Union in 1991, many Shia, especially in Iraq and Lebanon, looked to revolutionary Iran as the new alternative. Tehran replaced Moscow as their Mecca, the Soviet Big Brother gave way to the Supreme Leader. Adel Abdul Mahdi is a perfect example. He had been a central committee member of the Iraqi Communist Party for years. In the 1980s, he fled to Iran, became an Islamist, and joined an Iran-based party of Iraqi exiles. Comrade Adel would live on to become an Iranian-backed prime minister of Iraq in 2018. When Iran built an alliance with Putin's Russia, Moscow's Arabic-language media featured many such communists-cum-Islamists who had learnt Russian in their communist days and were now invaluable to the Tehran-Damascus-Moscow axis. The transition wasn't unique to the Shia.

The Iranian revolution had initially brought hope to some disillusioned communists. Some would continue to find inspiration in the dogged anti-Americanism of Tehran. Ilich Ramírez Sánchez, the Venezuelan revolutionary better known as Carlos the Jackal, was one example. In the 1970s, he worked with the Palestinian communists, helping to stage the legendary siege of OPEC's headquarters in Vienna in December 1975. In later years, the man infamous for his drink, drug, and womanizing problems turned to the Islamic Republic of Iran. From his base in Sudan, he was funded by Tehran before the Sudanese gave him up to France in 1997. Carlos had easily moved from the anti-Zionism of his communist years to Tehran's openly anti-Semitic hatred for Israel. In prison, he converted to Islam and married his lawyer, Isabelle Coutant-Peyre, whose clients included another notorious communist-turned-anti-Semite, Roger Garaudy.

Once a major Marxist philosopher and a senator representing the French Communist Party, Garaudy converted to Islam following his marriage to a Palestinian woman in 1982 and went down the path of Holocaust denial, for which he was convicted under French law. In Iran, and among its Shia partners, Garaudy became a favorite, praised by Hezbollah's Hassan Nasrallah and Ayatollah Khamenei, whom he met in Iran in 1998. Carlos the Jackal would, too, have his own fans in Tehran. In 2003, from his cell in Paris's Santé prison, Carlos wrote a book titled *Revolutionary Islam*, much of which is in praise of Tehran's Islamic Republic. His wife would offer to bring a lawsuit on behalf of Iran against Ben Affleck's film on the hostage crisis, *Argo*.

Could Tehran become the new Moscow? Could its internationalist Islamism replace the global communism of previous years? It seemed to have much going for it. It had a state seriously dedicated to foreign allies and spreading its ideology. It had shown resolute devotion to anti-Zionism, a cause that had excited the global left for decades. As Yasser Arafat shook hands with the Israeli prime minister, Yitzhak Rabin, in the Rose Garden at the White House, Iran led the "Rejectionist Front." To the chagrin of the PLO, the Iranian leadership denounced Arafat and his associates as sellouts and gave financial and diplomatic support to the PLO's Islamist rivals, Hamas and the Palestinian Islamic Jihad (PIJ), both with roots in the Muslim Brotherhood.

But one factor stopped Iran's internationalist project in its tracks. Unlike Soviet communism, it lacked a model that could be replicated elsewhere. At one point in the 1970s, one third of humanity had been governed by Soviet communism in one form or another: one-party rule, a nationalized economy, rapid social programs for women, and so on.

Iran's ruling doctrine, *Welayat al-Faqih* or "guardianship of the jurist," could only work in a Shia-majority society. Other than Iran, there were only three of those in the world: The Republic of Azerbaijan, whose population had been so heavily secularized during the Soviet years that there was hardly a Shia clergy to speak of; Bahrain, where a Sunni kingdom ruled with strong support from Saudi Arabia; and Iraq, where the Shia formed only a small majority (a little over 50 percent) and were geographically concentrated in the south.

If it could modify its "guardianship of the jurist" model, Iran's Islamism could theoretically be replicated in non-Shia contexts. After all, the revolution sometimes took pains to avoid sectarianism. Many, if not most, of its founders and leaders believed in the necessity of a united Ummah (Muslim world) and downplayed Shia-Sunni differences, even when the war with Iraq was raging. The Islamic Republic ran massive ecumenical institutions, trying to bridge the gaps in the Ummah. But the republic also lacked an attractive model of Islamist politics and economics to offer the world. In its first revolutionary decade, it oscillated between anti-capitalists and their pro-capitalist opponents. Under Khamenei, it took a capitalist turn in economic reality even if the Supreme Leader kept up the rhetorical claims to a third way between the deposed communism of the "East" and the decadent capitalism of the "West."

Hezbollah's trajectory shows this lack of a replicable Khomeinist model. In its early years the party had promised an Islamic republic, along with the guardianship of the jurists. Before long, it realized the folly of promoting a Shia theocracy for a society composed of many different religions and sects. After 1990, when the Lebanese civil war came to an end and an ethno-sectarian order was built which divided power between sectarian communities, including the Shia, Hezbollah effectively acquiesced. Gone were its dreams of Islamist revolution and it went out of its way to claim it wanted to do nothing to disrupt the careful religious mosaic of Lebanon.

In the 1990s, the Quds Force's first major post-Hezbollah project had also been a massive failure. In 1992, a civil war broke out in the newly independent Bosnia and Herzegovina, pitting the Muslim-led central government against two statelets funded and supported by Serbia and Croatia. The president of the new republic, Alija Izetbegović, had been an Islamist activist for decades, repeatedly imprisoned by Tito's Yugoslav republic. He had relied on help from the Muslim world and had sent emissaries to Iran as early as 1982. With the war now raging, he went to Tehran and asked for help. Bosnia's location in the heart of Europe was as attractive to Iranians as it was to other powers, and the beautiful land soon became a battleground for those who wanted to win over the hearts and minds of the Muslim Bosniaks.

The Quds Force led the energetic Iranian intervention. Using covers such as the Red Crescent, cultural and religious exchange organizations, and passenger flights, the Iranians flooded Bosnia. Representing Ayatollah Khamenei was Ahmad Jannati, a conservative cleric and then secretary of the Guardian Council, a key regime body tasked with vetting electoral candidates and reviewing legislation. The thin Shia cleric walking the streets of besieged Sarajevo, guarded by muscular Bosnian soldiers, became an iconic, if surreal, image of the era. Leading the military side of things was Mohammadreza Naqdi, a division commander during the war with Iraq who then led the country's police intelligence. Naqdi had helped manage some of the IRGC's external relations with Lebanon and Iraq, which explained his Bosnian posting. He faced a dilemma in Bosnia: The Islamists who had found their way to fight there were linked to Sunni extremists whose hatred of the Shia was fundamental. Pragmatism meant that the Shia state worked with them. On the state level, Izetbegović remained grateful for Iranian help, not least

Tehran's brave breaking of the international embargo to get arms to the Muslim forces, an event approved by the Americans and later mentioned in the Bosnian president's autobiography. The height of the Tehran-Sarajevo alliance was clear in the fall of 1993. As the newly minted soccer team of Bosnia played its first-ever international match against Iran in Tehran's legendary Azadi stadium, Izetbegović was in town, meeting with President Rafsanjani.

But a Bosnian Hezbollah never materialized. After so much financial and human capital had been spent, Iranian-Bosnian relations proved to be subject to the ups and downs of world relations. Izetbegović obviously went on to build not an Islamist theocracy, but a multiethnic federal democracy, with the Serb statelet being preserved as part of the 1995 Dayton Agreement brokered by President Clinton. In 1997, the Bosnian forces raided a training camp that turned out to be staffed by Iranians. In the years since, Iranian diplomats have been expelled when they go beyond their diplomatic remit, as some did in 2007. The expansive cultural center run by Iran in downtown Sarajevo is mostly quiet and to the degree that Bosniaks turn to Islamism, the much likelier candidate is the Turkish model, in line with their Ottoman heritage and with the context of parliamentary democracy. There is a lot of fondness for Iran in Bosnian society but a Hezbollah-style Islamist force has no chance of winning any appeal in Bosnia. Rafsanjani had boasted that Bosnia could be "Iran's gateway to Europe," but the door was firmly shut on Tehran.

Following such failure, the Quds Force's intervention in Afghanistan, under the leadership of Qassem Soleimani, used a wholly different model. Soleimani had encouraged unity between parties representing the small Shia minority in Afghanistan. But he had also worked with the Sunni Islamist leadership, banking not on Islamist internationalism or attempts to export the Iranian model but on the historical affinity between Iran and the Persian-speaking Tajiks of Afghanistan.

On the bloody battlefields of post-Saddam Iraq, the new model conceived by Soleimani's forces would combine anti-Zionism with Shia sectarianism and it would look little like the vision of Montazeri or Chamran. As we have seen, more than two decades before, Iran had avoided joining Saddam's fight against Israel, quipping that the path to the holy Quds (Jerusalem) must pass through Karbala. The road to

Karbala was now open and Iran now had an elite forced named after the eventual goal. In response to Bush's "Axis of Evil," a new term soon became popularized in speeches by Khamenei and Nasrallah: the "Axis of Resistance." It had first been deployed in a Libyan newspaper but it soon became synonymous with Iran's plethora of militia partners in the region. At around the same time, another term also became popular in academic and security circles: the "Shia Crescent." The US was leading a war on Sunni Islamists, and a symbol of the secular Sunni world, Saddam, had also fallen to its armies. The Shia were bound to rise in the post-Saddam Iraq.

The two terms had a sinister overlap. Officially, Iran emphasized the Axis of Resistance and insisted that this wasn't about Shia versus Sunni. This Tehran-led resistance club included Sunni Islamists such as Hamas and the PIJ and, theoretically, even non-Muslims willing to stand up to Israel. But Soleimani soon found the power and logic of Shia sectarianism to be a much more powerful organizing principle than the half-cooked ideology of the "oppressed" or even generic anti-Zionism, which had become staid and worn out. The powerful symbols and stories of Shia heroism and martyrdom had moved Soleimani and hundreds of thousands of his fellow Iranians to fight in the 1980s. He would now deploy the same to mobilize the youth across the Shia world: Whether they came from Iraq, Iran, Lebanon, Afghanistan, or Pakistan, the Shia, the most transnational of communities, were ready to fight for the shrines of the beloved Imams.

It helped that the latent anti-Shia hate of Al-Qaeda became a potent deadly force in the bloodbaths of the Iraqi civil war. The group's franchise in Iraq was led by Abu Musab al-Zarqawi, a Jordanian who had fought in Afghanistan and now pledged loyalty to Bin Laden. Zarqawi's group made its name with bomb attacks that followed the US invasion in 2003 before officially joining Al-Qaeda's global network in 2004. The US-led occupation forces were under attack from a plethora of sources: various Shia militias, the remnants of the Baathist army, local militias, and Zarqawi and fellow Sunni Salafi-Jihadists too. But the Jordanian distinguished himself by his willingness to engage in something that had been mostly taboo: a massacre of Muslims. The group was ready to declare Shia as *kafir*s or unbelievers and slaughter them at will. Zarqawi attacked not only the Shia but their shrines, repeatedly destroying the Sublime Gates, as in the February 2006 attack on the Eleventh Shia Imam's shrine in Samarra. Zarqawi's vicious violence put off even Bin Laden and the Al-Qaeda leadership, who would go on to break ranks with his political successors. The Jordanian himself was killed in June 2006 by US airstrikes.

But his legacy lived on in major ways. His anti-Shia crusade took sectarianism up a level and helped solidify Soleimani's attempts at mobilizing the Shia. The battlegrounds of Afghanistan in the 1980s had helped build the transnational forces of Salafi-Jihadism. The battlegrounds of Iraq in the 2000s helped develop the forces of Shia and Sunni sectarianism.

* * *

Anybody who thinks the Iraqi Shia naturally fall in line with the demands of Tehran clearly never attended a meeting of the Revolutionary Islamic Supreme Council of Iraq (RISCI) in its long years of exile in Iran. In theory, all the members of this association shared basic beliefs: They wanted an Islamic revolution in Iraq; and they believed in fighting alongside Iran in the war with Iraq. In practice, the Shia clergy, which had the leadership of this political body, had always been a discordant bunch.

Perhaps surprisingly, there is something deeply democratic and pluralistic in the world of Shia clergy. There is no central body, no organization tasked with appointing cardinals, no central dogma. There is not even a central system of deciding who is an ayatollah or who holds the lower rank of *hojjatoleslam*. You are an ayatollah if you call yourself one, and you are taken seriously as one if you are able to organize enough followers. The Shia faithful can pick which of the grand ayatollahs they wish to follow (a practice known as *taqlid* or "emulation"). Thus, one ayatollah might have wildly different interpretations of Islamic law from another and the faithful are free to follow whomever they want. The process of rising as a major Shia ayatollah has never been based on pure scholarship or religious credentials and has always had a political and material side to it. Since it is the ayatollahs who pay "tuition" to their students at the seminaries, the more financial resources the cleric has, the more potential students he can attract. It helps, of course, if the lessons are attractive. Students might then compete over becoming disciples of a particular ayatollah. In turn, the followers would pay a proportion of their income to the ayatollahs to be spent as they wished, traditionally for the upkeep of orphans and widows. But in the politicized world of Shia activism, the money could also be spent on politics.

The Islamic Republic of Iran did the most to suppress this pluralistic culture. Holding state power, Ayatollah Khomeini did not respect the unwritten rules of decorum for the Shia clergy, especially those with large followings. The Shah's regime had arrested many clerics but it had also often acted with respect towards the elder clerics. Khomeini's Islamic Republic would instead set up courts that prosecuted, jailed, and defrocked clergy. The new regime would institutionalize and politicize the Shia clergy in an unprecedented way.

Among the Iraqis, no such process had taken place yet. Much of the main Iraqi clergy continued to remain in Najaf even as Saddam's anti-Shia screeds reached a climax in the years of war with Iran. After the brutal murder of Ayatollah Sadr in 1980, many prominent clerics, especially those active in Sadr's Dawa Party, fled to Iran. Among these was Mohammad Baqir Hakim, who reached Iran in the early 1980s after a sojourn in Damascus and transit via Turkey. Around a dozen of his family members had been arrested or killed by Saddam and he himself escaped a life sentence after leading an Arbaeen protest march from Najaf to Karbala. The Sadrs and the Hakims had been both rivals and allies. Hakim's father had been a giant of Najaf. Born in 1889, Ayatollah Mohsen Hakim had organized the Shia to fight for the Ottoman Empire during the First World War. He maintained his major political role in the community from then to the end of his long life in 1970. After the 1958 revolution in Iraq, Hakim, like Sadr, helped fight the alarming growth of communist ideas within the youth. The younger Sadr did the intellectual work of writing pamphlets. The more conservative Ayatollah Hakim simply issued a fatwa in 1959 that banned membership of the Communist Party. He expanded his clout beyond Iraq and, by the time of his death, ran a multi-million-dollar empire with offices from Indonesia to India.

The political mantle of Hakim's family was left for the bookish Mohammad Baqir, fifth out of ten sons. He had been politically active all his life, helping to found the Dawa Party along with his father and Sadr in 1958, even though he was only nineteen. After his father's passing, he stepped up and took a more active role in Dawa's work.

By 1981, when he made it to Iran, he was senior enough to be expected to lead RISCI. This clerically dominated body was founded in 1982, at the behest of Tehran, by merging various exiled Shia revolutionary groups. The party's first leader was Ayatollah Mahmoud Shahroodi, a Najaf-born cleric who had lost three of his brothers to Saddam's repression. It's a sign of the highly flexible transnational Shia world that Shahroodi, RISCI's first head, took a different course in life and entered Iranian politics, despite racist chants that would see him heckled as "the Iraqi" for decades. He was elected to the Assembly of Experts, became the head of the Iranian judiciary and by the time of his death in 2018, was a major contender for the Supreme Leader position.

The leadership of RISCI passed to Hakim in the early 1980s. Although only in his mid-forties, Hakim was an experienced political hand, having lived through the tumultuous politics of Iraq for the two stormy decades of the 1960s and 1970s. This sharply contrasted with the young brash men of the IRGC, who soon took over the task of working with RISCI. Their aim was the formation of a brigade of Iraqis in Iran (exiles plus prisoners of war) to fight for Iran against their own country. Such actions had pedigree in modern military history. The communists around the world had, of course, seen no contradiction in being patriots of their own country but also working with the Soviet Union for revolutionary goals. In the Second World War, numerous nationals had fought against the armies of their own country based on ideology or convenience. German communists such as Fritz Schmenkel defected to the Soviet partisans and fought the Nazis. On the other side, the Nazis ran their own "Russian Liberation Army" led by Andrey Vlasov, a Red Army defector general. The Germans even organized a minuscule British Free Corps, formed of prisoners of war.

The Iranians now helped RISCI in organizing an Iraqi unit that would fight for Khomeini. It was called the Badr Brigade, named after the legendary battle of the Muslims under the Prophet Mohammad against their Meccan enemies in 624. Young commanders, chief among them the top IRGC commander, Mohsen Rezayi, wanted Badr to be a serious military force and would not stand for the oversight of Hakim and his colleagues. To the chagrin of the latter, the Iranians in khaki overcame the Iraqis in clerical robe. Badr was supposedly the armed wing of RISCI but the Iraqi clerical leadership had little real influence over it.

Quickly learning the art of war themselves, the Iranian IRGC commanders helped make Badr into an effective force. Esmayil Daqayeqi, a local boy from Khuzestan, had a major role. He had been an old comrade of Rezayi, friends with him since they both went to the national oil company's high school. They had gone to jail together during the Pahlavi years and cofounded a guerrilla group. In early 1985, the Badr Brigade played a key role in liberating a significant area of the Howayzah Marshes, which straddle the Iranian-Iraqi border. The Iraqis showed that they were ready to shed their blood for revolutionary goals. It went both ways: In 1988, as the Iranian forces of the PMOI, helped by Saddam, attacked the Iranian armed forces, the Iraqis of the Badr Brigade stood against them.

Badr owed most of its success to the young Iraqi Shia revolutionaries who took over from Hakim. Two men stood out in particular. Both born in 1954, Hadi al-Ameri and Abu Mahdi Muhandis were twenty-six when the war with Iran broke out. Ameri came from the province of Dialayah on the Iranian border and had joined the Dawa Party in his youth. He made it to Iran after the 1979 revolution, fleeing persecution and excited by the prospects of the new revolutionary Iran. He married an Iranian, gained Iranian citizenship, and quickly rose to become one of the most trusted leaders of the Badr Brigade.

Muhandis (who had been born Jamal Jaafar Mohammad before adopting his *nom de guerre*) hailed from the port of Basra. His father was Arab and his mother Iranian. He spoke fluent Persian. He studied engineering in Basra, getting a MA in 1977. At university, he joined the Dawa Party branch and fled to Iran after the events of 1979. In the early years of the revolution, Muhandis signed up for one of the most daring operations linked to Tehran: causing mayhem in Kuwait, the super-rich sheikhdom to the south of Iraq which had hundreds of thousands of Shia citizens, mostly of Iranian origin. The Khomeinists would quickly find out that Kuwait wasn't exactly ripe for revolution. The Kuwaiti Shia were about the most unlikely Shia in the world to set up a Hezbollah-type party: They suffered from discrimination but were still mostly affluent enough not to want to rock the boat too much. They were mostly connected to their own clerical networks, outside of the circuit of Khomeini, Sadr, or Hakim.

Muhandis's mission in Kuwait had hence been military not political. Helped by Imad Muqniyah, the military mastermind of the fledgling Hezbollah who had started his political life in the PLO, Muhandis helped organize the 1983 bombings in Kuwait. On December 12, six coordinated attacks targeted two embassies, Kuwait International Airport and a chemical plant. Hundreds could have died but faulty bombs meant that the actual death toll was no more than six, including one of the bombers. Muhandis fled the country to Iran, convicted in absentia by a Kuwaiti court. He rose to leadership positions in both RISCI and the Badr Brigade.

In 1986, as Iran staked all in Operation Karbala V, Muhandis and Ameri fought hard together with the man who had helped recruit them, Daqayeqi. This would be Daqayeqi's last operation. He was on a motorcycle when he fell to Iraqi airstrikes. Muhandis and Ameri were both nearby fighting under another commander, Hassan Danaeifar. In exactly twenty years, Muhandis and Ameri would become leading figures in the Iraqi government, while Danaeifar, now with the Quds Force, was appointed as Iran's ambassador to Iraq.

In addition to these Shia Iraqis, Iran also continued the old tradition of courting Iraqi Kurdish groups. Jalal Talabani's Patriotic Union of Kurdistan ended up becoming Iran's major partner despite the fact that many of Talabani's old Iranian comrades languished in Iranian jails or had been killed by its firing squads. Talabani's quasi-magical quality is that he remained popular, to his very last days, across the widest imaginable political spectrum, beloved both by Qassem Soleimani (who sent a heartfelt note to his funeral) and by many of the most radical of the Kurdish communists on either side of the Iranian-Iraqi border.[5]

In 2003, as Soleimani planned Iran's intervention in post-Saddam Iraq, he had formidable resources at his disposal: all the links built with Shia and Kurds throughout the hard years of the 1980–8 war. There were thousands of Shia Iraqis who wanted to work with the IRGC in shaping the developments of the new Iraq. But the Shia weren't to easily fall in line. In the new Iraq, they were to have a political base. There would soon be many contenders for their hearts and minds. Accounts written retrospectively can give the mistaken impression that once Saddam was gone, Iran's rising clout in Iraq was inevitable. But there was no such inevitability. The rising Iranian dominance in Iraq was the result of hard work by many men, but chiefly two: Ayatollah Khamenei, who made foreign interventions the main narrative of his reign; and Qassem Soleimani, who faithfully carried out his vision.

In the chaos of 2003, as Ahmad and his comrades finished their pilgrimage at Karbala and Najaf and headed to take up their posts at the Iranian mission in Baghdad, nothing looked guaranteed. They were faced with Shia discordance, a failing society, and the military forces of the world's sole superpower.

* * *

On May 12, 2003, Ayatollah Mohammad Baqir Hakim ended his twenty-three years of exile in Iran and went back to Iraq. Thousands greeted him as he crossed the land border and entered Basra in a long convoy. Was this a Khomeini-like return? Media commentators loved pointing out the similarities between 1979 and 2003: Here was a Shia cleric, head of a party that pledged a Khomeinist revolution, loudly ending his exile in the aftermath of the fall of a tyrant. But there was not much serious content to this comparison. Hakim had barely entered Iraq before going to some lengths to carefully show he no longer held his past beliefs. His speeches all emphasized Iraqi nationalism and the necessity for all peoples of Iraq to live together. In a press conference in the holy city of Najaf, he came out for "a system based on the will of the Iraqi people, elected by the Iraqi people." He emphasized that the new government should be a "modern Islamic regime to go along with today's modern world" and that he didn't support "extremist Islam." The new regime had to be a "democratic government which respects Islam . . . neither an Islamic government nor a secular administration."[6] Hakim did not live to carry out his vision in Iraq. In August, he was killed by Abu Musab al-Zarqawi's men. The leadership of RISCI passed on to his brother, Abdulaziz, who, in 2007, took the "Revolutionary" out of its name.

The Hakims were only one of the many Shia contenders for power in the new Iraq. The traditional rival family, the Sadrs, had lost many of its key members but a thirty-year-old firebrand cleric surprised all by emerging as a dominant figure. The Najaf-born Muqtada al-Sadr had lost his father and two of his brothers to Saddam's repression. The famous Ayatollah Mohammad Baqir al-Sadr was his father's cousin. Bint al-Hoda, the ayatollah's sister, who was killed alongside him, was an aunt of Muqtada's wife. Instead of following the path of Hakim and many others, the young Muqtada had remained in Iraq, conducting underground work. When Saddam fell, he was ready to burst into the open and organize hundreds of thousands of poor Shia, especially those in the public housing project in northeastern Baghdad. This suburb had been built as Revolution City in 1959 and had changed name to Saddam City in 1982. Soon, the world would remember it by only one name: Sadr City.

If Hakim liked to be mildly autonomous from Tehran, Sadr was fiercely independent. "Muqtada Sadr would not listen to anyone," Ahmad remembers. "In all my years in Iraq, there was one name that could send Hajj Qassem up the wall and that was Muqtada. Because he was unpredictable and not easy to charm." With his base in Sadr City, he quickly raised an impressive militia. By the time the Iranians started coming to Iraq, the Mahdi Army already boasted tens of thousands of members.

What would Iran do in this new Iraq? Soleimani adopted a three-pronged strategy: First, Iran would work with all Iraqi forces, even if they didn't agree with Tehran's Khomeinism, by giving them the type of support that a massive state like Iran could afford. Second, Iran would build militias that could be independent of the existing Shia political powerhouses like Hakim and Sadr. If Khamenei were to be a good Stalin, he couldn't have a Tito or a Mao on his hands. He needed devout loyal forces, like Lebanon's Hezbollah. Third, Iran would not stand in the way of Al-Qaeda and ex-Baathist attacks on American forces. It would conduct its own campaign against the American presence with two goals: strengthening its hands in negotiations with the Americans and ultimately driving them out of the region.

Soleimani hadn't come up with this policy on his own. But he had now risen to a level at which he consulted directly with Khamenei. His driver remembers him coming out of a meeting with the Supreme Leader in 2004. He had a somber look. "Aqa [an affectionate term for Khamenei] kissed my forehead," Soleimani told the driver. "What grave duty is on our shoulders. This revolution, this leader."

Soleimani was not to disappoint his leader. All three policies were followed. American forces were soon to discover that he was the source of the roadside bombs bedeviling their efforts.

When Iraqi politics were reorganized in 2005, the Iranians were instrumental in bringing about a system that looked awfully like Lebanon's: an ethno-sectarian division of powers. Only here the most important positions went to the Shia, the long-downtrodden people who were, after all, the country's majority. In the new Iraq, the prime minister was to be always a Shia, the president a Kurd (from the PUK, according to an unwritten agreement), and the speaker of the parliament a Sunni. The Badr Brigade changed its name to the Badr Organization for Reconstruction and Development. It became a powerful force in the new Iraq, holding key cabinet positions like the interior and transport ministries. The presidency went to Jalal Talabani, the man with whom Soleimani and the IRGC were on the best of terms. In the years to come, the chubby, smiling ex-Maoist would emerge as one of the main mediators between Iran and the United States, the two foreign countries that became, and have remained, kingmakers of Iraqi politics.

As Shia militias mushroomed in Iraq, along with those of other sects, Soleimani adopted a patient strategy. He would support them whenever they were needed—and he would stand out of their way when they attacked common enemies. He would also try to stay above their petty differences. It was clear that Badr couldn't be a central organization for all Shia militias. In 2006, the young Iraqi cleric Qais Khazali split to form his own outfit, Asaeb Ahl al-Haq. In the same year, Soleimani brought Muqniyah to Iraq and with the help of Muhandis they founded a new group: Kataeb Hezbollah. As shown by the name, the adopted color of yellow, and the group's logo, which sported an AK-47, it was proud of its association with Tehran and with its Lebanese namesake.

Soleimani here made a key decision of his career. His brainchild Kataeb Hezbollah would be exactly as he wanted: ideologically in line, with full loyalty to Khamenei, but also militarily competent and disciplined. The Quds Force would give full support to this new Hezbollah but it would not alienate other Shia forces. Around the same time, the difficult Sadr was taken to Qom and given assurances by Iran that his autonomy would be respected. Khamenei saw Sadr personally and assured him that Soleimani would not work against him.

In May 2006, when the Iraqi parliament was to pick a new prime minister, the Iranians got Sadr's consent for a candidate they backed: Nuri al-Maliki. Maliki was the type of candidate that could be accepted by all sides. Born in 1950 in Karbala, the mild-mannered, half-bald, bespectacled political activist seemed like the type of man you could control. Not only Sadr but the Americans came to agree with the choice of Maliki too. Their efforts in Iraq were led by a man who liked to work with Iranians: Ambassador Ryan Crocker, who sat down with Soleimani's men once more. On his side Crocker had General David Petraeus, head of the multinational force, who would come to develop his own indirect channels of communication with Soleimani—and develop something of an obsession with him. Both Crocker and Petraeus were heartily sick of Ibrahim Jaafari, the professorial Dawa Party man who had become Iraq's first post-Saddam prime minister (not counting the interim prime minister, Ayad Allawi). He seemed to be clueless about the gravity of the tasks at hand. The Americans figured they could work with someone like Maliki, who would have greater influence on the ground. Yes, Maliki had fled to Iran in 1979 and spent much of his twenty-plus years of exile there or in Syria. But if the Americans were to bring about stability, and ultimately reduce their forces in Iraq, they needed someone more effective than Jaafari. From the White House, Bush said Maliki's ascent marked "a victory for the cause of freedom in the Middle East" and praised the "strong leaders" now in charge of Baghdad. He mused that years later people would look back to see Maliki's ascent as "a decisive moment in the history of liberty."

May 2006 indeed marked a "decisive moment" but not the one imagined by Bush. The implicit agreement between Tehran and Washington over Maliki became a tradition that has been maintained more or less to this day. Like two colonial overlords, Iran and the United States decide who should be the prime minister of Iraq. In 2007, Crocker and Hassan Kazemi Qomi met in Maliki's office—the highest-level talks between

Iran and America in a quarter century. The official talks excited media but they had been taking place confidentially for over a year.

The course of events soon went in Tehran's favor. In 2005, Ahmadinejad came to power in Iran and Soleimani could now count on more IRGC influence over the government and less interference from the foreign ministry. In 2008, Barack Obama was elected president in the United States. He had opposed the Iraq War as a senator and he immediately scaled back US presence and prepared withdrawal.

Meanwhile Soleimani's mixture of charismatic relationship-building and kinetic military action proved best suited for the soil of Iraq. Soon, his forces didn't have to tell Maliki what to do. It was Maliki who would come to Hajj Qassem, asking for advice. The meetings would often happen in Maliki's home.

"Hajji would be sitting on the ground, humbly playing with Maliki's kids, bringing them gifts from Iran," Ahmad remembers. "Maliki wasn't used to such military commanders. He was taken by Hajji like so many of us."

In 2008, when Maliki was negotiating for a security agreement with the US, in the last months of the Bush administration, Soleimani was updated daily. He helped convince the Iraqi prime minister to not accept permanent US military bases under any conditions. After spending billions of dollars in Iraq, the US was now forced to contend with a prime minister who often took orders from the most mortal enemy of the United States—and a man whom the US had helped designate as a terrorist in a March 2007 United Nations Security Council resolution.[7]

Soleimani was careful to not cut ties with Sadr either. In 2007, the hands-on commander was sighted in Sadr City. As Muqtada's forces were fighting those of the central government in Najaf, Soleimani was there to mediate.

A much more significant mediation came a year later. In March 2008, as the British started leaving the port of Basra, Sadr's Mahdi Army fought the forces of central government for control of the city. More than 500 were killed in the Battle of Basra and hundreds more injured. It was a sign of Iran's place in the country that the talks to end the bloodshed happened not in Basra, Najaf, or Baghdad but in Qom and Tehran. Sadr was once more brought to Iran where he met representatives of the Dawa

Party and Hadi al-Ameri from the Badr Organization. Soleimani attended the meetings and had a major role in bringing about a truce. Sadr declared that he was ending his military presence not just in Basra but all over Iraq. Upset with losing to Maliki, he criticized Iran in an Al Jazeera interview. Even the opponents of Soleimani in Tehran praised Qassem for bringing about an obvious victory.

Testifying in the Congress in September 2007, Petraeus had reassured the Americans that the Quds Force and "Hezbollah trainers" had "by and large . . . been pulled out of the country." A few months later, Soleimani's forces had humbled the American general. As successful as the US's policy of a "surge" in troops or its campaign to recruit Sunni tribes to fight Al-Qaeda were, Iran's role in Iraq was not about to decrease. The Quds Force was not going anywhere. In the heat of the Battle of Basra, Soleimani made this clear to Petraeus, in a message sent through Talabani: "General Petraeus, you should know that I, Qassem Soleimani, control the policy for Iran when it comes to Iraq, Syria, Lebanon, Gaza, and Afghanistan."

Soleimani was not bluffing. The foreign ministry had now moved aside and given all these portfolios to him. The ambassadors to these countries were all Quds Force members who answered first to Hajj Qassem. Petraeus was not to forget his Iranian counterpart. In 2015, when visiting Iraq in a personal capacity, the American general remembered him as a "very capable and resourceful individual, a worthy adversary [who had] played his hand well." Upon Soleimani's assassination in January 2020, Petraeus recalled the 2008 story, which had clearly stayed with him despite the passing of the years.

This was not the first or last message sent by Soleimani to Petraeus. In the summer of 2006, as violence seemed to ebb in Iraq, he is known to have sent a message to the Americans: "I hope you have been enjoying the peace and quiet in Baghdad. I've been busy in Beirut!"[8]

Again, the Iranian wasn't bluffing. The Quds Force had been established to oversee all IRGC operations abroad, but in practice, things were usually left to local commanders. The ever-moving Soleimani changed this. Stories went around of him having breakfast in Beirut, lunch in Damascus, and dinner in Baghdad. Building a transnational army, he moved forces from one country to another, a practice he later elevated to new heights in Syria. His desire to be on the scene, the thing which had driven him to go fight the Iraqis on the frontlines all those years before, remained with him to the very end of his life. In the summer of 2006, he defied all security recommendations by being present in Beirut as Hezbollah, under his overall command, took on a task of the highest order: fighting Israel. Hajj Qassem would now directly face off the Zionist enemy he had talked about for years.

Chapter 10

Busy in Beirut

The port city of Haifa is most pleasant in the fall. The scorching humid heat of the summer is over and, if it doesn't rain, you can sit by the sea and enjoy the Mediterranean breeze. On Saturday, October 4, 2003, hundreds of Haifans were having their lunch by the sea. Some had come from out of town. The extended Zer-Aviv family from the nearby kibbutz of Yagur were spending their holy Shabbat shopping in Haifa. For lunch, they went to Maxim, a beachfront restaurant near the southern end of the city. At the top of the table sat Bruria, 59, not far from her two little grandchildren: Liran, who was to soon have his fourth birthday in the kibbutz's communal nursery, and Noya, who was just fourteen months old, able to say a few phrases like "thank you" but not yet able to eat any of the plates of hummus generously spread around by Maxim's waiters. In addition to Bruria, Liran and Noya were joined by their parents, Bezalel and Keren, although their grandfather, Freddy Zer-Aviv, an orthopedist at a Haifa hospital, had not come. He didn't like shopping.

Like many families in Israel, the Zer-Avivs came from many places, near and far. Bruria was born in Haifa, not far away from the restaurant, but had grown up in the embarrassingly provincial city of Netanya. She had met the Algerian-born Freddy when they both worked at a clinic.

Their first son, Bezalel, was born in the difficult year of 1973, when Israel fought a gruesome war with its neighbors Egypt and Syria. They used Freddy's French background and moved across the Mediterranean to Nice, right in the heart of the heavenly Midi, long a haven for those fleeing the chaos of the Middle East. Bruria and Freddy had two daughters there but in less than a decade they moved back to Israel. France was a wonderful place but Israel was home. They were able to get a place in the venerable Yagur kibbutz, founded in 1922 and one of the largest in the country with more than 1,300 residents.

By the time of that pleasant Saturday, they had lived in the kibbutz for eighteen years. Bezalel was now thirty years old. He had met his beloved Keren in the army and they had started a family in the kibbutz, near the grandparents who loved spending time with the little ones. Bezalel was in a cookery school and dreamed of becoming a chef.

Not only was the food at Maxim sublime, it had always stood for the best of Israel even in the darkest times—and with the failure of the Israeli-Palestinian peace talks at Camp David and the alarming increase of suicide bombings, these were indeed dark times. Maxim had been founded in 1965 by two men both of whose families had roots in the culinary paradise of Lebanon: the Jewish Mattars and the Arab Palestinian Tayars. Their ancestral land was so near, less than 50 kilometers away, and yet so far. But there was no city like Haifa to make one feel that Arab and Jew could get along. Working in the kitchen that day was Osama Najar, a 28-year-old Palestinian and a Christian like the Tayar family. Osama loved Maxim. When he wasn't cooking, he was playing poker by the sea, with his friend Jamal Khouri, a man with a big laugh and the most typical Arab surname there was.

Although the locals didn't know it, their ordinary lunch that day was a subject of attention in several foreign capitals. In Tehran and Damascus, the Quds Force officers reporting to Qassem Soleimani were told of an operation there that had gone ahead as planned. It had been the work of a bright young Palestinian woman the Iranian officers had been previously told about. Hanadi Jaradat came from the village of Silat al-Harithiya, near Jenin, deep in the occupied West Bank. She had gone to a university in northern Jordan to study law. That October, the 28-year-old Hanadi was only a few weeks away from being called to the bar. Her family expected her to graduate and work as a lawyer in Jenin. She already had prospects for a job in a local law office. But Hanadi had secretly planned a different life goal.

The people of Jenin had long been harassed by the occupying forces of the Israeli army. Silat al-Harithiya was one of the very few villages where the Palestinian Islamic Jihad (PIJ), a minor group compared to the dominant Hamas and Fatah, had put down roots. Worried about this new threat coming from Iran's favorite Palestinian organization, the Israel Defense Force (IDF) swept the area often. Almost every family knew an incident involving the IDF, and the Jaradats were no exception. Hanadi had seven sisters and two brothers. But in June of that year, one of the brothers, Fadi, had been killed by the IDF. He was only twenty-five. Also killed with him was his cousin, Salah, 34, a ranking member of the PIJ who had helped recruit Fadi. Hanadi was in the same house when it happened. She went into something of a trance and pledged to take revenge. It wasn't hard to contact the PIJ local leaders in Jenin. It all happened so fast. In just a few months, she was ready.

On that Saturday, October 4, Hanadi Jaradat was able to get past the security cordon and enter Haifa. A beautiful Palestinian woman in Haifa was not a sight that aroused suspicion. By lunchtime, she'd made it to Maxim. She detonated the belt of explosives she was wearing right in the middle of the restaurant. The explosion was so powerful that only Jaradat's head remained intact. Some of the patrons died at their dining tables. Some were splattered on the walls. All five Zer-Avivs, from Grandma Bruria to the one-year-old Noya, were dead, as was Osama Najar, the Palestinian cook. In all, counting Jaradat herself, twenty-two people were dead: eighteen Jews and four Arabs.

In her will, written one day before the attack and left in care of the PIJ, Jaradat had made it clear why she was sacrificing her life as "the sixth martyrdom-seeking woman who is exploding her own body to kill Zionists." "It is not enough for our mothers to stop mourning for their children. We must do something so that the mothers of the Zionists will mourn theirs," she wrote. "Putting my trust in God, I have decided to kill the Zionists who have surrounded us. Like this, I will be the one putting them under siege, making their mothers shed tears. I ask the Almighty to send us to heaven and put them in hell."

In Damascus, the news of the operation's success led to rounds of "Allah is Great" from the Syrian, Palestinian, and Iranian officials who were in the Quds Force's safe room.[1] The energy of the leadership was all focused upon Iraq, where Soleimani was planning an extensive intervention. But the new commander of the Quds Force insisted his forces had to learn to be involved in more than one front at a time. They were not directly involved in the Haifa operation but their constant financial and moral support of the PIJ had equipped it with the confidence it needed to plan a daring attack in the heart of Israel, and in a major city which was a particular obsession of the Quds Force due to its proximity to Hezbollah's forces in southern Lebanon. For Soleimani's Quds Force, Israel would always have a special significance. The force, after all, had been named "Quds" for a reason. This was the greatest PIJ operation so far—and it was seen as a victory specific to Iran. As Yasser Arafat condemned the attack in the strongest terms, the Iranians were jubilant at the credibility it would bring them.

* * *

Throughout the years of the Oslo-framework peace process, which had kicked off in 1993, Iran had been a steadfast supporter of the anti-Arafat forces that rejected any compromise with Israel. Radical Arab states like Algeria and Gaddafi's Libya had sometimes equivocated. Even Hafez al-Assad had directly negotiated with the Israelis, spurred on by Bill Clinton. But not Iran. The Islamic Republic had remained constant. It had helped fund Hamas despite its ideological origins in the Muslim Brotherhood, whose Sunni Islamism had clashed with Khomeini's version, especially after Iran backed Syria's slaughter of thousands in Hama in 1982.

Iran established much closer ties with the PIJ. This organization's roots went back to Gaza, the little enclave sandwiched between Egypt and Israel, run by Cairo from 1948 to 1967 and occupied by Israel since. It had been founded there in 1981 by two Palestinian activists in their early thirties, both of whom had been born in Gaza when it was still under Egyptian rule. One came from a family who fled to Gaza from the Palestinian city of Ramlah after it was ethnically cleansed by the Israelis in the 1948 war. The other was a local preacher in a village south of Gaza

City. The former, Dr Fathi Shaqaqi, became a physician and a Muslim Brotherhood activist. The latter, Sheikh Abd al-Aziz Awdah, studied Islam in Cairo and became the imam of his local mosque. The two men had been active in nearby Egypt and were radicalized by the Iranian revolution and the storm that followed the assassination of Egypt's President Sadat in 1981. Sadat had made peace with the Zionists and had been slain. The doctor and the sheikh now sought inspiration in the revolutionary Iran that not only decried the Camp David Accords but openly praised Khaled Islamboli, the Islamist assailant who had killed Sadat. A major street in Tehran was named after him.

But it wasn't ideology that bound Tehran and the PIJ together. Dr Shaqaqi and Sheikh Awda liked Khomeini's Iran for the same reason that it liked them: They wanted military action against Israel and total rejection of all negotiations. When Assad's Syria helped set up the Alliance of Palestinian Forces (APF) in 1993, the PIJ had been a central force, one of the ten Islamist and leftist organizations pledging to fight Israel with arms and reject all negotiations. But with the advent of time, the APF, better known as the Damascus Ten, had proved to have more bark than bite. Many of its leaders loved giving speeches from their bases in the Yarmouk refugee camp just outside Damascus, where tens of thousands of Palestinian refugees lived, but only Hamas and the PIJ were ready to take significant action.

By the time the Camp David summit of 2000 failed and the Second Intifada broke out, the Damascus Ten had become irrelevant. Hafez al-Assad died a month before Camp David and was replaced with his inexperienced, young, and shy son, Bashar. Amid hopes for a Damascus Spring and political opening in Syria, it wasn't clear what Bashar's ultimate policy on Hezbollah, Iran, and anti-Zionism would be.

Iran had no such ambiguity. While Israeli civilians were continually being attacked during the Second Intifada, Iran kept up its support of Hamas and the PIJ. With its twenty-two fatalities and sixty injured, deep in Israeli soil and in a major city, the Maxim restaurant suicide bombing was a boon to the PIJ. It could now hold its head high next to Hamas. It had also made Iran proud.

"We had to overcome so much suspicion," a Quds Force member who was part of Iran's Damascus team in the late 1990s remembers. "They really saw us as outsiders, Persians, Shias, even if they didn't say so. Especially the Hamas folks! They were really too doctrinaire. But the PIJ, not so much. For them, action came first and they knew we Iranians were men of action. We didn't just talk."[2]

Iran had used Hezbollah to build links with the Palestinians. It helped that the Lebanese party boasted the presence of Imad Muqniyah, a man who had started his military life with Fatah and was widely respected as an operational genius. In the days when Iran had no ambassador in Beirut (although the IRGC still had its heavy local presence), Mohammad Hassan Akhtari, Iran's ambassador to Damascus from 1986 to 1998, prioritized the building of links with the PIJ and Hezbollah's increasing independence from Amal (with which it violently clashed at times) and Damascus.

In 1998, when Qassem Soleimani took over the Quds Force, he oversaw personnel changes. Akhtari was replaced by Hossein Sheykholeslam as Iran's ambassador to Syria. Sheykholeslam had been an Islamist student activist at Berkeley when the 1979 revolution broke out. He had held high positions in the foreign ministry from the outset, leading its political department for much of the 1980s.

"Hajj Qassem wanted things to be more professional," a Quds Force member remembers. "The 1980s had been a big mess and things were done locally in ways that weren't acceptable to a disciplined military commander like Hajj Qassem. Someone like Akhtari wouldn't have listened to Soleimani the way his own appointees would. At the same time, Sheykholeslam had a deep knowledge of Hezbollah that could help Hajji."[3]

* * *

Prior to his posting as Quds Force commander, Soleimani had had zero input into the Lebanese file. Iran's operations had been led by experienced hands like Akhtari, who was among the founding fathers of Hezbollah. By the time Soleimani took the reins, the Lebanese militia-party was a major force and one of the most feared terror organizations in the Western capitals. What could a man whose entire diplomatic experience was limited to dealing with some Afghan warlords bring to Iran's most sensitive file abroad?

Soleimani took the first step by leaving for Beirut. He had to meet the men he was going to work with. In a meeting in Dahiya, the Shia-populated southern suburb of Beirut doubling as the operational and spiritual heart of Hezbollah, Soleimani sat with a dozen Iranian and Lebanese men. Not a single one of the Hezbollah members present had ever met Soleimani, who spoke Arabic with a heavy Persian accent, making it unintelligible to some.

At the top of the table sat Hassan Nasrallah, the 38-year-old cleric who had led the force since the 1992 Israeli assassination of Abbas al-Musawi, his predecessor as secretary-general. On either side sat his two most prominent military lieutenants: Imad Muqniyah and his comrade, cousin, and brother-in-law, Mostafa Badreddin. Muqniyah and Badreddin had known each other since their activities in Kuwait in the 1980s. Under Nasrallah, and with increased support from Tehran, they aimed to turn Hezbollah into a more serious military force than it had ever been. Even though they had never met, Nasrallah trusted Soleimani because he had been especially recommended by Ayatollah Khamenei.

It didn't take long for the four men to take a liking to each other. Nasrallah, Muqniyah, and Soleimani became particularly close. Despite their differences, they had important commonalities that made for one of the most consequential and fruitful triangles in the history of the Islamic Republic. They were all relatively young. They all came from marginal Shia backgrounds, far from the main cities of their countries. They were all less interested in books and ideology than in efficacy and military action. They all had disdain for men who talked the talk but didn't know what it was like to be in a battleground. They were also all obsessed with Israel—not as an abstract Zionist enemy but as a real foe that must be understood if it is to be fought.

Twenty-two years later, days after Soleimani's killing, Nasrallah remembered that first-time meeting in Dahiya. "From that very first meeting, I felt I was spiritually, psychologically, and intellectually close to him," he said in an interview with Tehran's al-Alam TV. "It was like we had known Hajj Qassem for ten years and he had known us. As you know, first impressions matter. The first image, the first hour, the first meeting between Hajj Qassem and the brothers in charge and Hezbollah's jihadi and political commanders went very well and augured well for our cooperation. Our relationship with Hajj Qassem started from that very meeting and it only ended with his martyrdom."[4]

The personal close ties between Soleimani, Nasrallah, and Muqniyah (and, to a lesser degree, Badreddin) laid the groundwork for the rise of the Quds Force as the integrated transnational army Khamenei had once dreamed of. The other important triangle was the one between Khamenei, Soleimani, and Nasrallah. They got used to meeting regularly, often in the holy city of Mashhad, Khamenei's hometown and the only place outside Tehran frequented by the paranoid leader. All three men spoke Persian and Arabic and could interact in a mix of the two languages. Soleimani's Arabic improved rapidly and he could now even tease Nasrallah in the local Lebanese dialect. Nasrallah's Persian had long been near-native. Khamenei's Arabic remained wooden and bookish and he relied on translators for talking to Hezbollah commanders.

In late 1999, more than a year after the initial meeting, Nasrallah, Soleimani, and Khamenei met in Iran. A large Hezbollah delegation, consisting of about fifty commanders led by Muqniyah and Badreddin, had come to Iran for a broad meeting. Khamenei led the communal prayers for the men, who considered this to be a crucial spiritual experience. Following the prayers, he and Nasrallah spoke jointly to the men present, with the Lebanese commander translating for the Supreme Leader. The purpose of the meeting was twofold: to establish that Soleimani spoke for Khamenei and had to be obeyed; and that Hezbollah needed to be more sophisticated and plan for eventual skirmishes with Israel.

"Aqa [Khamenei] looked directly into everyone's eyes and said: 'You should have faith that Israel will cease to exist,'" an Iranian present at the meeting remembers. "He said: 'You have to have faith. Some of us might be too old but you'll see with your own eyes.'"[5]

A few months after the meeting, in May 2000, Israel's Labor Party prime minister, Ehud Barak, withdrew his forces from Lebanon, ending an occupation that had lasted more than two decades. The move was mostly the result of Israeli domestic politics. Responding to a clamoring for peace, Barak had gone into the 1999 prime ministerial election promising to bring the troops home and do better than the right-wing incumbent, Benjamin Netanyahu, in making peace with the Palestinians. Barak was handed a landslide victory by the voters and followed through on his promise: He pulled his forces from Lebanon and, a few weeks later, went into the Camp David summit with Yasser Arafat.

But from the perspective of Tehran and Hezbollah, this marked a retreat by the Israelis. On May 24, just as the Israeli forces were leaving, Soleimani, Nasrallah, and Muqniyah sat in an operational room in Dahiya. Hossein Sheykholeslam, then Iran's ambassador to Syria, had joined them from Damascus.[6] What should the Iranians do in the face of the Israeli withdrawal? The diplomat resorted to *estekhare*, a Quranic divination in which you open a page of the Quran and decide by the nature of verses whether it is the right time to do something. He suggested to the commanders that the Israelis should be attacked as they were flee-ing. Soleimani firmly disagreed: The Israelis were leaving on their own accord and shouldn't be engaged with. Nasrallah and Muqniyah agreed with Soleimani. Under his leadership, military decisions were to be taken with what came to be known as "strategic patience." They would not strike Israelis based on Quranic whims.

* * *

The Israeli withdrawal from Lebanon was not followed by a negotiated peace at Camp David. The summit became a "tragedy of errors" in which the two sides failed to agree despite having come very close to a total agreement on all terms. Following the election of George W. Bush, it became clear that, with the Democrats out of the White House, the peace process, in which Clinton had invested so much, wouldn't be easily resumed. In the final weeks of his term, in December 2000 and January 2001, the outgoing president offered a set of "Clinton Parameters" that could have achieved a last-minute agreement. Barak accepted a version of these but Arafat did not. In February 2001, Barak went down to a humili-ating defeat in prime ministerial elections in Israel and the hawkish new leader of Likud, Ariel Sharon, became the new head of government.

Sharon was infamously known to the Iranians and Hezbollah as the minister of defense under whose watch the Sabra and Shatila massacre of

1982 had taken place. His victory was a gift to the "Rejectionist Front," now proudly led by Iran and Hezbollah. Arafat's peacemaking path had been abandoned. With the death of Hafez al-Assad in 2000 and Jordan's King Hussein in 1999, new young leaders came to power in Damascus and Amman. It would take time for them to cement their strategies toward the complex web of Middle East politics. The Iranians, on the other hand, were now able operators. They were going to leave their mark.

Iran continued its campaign against Arafat and blessed even the most egregious terrorist attacks during the Second Intifada with its full support. Killing rabbis, bombing markets, slaughtering women and children, and blowing up buses were not just supported but funded by Iran, who made it clear that both Hamas and Islamic Jihad, and any other force that would attack Israel, could count on its support. It helped that Bush declared Iran to be part of the Axis of Evil just before another component of the axis, Saddam Hussein, was overthrown. The Islamic Republic now walked into the vacuum by declaring the aforementioned Axis of Resistance. In 2004, both of the main leaders of the Palestinian movement died: In March, Israel assassinated Hamas's spiritual leader, Sheikh Ahmad Yasin, in a widely condemned move, and in November, Arafat died in a military hospital in Paris, having spent the last two years of his life under a siege by Israel of his compound in Ramallah.

The deaths of Yasin and Arafat further helped Iran position itself as the main anti-Zionist force in the world. For decades, Israel had attempted to defeat the Arabs by establishing ties with its fellow non-Arab countries in the region, chiefly Iran, Turkey, and Ethiopia. Iran had now turned into the most committed anti-Israel state in history.

* * *

The Second Intifada is considered to have come to an end by the time the leaders of the Middle East came together in a summit held in the resort town of Sharm el Sheikh in Egypt in February 2005. There, Egypt's President Hosni Mubarak hosted Jordan's King Abdullah, Israel's Sharon, and Arafat's successor, Mahmood Abbas. A topic not mentioned in any of the official reports but known to have been part of the private discussions was a regime that was hated by all four participants: the Islamic Republic of Iran.

Iran was threatening Israel and intervening in the internal affairs of Arab countries. Worse, it was developing nuclear weapons. Abbas and Mubarak were angry at no longer being the main leaders who called the shots in the Palestinian struggle. Emboldened with Iranian support, Hamas was now using its bases in the West Bank and Gaza to organize its own independent policy. It was widely popular on the street in Palestine, perceived as clean and daring, a far cry from the corrupt fat cats of the PLO.

But the Iranian sponsorship of Hezbollah and Hamas was also cautiously seen as probable good news. The more seasoned military and intelligence officials knew that states were prone to act more rationally than more unfettered organizations. The clerics of Iran had proven to be cunning negotiators when need be. A common understanding in Tel Aviv was that Iran would restrain its so-called proxies. On the other side of the equation, Iran expected Israel to not jolt into action so easily.

The year 2006 started with a serious stroke suffered by Sharon. He was replaced on January 4 by his colleague Ehud Olmert, as acting prime minister. In March, new elections were held and Olmert's centrist Kadima won. The new party had been founded by Sharon and it included senior defectors from the Labor Party, such as the former prime minister, Shimon Perez, who wanted to give support to Sharon's daring withdrawal from Gaza, which had taken place in the spring of 2005. The Labor Party itself joined Olmert's governing coalition with the most important portfolio, the defense ministry, going to Labor's leader, Amir Peretz, a Moroccan-born trade union leader with an iconic moustache that gave him a resemblance to Lech Wałęsa.

Israel's withdrawal from Gaza, which included the dismantling of twenty-one illegal Israeli settlements there, was seen as another retreat in Tehran. Buoyed with confidence, Hamas forces in Gaza used the tunnels they had made with the help of Iranian expertise and finance to attack a tank battalion on Israeli soil on June 25. They killed two Israeli soldiers and took a corporal named Gilad Shalit hostage. The Israelis had been surprised and Olmert was livid not only with Hamas but also with Abbas.

A few weeks later, the IDF attacked a safe house where Hamas leaders had gathered, aiming to kill its military commander, Mohammad Deif.

On July 12, as Israel's security cabinet gathered to assess the ramifications of hitting Deif, a note was brought in about a similar raid in the north of the country. This time the guerrillas of Hezbollah had ambushed a patrol in Galilee, killing three soldiers and taking two prisoners. This had been an unusually sophisticated operation. The Hezbollah forces hadn't just sneaked across the border. They had fired rockets and ambushed two Israeli army vehicles in what they called Operation Truthful Promise. The declared aim of the operation was to achieve the release of Lebanese prisoners in Israeli jails, and at the top of the list was a non-Shia fighter whose arrest predated the formation of Hezbollah. Samir Kuntar came from the community of Lebanon's Druze and had been a fighter with the left-wing Palestine Liberation Front. In April 1979, the sixteen-year-old activist joined three of his comrades in an attack meant as revenge for Sadat's peace with Israel. They used a small boat to get to Israel from the southern Lebanese port of Tyre. In a clumsy attack on the northern Israeli province of Nahariya, Kuntar and his companions killed a young father and his daughters, aged four and two (the latter had been mistakenly smothered by her own mother who was trying to hide her from the assailants). Hezbollah now wanted to secure the release of a man considered by the Israelis to be a derided killer of infants. On the other hand, Hezbollah could buy itself clout by showing that it cared not only for its fellow Shia but for all fighters against Israel. With the help of Iran, it wanted to establish its hegemony in the anti-Israel camp.

Less than a year into his premiership, Olmert was now faced with a harrowing situation. Within a matter of weeks, the Jewish State had come under attack from Iranian-funded groups on both its northern and its southern borders. Iran's newly elected President Ahmadinejad openly denied the Holocaust and spoke against Israel with an unprecedented vehemence. He promised its disappearance. This was the same president who championed Iran's nuclear program, while sticking to the official claim that it was for peaceful purposes only.

Olmert and Peretz resolved to do what Israelis have often done when faced with danger: They went on the offensive. If Hezbollah wanted to use its bases in Lebanon to attack the Jewish State, the whole country was going to pay. The IDF invaded southern Lebanon, brought the country under siege by air and sea, and sent their long-distance Heron drones to bomb not just Hezbollah's bases in the south but Beirut's Rafiq Hariri International Airport. A storm of hell rained over the suburbs of Dahiya, where Hezbollah's buildings exploded one after the other. The latest generation of Israel's precision missiles successfully targeted Shia villages that were Hezbollah strongholds while sparing Christian or Druze villages nearby. Six years after the 2000 withdrawal, the full might of the Israeli army had been unleashed on Lebanon—precisely the scenario that Hezbollah had long hoped to avoid.

In his base in Dahiya, Hassan Nasrallah was experiencing the worst time of his life. Had he committed a grave miscalculation? Hezbollah was already reeling from the widespread accusation that it had organized the assassination of the popular Sunni prime minister, Rafiq Hariri, in February 2005. The massive backlash to the attack led to Lebanon's Cedar Revolution and the expulsion of the Syrian army from Lebanese soil after thirty years of occupation. Would Hezbollah now be accused of having frivolously brought war on Lebanon? Worse, would the Israelis kill Nasrallah just like they had killed Musawi, Yasin, and so many of the leaders who had stood up to the Jewish State? Was this the end of Hezbollah? There was no doubt that Nasrallah had blinked.

Nasrallah himself later remembered the immense pressure he was under: "It was a very terrible war. Many had been displaced. Many houses, shops, markets, and schools were destroyed in the first days. All the world was set against the Resistance. In a statement on the first day, the US, Europe, Russia, and China all stood against us. Most Arab states also had very negative reactions. Even inside Lebanon there was a divide."

Qassem Soleimani had been in Beirut just one day prior to the operation. By then he had made it a habit to shuttle quickly between Iran, Iraq, and the Levant as he directed the increasing forces that came under his command. He was in Damascus when the surprise Israeli attack came. He spoke to the panicked Nasrallah on the phone and went on to do what had already become a hallmark of his career. He made arrangements to get himself to the heart of the battlefield, to calm Nasrallah down and to plan an operation patiently.

Nasrallah couldn't believe his ears when he heard Soleimani's offer. Damascus was only a few hundred kilometers east of Beirut—but how could he get there under constant Israeli fire? The border post at Masnaa had been closed.

"We told him this was impossible," the Lebanese leader later recalled. " 'All the bridges have been hit, all the roads are closed, the Israeli warplanes are hitting every target. It is total war. You can't get yourself to Dahiya or Beirut.' But Hajj Qassem insisted. He said he would walk if we didn't send him a car."

Imad Muqniyah understood Hajj Qassem better. A commander couldn't lead from afar. The two men coordinated together. Muqniyah got himself into Syria, picked up Soleimani and got him to Dahiya via an arduous route that was a mixture of walking and getting rides. Nasrallah expressed a sigh of relief when the two commanders returned together.

The shadow commander was now ensconced at Dahiya, Hezbollah's beating heart, under ferocious and unprecedented Israeli attack. At the center of the battle, Soleimani would now directly face the Zionist enemy that constantly haunted him. It would be the confrontation of a lifetime.

* * *

"Dahiya" is the Arabic word for "suburbs" but the term is now mostly associated with one particular neighborhood: "Dahiya al-Junubiya" or the "Southern Suburbs" of Beirut. Filled with low- and mid-rise apartments and busy streets, Dahiya has been a Shia-majority area for decades. In normal times, before the 2006 war, it was an area full of life and commercial activity. Soccer tournaments engrossed the area's youth, shopping malls were frequented by the rising Shia middle class, and the old men did what the old men of the Mediterranean have long done: watch the neighborhood from the comfort of a chair. Hezbollah had mastered the art of hiding in the plain sight of this bustling district. Here its commanders gave speeches in amphitheaters, its Ashura processions

mobilized everybody, and young men were recruited to the organization. After his role in the 1983 Beirut bombings became clear, Muqniyah,
who was barely twenty years old at the time, became one of the most
secretive operatives in the Middle East. In fact, he was the true shadow
commander whose name and bearings were unknown to most Hezbollah
operatives. But the same Muqniyah played soccer on the streets of
Dahiya. Nasrallah was famous for stealthy tours of Dahiya in disguise,
not too hard for a cleric who can hide behind the garb. Stories of
Nasrallah and Muqniyah having ice creams together in Dahiya, while
intelligence organizations looked everywhere for them, have become
part of Hezbollah lore.

But on July 12, 2006, as Israel rained down on Dahiya, it quickly
turned into a ghost town. "I thought this was the end of Dahiya and the
end of Hezbollah," says an Iraqi operative who has lived in the area for
years. "The first day, second day, third day. They just didn't seem to stop."7

This was the Dahiya that Soleimani entered with Muqniyah. Hundreds
of the area's residents were being killed and hundreds of thousands of
Shia were being displaced. In one of the first nights, Soleimani remembered being alone in an operations room with Muqniyah and Nasrallah
as they watched building after building collapse around them. A twelve-
story high-rise right next to them was hit by Heron drones and the three
men watched it come down in flames. Soleimani and Muqniyah knew
that they had to do whatever it took to save their leader. It was almost
midnight. They overcame Nasrallah's resistance and fled from the building on foot. It was a risky move. Scarcely a single soul was venturing into
the streets—a far cry from the usually bustling evenings of Dahiya,
where men and women enjoy barbecues, tea, and hookahs. People were
afraid of the seemingly endless Israeli raids.

The three men left the area on foot and sat under a tree. Soleimani had
taken off his camouflage uniform and was in his underwear. On the
suggestion of Muqniyah, they spent hours under the tree. No one would
have believed that the three most wanted men of the Axis of Resistance
spent the long night not hiding in an underground bunker but under a
tree in the open in Dahiya.

Nasrallah regained his nerves when faced with the calm and confident duo of Soleimani and Muqniyah. The two of them gave him hope.

As they climbed onto motorcycles and visited the front, spent nights in villages under fire, and carefully planned the comeback, the secretary-general got a much-needed boost. Hezbollah now rained its own rockets on Israel. Some days, more than a hundred rockets hit Israeli towns and villages. Up to half a million Israelis were displaced. In the Jewish-Arab town of Maalot Tarshiha, three Palestinian citizens of Israel were killed in the very first days. They had gotten out of their car after hearing a bomb alarm and a rocket had hit them.

Hezbollah hit Israelis wider than ever before. It hit Ein Qiniyyeh, a Druze village in the illegally occupied Golan Heights. It hit the ancient holy city of Tiberias on the western shore of the Sea of Galilee, the very lake Jesus Christ had once walked upon. It hit Nazareth, Jesus's childhood home and now an unofficial capital of Arab Israel. A Hezbollah rocket killed Rabia and Mahmoud Taluzi, two Palestinian children, aged three and seven, walking to their cousin's home. A Palestinian home in Haifa was hit by another rocket. Hezbollah's rockets went as far south as Atlit, a coastal town 20 kilometers south of Haifa.

The rockets were having their effect on Israel. The population was sick and tired of years of terrorist attacks and they now faced rocket attacks unlike anything they had seen in years. Worse, Israel seemed to be not as invincible as it had gotten used to being. Despite three sustained attempts, the IDF failed to occupy the Shia town of Bint Jbeil. Although it had only 20,000 inhabitants, the town had acquired a symbolic importance for both sides. When the Israelis withdrew in 2000, Nasrallah gave his famous victory speech here, bellowing to a crowd of 10,000 that "Israel might own nuclear weapons but it is weaker than a spider's web." The speech became notorious in the ranks of the IDF. Six years later, the army's chief of staff, Dan Halutz, and regional commander, Gadi Eizenkot, wanted to teach Hezbollah a lesson. The IDF's first assault on the city, on July 23, was codenamed Operation Webs of Steel, a clear reference to the Nasrallah speech. But Bint Jbeil would not fall. Dozens of Hezbollah fighters (and seventy-six Lebanese civilians) died defending the town. Israel's claim to have "total control" of the town turned out to be a lie. It lost seventeen soldiers there, including Major Roi Klein from the prestigious Golani Brigade, the 31-year-old son of two Holocaust survivors. Four years later, Iran's President Ahmadinejad received a hero's welcome when he spoke in the city and praised it for standing up to Israel.

In the liberal *Haaretz* newspaper, columnist Ari Shavit saw doom and gloom: "Despite the media euphoria and the patriotic spin, the aerial war . . . is not heading for victory . . . There will be no resolution from the air, even if the pilots ultimately manage to locate Hezbollah leader Sheikh Hassan Nasrallah and kill him."

Israeli society was livid. Despite having a very broad parliamentary base, Olmert's coalition government was coming under attack from all sides. The leader of the opposition, Benjamin Netanyahu, whose party had received less than 9 percent in the March elections, went ballistic on the government and accused it of being weak. At his side, Netanyahu had Uzi Dayan, nephew of Moshe, the storied, eyepatched defense minister of the 1967 and 1973 wars. After serving in the army for thirty-six years and heading the National Security Council for two (2003–5), Dayan's first attempt at politics had failed shortly before the war when his party got less than 1 percent of the vote. Unlike his Labor Party uncle, Dayan now went to the right wing of Israeli politics and became a military advisor to Netanyahu, echoing his criticism of the war effort with the credibility that came with a decades-long military career and that last name. In the occupied territories, the West Bank settlers used their umbrella Yesha Council to wage a nationwide campaign aimed at bringing down the government. A soldier then fighting in the war became key to Netanyahu's political comeback plans. Naftali Bennett, a 34-year-old Orthodox Jew who had given up a tech career in Manhattan to get into Israeli politics, became Netanyahu's chief of staff shortly after the war. He would help make the stories of the Olmert government's failure in the war a fixture of Netanyahu's rage against the old Zionist elites of Israel.

The one million Arab citizens of Israel also joined in attacking their own government. After the killing of the Taluzi children by a Hezbollah rocket, the mayor of Nazareth, Ramez Jaraisi, a Palestinian from the Communist Party of Israel, asked for Israel to accept a ceasefire. Ahmed Tibi, a popular and highly respected Arab member of the Knesset, brought a bill to the parliament that sought the same thing. Only Arab MPs voted for it but Tibi, who was against Hezbollah's rockets, continued his opposition to the war effort: "I cannot accept this destruction of another country by Israel. War crimes are being committed." As the number of civilian deaths rose, Israel gave its classic response. Tzipi Livni, the foreign minister who had made her career on wanting to make peace with the Palestinians, said: "Unfortunately civilians sometimes pay the price of giving shelter to terrorists."

* * *

After about ten days on the battlefronts, Soleimani arranged to return to Iran to report back to Khamenei. He went to Mashhad and, not far from the holy shrine, met his commander-in-chief to brief him on the war in Lebanon. Khamenei was flanked by all the highest political and military leaders of the Islamic Republic, who had descended upon Mashhad for the occasion: President Ahmadinejad, the chief of the judiciary, the speaker of the parliament, the chief of staff of the armed forces, and the leaders of the army and the IRGC.

"It was a bitter report," Soleimani later remembered. "My observations showed no horizon for victory. This was a different war. It was a war of technology and precision."

When the meeting broke at prayer time, all the leaders went for their ablution, the ritual washing of hands and feet necessary prior to the prayer. Khamenei gestured to Soleimani, asking to speak to him privately. If Soleimani had reassured the panicked Nasrallah, the Supreme Leader now wanted to reassure his commander, whose report had had an unmistakably pessimistic tone. Khamenei resorted to the usual tool of Islamic tales. He told Soleimani that the 2006 war was going to be a modern-day version of the Battle of the Trench. Soleimani trembled. That battle had been led by the Prophet Mohammad himself in 626, just five years after the establishment of the Muslim community in Medina. The similarities were uncanny. Mohammad's Medina had been besieged by a deadly coalition between the elders of the holy city of Mecca and the area's Jewish tribes. An army of 10,000 had put Medina under siege and the city only had about 3,000 active fighters to defend itself. The war had turned when a genius tactic was suggested by the Prophet's top Iranian advisor, Salman the Persian, a Zoroastrian-born convert to Islam who suggested digging trenches around the city to stop the charge of the enemy's cavalry. The tactic worked and the Muslims won. Mohammad's top fighter on the ground had been his cousin, Ali, later the First Shia Imam. Was Khamenei slyly asking Soleimani to be a 21st-century Salman to Nasrallah? It was too much of a weight for a man to bear.

Soleimani overcame renewed objections from Nasrallah and once more made it back to Beirut. He brought with him a personal letter from Khamenei that did much to boost the morale of Hezbollah's leadership. "Send my regards to each and every one of the brothers in this difficult war," Khamenei's letter read. "Trust in God and stand your ground. We have full faith in the victory of the resistance. The resistance will win and it will become a regional power. We are with you and will defend you in every way. You will turn into a power that no force could stand up to."

Khamenei didn't just offer words of support. More importantly, he gave Hezbollah a great political cover. He claimed that Iranian intelligence showed that the Israelis had planned to attack Hezbollah by the fall and were just looking for an excuse. In other words, Nasrallah shouldn't think that his cross-border raid had caused the war.

* * *

On August 11, the United Nations Security Council finally approved a unanimous resolution calling for a ceasefire. A full month of war had passed before the UN's highest body took action. The US's hawkish ambassador to the UN, John Bolton, had deliberately delayed UN action in the hope of seeing Hezbollah destroyed. In the final days of the war, it was Hamad bin Jassem, the foreign minister of Qatar, then the Arab member on the security council, who did much to convince Bolton.[8] Hezbollah and the Lebanese government accepted the offer a day later. The Israelis followed the day after on August 13. On August 14, at 8 A.M. local time, the ceasefire went into effect.

Militarily speaking, Hezbollah had not won this war by any stretch of the imagination. It had lost hundreds of men, including some of its valued regional commanders. More than a thousand Lebanese civilians had died and up to a million of its constituency, the Shia, were internally displaced. On the other side, Israel had lost 121 soldiers and 44 civilians (plus an American and an Argentine visitor). One could even claim that

Israelis had won since subsequent events have shown they reached one of their key war goals: Hezbollah was effectively deterred and has barely attempted to attack Israel again. The Israelis of the north could now safely swim in the Sea of Galilee or go for hikes in the occupied Golan Heights without the fear of rockets.

But the Axis of Resistance, headed by Iran and Hezbollah, turned the stalemate into an indubitable political victory. The Lebanese militia, which had been perceived by many, including some of its own leadership, to be on the verge of destruction in the first days of the attack, had survived. It had fought the mighty army of the Zionist enemy to a draw. It had exploded its warships with the missiles that were increasing in number thanks to Iran's largesse. In 1973, Egypt and Syria had turned an obvious military defeat in the Yom Kippur War into a political victory for themselves. Thirty-three years later, Iran and Hezbollah made the so-called 33-Day War the subject of a massive propaganda campaign.

Supporters of Iran now glowed that Hezbollah, a paramilitary body, had achieved what no mighty Arab army ever had: It had humiliated Israel. All the might of the Arab world, backed by the superpower Soviet Union, had lasted six days faced with the Israelis in 1967. But Hezbollah had lasted more than a month. In less than a year, Hezbollah solidified its gains when it swapped the coffins of the two Israeli soldiers whose kidnapping had sparked the 2006 war with five Lebanese militants, including two of the four people it had demanded during the initial raid (Israel denies holding the other two). These were Samir Kuntar and Nasim Nisr, a Lebanese Jew who had made *aliyah* (immigrated to Israel) and gained Israeli citizenship to help Hezbollah spy. The infant killer Kuntar was met with jubilant celebrations in Beirut to the disgust of his fellow Druze, including Israel's deputy foreign minister, Majalli Wahabi, who attacked "Kuntar's fans [who] praise a man who is proud of smashing the skull of a child."[9] The militant's "fans" included Ayatollah Khamenei. In early 2009, Kuntar traveled to Iran as part of a delegation of militants freed from Israeli jails. In meeting them, Khamenei praised them for their "patience in prison" and "all you've done for the massive and global movement of Islamic awakening."

It helped that many on the Israeli side seemed to agree with this assessment of their own failure. The war was widely considered to have been a shameful disaster. Olmert and Peretz never quite recovered and the Israeli right wing received a monumental boost. In the next elections in 2009, following Olmert's resignation due to corruption allegations, Netanyahu scored a historic victory: Despite his party coming in second with 21.61 percent of the vote, he was able to form a coalition and come to power. At the time of writing (summer 2020) he remains prime minister, having outlasted David Ben-Gurion as the longest-serving prime minister of Israel. The left-of-center parties of Israel are now a shadow of their former selves. The people who had helped Netanyahu pummel Olmert due to his wartime performance have all been richly rewarded during his long rule. Uzi Dayan came to head Mifal Hapayis, the national lottery organization. Naftali Bennett became a top cabinet minister and political ally of Netanyahu. The West Bank settlers got the most pro-settlement prime minister they could have dreamed of.

At this time, just when the Iraq War was raging and the US had tens of thousands of forces across the Middle East, the conservative press in America lambasted Israel for having become a slothful nation, having lost its militant edge. The Jewish-American writer Max Boot led the charge with an influential editorial published in September 2006 in *the Washington Examiner*.

"Many Israelis now lament that the frontier spirit that kept their country strong enough through decades of adversity has disappeared, killed by rampant individualism, materialism and liberalism," Boot wailed.[10] He warned that "Iran and its terrorist proxies [were] growing powerful and increasingly impudent while the Western democracies lick their wounds," and suggested that the mass murder of civilians, on the scale of the nuclear bombing of Hiroshima, might be now necessary.

Boot also quoted Ari Shavit, who now lamented the fact that "masculinity" had been "publicly condemned" in Israel, seeing this as a reason for Israel's failure in battle. (Shavit's obsession with preserving the "masculinity" of Israel didn't age well since he had to resign a mere four years later from his position at *Haaretz* due to allegations of sexual misconduct. He later wrote a report for *Haaretz*, entitled "I was blind to the power I had as a privileged white man."[11])

As Tel Aviv soul-searched, Tehran glowed. Soleimani, who had remained in Beirut to the very last day of war, made his way back to the

Iranian capital. In another meeting, he met the same crowd as he had in Mashhad, all the top leaders of the Islamic Republic. Gone was the pessimistic tone of only a couple of weeks before, although the commander kept his usual calm and quiet tone. Khamenei praised him lavishly in front of all the top political and military officials of the country.

The Quds Force's help to the frontline organizations facing Israel only increased. In June 2007, Hamas was able to kick Fatah out of Gaza and take over the strip. This followed Hamas's shocking electoral victory the year before. Hamas-run Gaza now became subject to a brutal Israeli siege and constant military operations. Israel adopted a "Dahiya doctrine," named for its actions during the 2006 war. Formulated by Gadi Eizenkot, Israel's commander of the northern front during the Lebanon war, who rose to become chief of staff in 2015, the "doctrine" was a barely concealed attempt to justify war crimes: Israel would no longer allow Hamas and Hezbollah to hide in plain sight. It would hit civilian infrastructure used by combatants.

In December 2008, Olmert's government, with the Labor Party's Ehud Barak as minister of defense, attacked Gaza for three weeks with the stated goal of stopping Palestinian rockets. Operation Cast Lead killed close to 1,500 Palestinian civilians, compared with three Israeli civilians dead on the other side. A subsequent UN mission accused both sides of war crimes. By this time, Iran didn't even try to hide its involvement. Hamas used Iranian-engineered missiles, many of its commanders had been personally trained by Soleimani in Iran, and Iranian arms were funneled to Gaza using Sudanese ports and tunnels in the Egyptian Sinai. Shortly following the war, Israel staged two airstrikes on Sudan and one on a ship in the Red Sea to stop the smuggling of arms to Gaza.

"The day of the Israeli air raids on our missiles getting into Gaza was actually one of our happiest days," an Iranian Quds Force officer said years later. "We had proven that we could get arms to the Palestinians while the likes of traitor Mubarak sat down and watched Palestinian children die in Gaza." The officer also made the claim that Soleimani and Muqniyah had both made it into Gaza during the conflict, using the Hamas tunnels—a claim, whispered here and there, that is likely to be a propaganda fabrication.[12]

As Iran's confidence grew, it now publicly boasted about its anti-Israel actions. During the next conflict in Gaza, the biblically named Operation Pillar of Cloud in November 2012, the IRGC's top commander, Mohammad Ali Jafari, boasted: "Iran will technologically help the Muslims and the oppressed of the world to stand up to tyranny and the regime of arrogance," before adding that Tehran hadn't sent its Fajr 5 missiles to Gaza "directly" but had given the Palestinians "its technology" and, as a result, "an innumerable amount of these missiles [were] being produced."[13]

As the Middle East was engulfed in military action on all sides, Soleimani's armed men gave Iran clout. The infamous Shia Crescent was already operational. It was typical for a Quds Force soldier to get training in Hezbollah's increasingly sophisticated camps in the Beqaa valley, before seeing action in the quagmire of sectarian and anti-American conflict in Iraq or in Gaza. Under Soleimani's leadership, the Quds Force became more than the sum of its parts. On January 26, 2011, Soleimani was promoted to the rank of major general, making him one of the very few Iranian commanders allowed to wear two stars on their shoulders, the maximum available in the Iranian insignia system.

These years of flourishing and thriving also came with an event that soured the taste of success for Soleimani. In February 2008, the Israelis finally got to Soleimani's fellow shadow commander. Imad Muqniyah was killed by a car bomb in Damascus, minutes after he had met Soleimani. Bashar al-Assad reportedly asked Nasrallah not to reveal the identity of the slain commander but the Lebanese leader went on to do the opposite:[14] Muqniyah, who had previously lost two of his brothers, would now become a poster boy for the Axis of Resistance. Media reports now listed all the operations attributed to him including some as far away as Latin America: He was noted as being responsible for the 1992 explosion in the Israeli embassy in Argentina and the 1994 bombing of a Jewish community center in Buenos Aires, the latter killing eighty-five civilians, making it the deadliest terrorist attack in Argentina's history.

In the midst of invasions, terrorist attacks, missiles, and warships, one could be forgiven for believing that the history of the Middle East was now solely made through the barrels of guns. In 2009, a mass movement for democracy was crushed in Iran, with Soleimani's comrades in the

IRGC playing a key role. Men with guns seemed to rule the roost. What hope could possibly lie with the ordinary people?

In December 2010, the people of the Middle East once more surprised the world. They unleashed a force unpredicted by the strategists in Washington, Tel Aviv, Tehran, or Riyadh. As the Islamic Republic plotted its response, Major General Qassem Soleimani led its efforts.

Chapter 11

Islamic Awakening, Sectarian Degeneration

In his sixty-two years of life, Qassem Soleimani visited many lands, near and far, but nowhere ever felt like his home province of Kerman. Here was home. He knew every patch of the desert; he had climbed every hill. Here he knew the people in a deep way; they were the ones he had mobilized and sent to die in wars near and far. He had built his career on these people's lives—and he loved them dearly.

On August 27, 2011, Qassem Soleimani went up onto the podium in Kerman's Grand Imam Ali Prayer Hall. Built on the city's Ashura Square, the hall could fit up to 50,000. Right next door there sat a unique Iran-Iraq War museum. These institutions were all the work of Soleimani and his fellow Kermani, President Rafsanjani, who spent the 1990s marking their city with the regime's adornments.

On that hot summer day, around 50,000 Basijis filled the hall. These were members of the IRGC's auxiliary volunteer arm, once known as heroes for having fought Iraq on the battlefields but now notorious for their thuggish behavior on Iranian streets. The Basijis had had a key role in drenching the 2009 Green Movement in blood. During the war years, the left-leaning prime minister, Mirhossein Mousavi, with his devotion to the revolution and his belief in socialist economics, had been an idol for many Basijis. But in 2009, the Basijis helped rig the election against Mousavi, who was now allied with the pro-democracy reformists, and in favor of the incumbent conservative, Mahmoud Ahmadinejad. When a mass movement erupted following the elections, the same Basijis helped put it down with hair-raising violence. Foreign observers compared them to the Nazi Brownshirts.

In the last decade of his life, as Soleimani rose to become a household name in the country, he carefully presented an image of himself as someone uninterested in internal political divisions, a national military hero all Iranians could love. There was little truth to this alleged impartiality. Soleimani had dedicated his life to the IRGC and to absolute obedience to Ayatollah Khamenei. When the reform movement threatened the rule of the ayatollah, Qassem knew which side he would take. He loved the Basiji boys who had defended the leader. He didn't care what anyone called them.

Young boys in the crowd were eager to catch a glimpse of the quiet commander about to address them. He was yet to become a celebrity in Iran, let alone abroad, but for Kermanis, few names were as exciting. They might not have known it but their local boy was about to give a speech of historical significance.

The events of the region in the preceding few months had shaken the whole world. For the first time in the history of the Arab world, a mass movement of people had overthrown a dictator. And then another one. And then another one. By the time Soleimani went onto the podium, Tunisia, Egypt, Yemen, and Libya had brought down dictators who, between them, had been in power for more than 125 years.[1]

The blustering wave of the Arab revolution seemed to have emerged out of nowhere. Middle Eastern analysts were busy eating their hats. Few had done anything to predict the possibility of such a movement. When it started in Tunisia in December 2010, many had been quick to point out that maybe it could take place in a small and relatively developed country of ten million but that it would never hit the heart of the Arab world, the grand nation of Egypt, most of whose population were not even connected to the internet. Wasn't this a Twitter revolution after all?

They were in for a surprise. The combined power of the Egyptian social activists and the mighty working class of the country was a force no one could stop. On February 11, 2011, Egyptian president Hosni Mubarak stepped down.

The rulers of Iran were not prepared for this. They could hardly believe their eyes. Old Egypt hands in the Iranian foreign ministry had been pushing for better ties between Cairo and Tehran. They had not foreseen the historic fall of the pharaoh. Khamenei and Soleimani might have been as surprised as Barack Obama and Hillary Clinton. But unlike the latter pair, the Iranians were quick to come up with an approach and stick to it.

Khamenei would have been excited by the massed throngs bringing down leaders not unlike the Shah he had once fought. He must have felt like many Soviet leaders in the wake of the 1959 revolution in Cuba. On a visit to the tropical island, the then 64-year-old Politburo member Anastas Mikoyan had been excited to meet Fidel Castro and his comrades. They reminded him of his own days as a revolutionary in old Armenia. The Egyptians on the street will have reminded the old ayatollah of his days in the Mashhad of the 1960s, when he smoked a pipe, hobnobbed with Marxist intellectuals, and admired Cuba and Vietnam. But just like the Soviet leaders in 1959, Khamenei's enthusiasm was quickly replaced with a cynical realism that sat well with his position: not a revolutionary but a dictator like the one he had once overthrown. The ayatollah, after all, had just violently put down a revolution in his own country. Iran would orient itself to the Arab Spring not in the spirit of revolutionary fraternity but with cold calculation worthy of a scheming monarch. Despite the words that came out of his mouth, Khamenei was now more of a sultan than a revolutionary.

On February 4, 2011, a week before the anniversary celebrations of the Iranian revolution, Khamenei gave a sermon half in Persian and half in his stilted Arabic. Mubarak was yet to fall but the writing was on the wall. Khamenei defined Iran's attitude in no uncertain terms. This was an "Islamic Awakening." The people of the Arab world had "woken up" just like the Iranians had in 1979. They needed to discover that Islam was their only solution.

Khamenei told a historical story. The powers of Europe and the US had long kept the countries of the region weak and divided. They had promoted Arabic, Turkish, and Iranian nationalism to keep up the divisions. They had corrupted the people's morals and kept religion away from them. But the Iranian revolution had changed everything because of "a wise man, a remarkable man, a sage, a jurist, a fighter, a brave man, a man who took risks, a man who spoke eloquently, Imam Khomeini." Now the new Iran of the Khomeinists should be an example for all other nations in the region. With its Islamic ethos and independence from the West, it could be the "foundation of a new civilization." The message was simple: Egyptians and Arabs must adopt Islamism and fight Israel. Khamenei called on the Al-Azhar clerics to "take a prominent role—people rightly expect it from you."

Soleimani took his cue from the Supreme Leader. As the commander of all the IRGC's operations abroad, he had been tasked by the leader with directing Iran's intervention in these revolutions. Six months after Khamenei's speech, when Soleimani went up onto the podium in Kerman, he knew what to say. "In our region today, we have more than one Iran. Today, Egypt is Iran, whether you like it or not. The nation of Egypt is the second Iran, whether you like it or not."

The commander boasted about the success that Rachid Ghannouchi's Islamists had had in the Tunisian elections. He predicted that Islamists would also take over in Egypt. Eighty percent of the future Egyptian parliament "will belong to the Muslims," Soleimani boldly predicted.

"All the Arabic governments will fall by the actions of their nations," Soleimani boasted. "The strongest and most oppressive governments have fallen and so will the rest. You cannot keep a country under the rule of a single family or a tribe anymore. Today a new order is taking shape in the world. Its main foundation will be spirituality and justice."[2]

* * *

Iran's support was not limited to words. Just as Soleimani gave speeches in defense of the Arab uprisings, the Quds Force made contact with the Muslim Brotherhood in Egypt and its sister parties, like Ghannouchi's party in Tunisia. Tehran wanted collaboration. A lot had to be overcome. There had been some bad blood between the Brotherhood's Sunni Islamism and Iran's revolutionary Shia version. Nonetheless there was hope for common ground. The Brotherhood leaders in Cairo liked

Ahmadinejad. They knew of his popularity with the youth in their own country. With his constant grabbing of headlines and his theatrical anti-Americanism, Ahmadinejad had built himself a global brand. When the Brotherhood's man, Mohammad Morsi, won the Egyptian presidential elections in June 2012, Iran welcomed the news. But, just like in 1979, there were very real conditions on the love between Iran and the Muslim Brotherhood.

Ghannouchi, after all, still remembered how sternly the IRGC papers attacked him in the early days of the Iranian revolution. He was called a conciliatory liberal—which is exactly what he was. Ghannouchi's Ennahda Party had its own extremists but he was able to drive it toward a liberal approach overall. Tunisia remains the only successful democratic transition that came out of the Arab Spring, largely because Ghannouchi refused to attempt a power grab at the expense of the country's institutions. In 2016, he would declare that his party had moved "from political Islam to Muslim democracy."[3] The last thing they wanted was IRGC interference in their small country.

In Egypt, too, there was limited enthusiasm for links with Iran and a serious aversion to letting the Quds Force operate in the country. Iran's dream of building a Sunni-Shia Islamist bloc in the region would get nowhere. Iran might have been proud to name a street in Tehran after the Islamist terrorist who assassinated Anwar Sadat in 1981 but the same process of Islamist radicalization had also heightened the anti-Shia rhetoric in the country. Gone were the days when the grand sheikhs of Al-Azhar embraced ties with the Qom seminary in an ecumenical spirit. In February 2013, Ahmadinejad became the first Iranian leader to visit Egypt in decades. He was there to attend a summit of the Organization of Islamic Cooperation and to return a previous visit by Morsi, who, in August 2012, had attended a summit of the Non-Aligned Movement in Tehran. Ahmadinejad's visit aroused enthusiasm but also suspicion. The Egyptian yellow press was full of tall tales about the secret plots behind the visit. Al-Azhar's Grand Sheikh Ahmed al-Tayeb warned Iran that it shouldn't attempt to spread the Shia religion in Egypt.

The Muslim Brotherhood had spent more than eight decades in opposition before Morsi took power. It still remembered the severe repression it had experienced during the presidency of the socialist Nasser. It moved cautiously and Morsi's cabinet included many non-Islamists. He had been at pains to promise not to repeal the peace treaty with Israel and not make major shifts in alignment. Cairo was in no hurry to get too close to the disruptive rulers of Tehran. During Ahmadinejad's visit, the foreign minister, Kamel Amr, pointedly declared: "The security of the [Persian] Gulf countries is a red line for Egypt." Iran's implicit attempt to build an Islamist Cairo-Tehran axis against Riyadh would find no support in Cairo. The Brotherhood had a much more relevant model at hand. Since 2002, Turkey had been ruled by the Justice and Development Party, a Brotherhood-inspired force whose leader, Recep Tayyip Erdoğan, became a key ally.

The Arab revolution had been fought on universalist slogans. It fought for bread and freedom. It had been led by trade unions, youth, and feminist associations. But the Muslim Brotherhood–style Islamists were the most organized political force and they entered the vacuum. Decades of erosion of leftists and progressive forces, together with a mushrooming of various Islamisms, now became apparent. The main beneficiary of the movement had become the "Turkish model" of Erdoğan. It had its own revolutionary media: the wildly popular Al Jazeera, which broadcasts in Arabic and English all over the region and the world. It was owned by the royal family of the tiny kingdom of Qatar, which had shown long-term interest in the bourgeois Islamism of the Brotherhood.

Al Jazeera English had proven popular throughout the years of the Iraq War when the American media failed basic tests of reliability. It was Al Jazeera that would lead exposés of American war crimes. But the Arabic channel had also promoted sectarian voices. Not only did the Muslim Brotherhood and its allies reject Iran's incendiary revolutionary approach in favor of a more measured strategy, all regional affairs soon took on sectarian colors—sectarianism that Iran and Al-Qaeda had been fanning in the gruesome battlegrounds of Iraq. This made any alliance between the Sunni-led Muslim Brotherhood and the Shia Islamists of Iran more difficult.

The small Persian Gulf island of Bahrain demonstrated the new politics of sectarianism better than anywhere else. Iran had given up its claims to sovereignty over Bahrain only in 1971 when, as the British evacuated the Gulf, the Shah accepted a UN process that gave independence to the island. With its majority Shia population ruled by a Sunni monarchy, Bahrain had long been an object of desire for Iranian Shia Islamists. In the early years of the revolution, several schemes to foment a Shia-led revolt failed. Throughout the 1990s, Bahrain's Shia Islamists were part of a wide coalition against the monarchy. It was only natural for this legacy of dissent to be reawakened in the stormy year of 2011.

But things got ugly very quickly. Saudi Arabia and other Sunni countries in the region sent forces there to put down what was considered a sectarian Shia uprising encouraged from Tehran, despite the years of dissent on the island, often completely unrelated to any foreign government. When Ahmadinejad visited Egypt, Al-Azhar's grand sheikh made a point of asking Iran to "respect Bahrain as a sisterly Arab state." The seminary that had been founded by a Shia dynasty more than a millennium ago now asserted its status as the leader of the Sunni world. In Tehran, when the popular local soccer club Persepolis played a match against Jeddah's Al-Ahli, many hardline pro-government protesters filled the Azadi stadium with slogans in support of the Bahraini Shia. "God curse the Saudi family" and slogans in support of Fatima, daughter of the Prophet and a symbol of Shia as the maternal ancestor of all imams, gave a clearly sectarian flavor to the protest.

The sweet hopes of the Arab Spring turned sour for all sides who hoped for change. Dictatorship, sectarianism, and armed conflict buried the memories of that brief moment of yearning for freedom. Fears of the Muslim Brotherhood in power helped millions join a popular movement against Morsi. But the movement ended not in liberal democracy but in a coup in 2013 led by Morsi's defense minister, Abdel Fattah al-Sisi, representing the worst possible iteration of decrepit military rule. The former director of military intelligence would lead Egypt to one of its darkest periods in recent history. Both liberals and Islamists lost out to the old military elites.

It soon became clear to Iranians that no "Islamic Awakening" was coming, no joint Shia-Sunni Islamist arch would be shaped. Millions of people in the Arab world had not arisen to replicate a system that could only sustain itself by severe repression. Iran's experimentation with democracy might have attracted some during the Khatami years (1997–2005). But by 2011, the regime was mostly associated with the brutal 2009 repression of the Green Movement and its international isolation and failures. If there were any leaders of the Islamic Republic that the revolutionaries of the Arab world could relate to, these were not the sultanistic Khamenei or his henchmen in the IRGC, but Mousavi and his fellow leaders of the Green Movement, Zahra Rahnavard and Mehdi Karoubi. But these three were put under house arrest when they called for a march in solidarity with the Egyptian and Tunisian revolutions in early 2011. At the time of writing (summer 2020), they remain in detention.

The experience of Lebanon and Iraq was reproduced on a grander scale. Iran's transnational Islamism had started out by wanting to defend all the oppressed of the world, from Ireland to the Philippines. Despite its sectarian basis, Lebanon's Hezbollah could have still claimed something of that universalistic legacy, seeing that it often couched its struggle in terms of fighting the Israeli occupation. The party did have the support of millions of non-Shia on this path. But in the battlegrounds of Iraq, imperialist sectarianism swiftly took the place of revolutionary transnationalism, as Soleimani rediscovered just how potent it was. The Quds Force might still claim that it was a "voice of the oppressed," but in practice it had become an instrument of Iran's state-based foreign policy of extending Iranian influence in the Arab world and doing so through sectarian Shia proxies. Before long, it embraced the use of such language too. Not for nothing did the Shah's former foreign minister, Ardeshir Zahedi, become a great fan of Soleimani and the Quds Force from his exile in Montreux, Switzerland. He might have not wanted any of the revolutionary Islamism of Tehran but he was happy to see the growth of Persian power in the Arab lands.[4]

For a few years after 2011, the Quds Force did attempt to supplant this sectarian approach with a possible alliance with the main Sunni force of the region, the Muslim Brotherhood. In a secret meeting in Turkey in 2014, Quds Force officials met the key leaders of the Egyptian Muslim Brotherhood to discuss a pact against the main bulwark of the status quo in the region, Saudi Arabia. Something of a tacit alliance did come to exist, especially as the Saudis went on to break diplomatic relations with Iran in 2016 and with Qatar in 2017. In the forever-changing map of Middle Eastern alliances, Iran's Axis of Resistance now has a working collaboration with Qatar, Turkey, and the Muslim Brotherhood. The basis of this alliance, however, is not ideology but the shifting power blocs of the region. This is not an Islamist bond between revolutionaries but a scheme between statesmen, of exactly the sort that both Khomeinists and Muslim Brothers had denounced throughout their history.

But Iran's tacit alliance with the Brothers did not extend to all countries. In two key countries of the Arab revolt where Iran carried out the most extensive interventions, it directly fought the forces of the Brotherhood. Here the Iranians cared not for an Islamic Awakening but for their crude survival interests. In the battlegrounds of Iraq, Khomeinist Islamism had degenerated into imperial designs of domination and sectarianism. In the battlegrounds of Syria and Yemen, this would escalate to gargantuan proportions.

* * *

Even as Soleimani promised to aid the oppressed everywhere, even as he declared that countries shouldn't be ruled by "a single family or a tribe anymore," he knew he was lying. Iran's policy was not consistent support for Islamists. It was not to foster revolutions against dictators. It was to preserve its own regime and spread its influence by any means necessary. Had Ayatollah Khomeini not said that all the rules of Islam could be broken to protect the Islamist state? Had the Islamic Republic not bought arms from Israelis to defeat a fellow Muslim nation when it was in its interests to do so?

When the wave of Arab revolutions hit Syria in March, there was never any doubt as to which side Iran would be on. "Hajj Qassem came to meet some of us, straight from a meeting with Aqa [Ayatollah Khamenei]," an Iranian Quds Force operative remembers. "This was in the summer. The protests were getting serious in Syria. He reminded us of the Assad family's help to us during the war with Iraq. He spoke about the brothers we had lost in the war. He said we had to stick by Bashar and defend him at all costs."[5]

The swift fall of Mubarak and Zine Ben Ali in Tunisia had awakened hopes in the region. Khamenei understood this well since the Iranian protesters were greeting him with a catchy slogan: "Mubarak, Ben Ali, now it's the turn of Seyyed Ali."[6] It rhymed in Persian. In the small southern city of Daraa in Syria, a teenager was arrested because he had dared to graffiti the same message. "It's your turn, doctor," he had written about the lanky ophthalmologist who was now Syria's president. The boy's arrest led to marches in the country's two main cities, Damascus and, to the north, the gorgeous ancient city of Aleppo.

Iran watched Syria closely. The Quds Force officials met with Ahmadinejad and made it clear that they had a mission from Khamenei to direct all Syrian-related affairs. Iran's ambassador in Damascus, Arabic-speaking Ahmad Mousavi, was soon replaced with Mohammdreza Rauf Sheybani, who was going to justify Iran's support for Assad.

"We knew Assad was a dictator with no religion," a Quds Force member says. "Some people grumbled about this early on. But when it became clear that the leader had decided personally on this strategy, we all obeyed."[7]

The well-spoken Sheybani took to Arab media to defend the Iranian approach. He said Iran continued to support the Arab revolution but the only genuine revolutions were those that were anti-American and anti-Zionist. The Syrian rebels, he claimed, were linked to the West and Israel. They didn't deserve support.

By the fall of 2011, when Sheybani was sent to Damascus, the civil uprising in Syria had turned into an armed movement. The shockingly brutal crackdown on the unarmed population killed hundreds of people. Armed forces were split and on July 29, the Free Syrian Army (FSA) was born. A haphazard collection of defected officers, the FSA was more a motley of anti-regime armed groups around the country than a united body. A specialist group in the Quds Force was tasked by Soleimani to liaise with the Syrian Arab Army (SAA) at all levels and to prepare it for the battles to come.

Was it Soleimani's advice that led Assad to adopt the murderous tactics such as dropping barrel bombs on residential neighborhoods, which came to kill hundreds of thousands of Syrian civilians? The passing of time and the opening of historical archives will help answer that question by showing us the details of Quds Force-SAA meetings. But if the details turn out to be wanting, there is no doubt about Tehran's role overall.

Iran would later link its massive armed intervention in Syria to the rise of ISIS. Evidence suggests otherwise. From the very moment Assad faced popular protests, the Quds Force and Tehran were ready to do all they could to save the rule of the Baath Party. There would be no equivocation in Iran's firm policy. Iran made different noises in the first few months of this uprising that turned into a civil war. It spoke of the need for reforms in Syria; it attempted to portray itself as a neutral country in the region. The joint envoy of the UN and the Arab League, Kofi Annan, came to note Iran as "part of the solution" in April 2012, a few months before he became the first in a long line of international diplomats tasked with solving the Syrian question to resign in frustration. But, all along, Iran had no interest in reconciliation in Syria, no interest in democratic reform. In fact, its emissaries were pushing on Assad to suppress the uprising mercilessly. It was the only way for the regime to survive.

* * *

In November 2011, an official in Yemen's Al-Islah Party received a worrying report from Turkey.[8] Turkish intelligence had revealed the content of a confidential conversation between an official in the Quds Force and a Yemeni party called Ansarallah. Al-Islah belonged to the global movement of the Muslim Brotherhood whereas Ansarallah was an Iran-backed movement of Yemen's Shia, better known by its colloquial name of the Houthis, after the main family buttressing the movement. According to the Turkish report, the Iranians were telling the Houthis not to accept a political transition that was being engineered in Yemen with the help of the Gulf Cooperation Council (GCC), a body that brought together the six Arab states around the Persian Gulf, chiefly Yemen's grand neighbor, Saudi Arabia.

As the Arab revolution had been spreading around the region, bets were high on Yemen's authoritarian president, Ali Abdullah Saleh, soon losing his position. Ever since the end of the Cold War had brought about the unification of North and South Yemen in 1990, Saleh had been its president. Prior to that, he had been in charge of North Yemen from 1978. He had mastered the art of keeping different foreign interlocutors happy. In the long years of conflict that marred this poorest country of the Arab world, Iran, Saudi Arabia, Egypt, the US, China, Cuba, and the Soviet Union had all done their bit to intervene. Saleh had learnt how to keep acquiescence for his rule as the first-ever president of a united Yemeni Republic. His influence in Washington was great enough that on January 11, 2011, as the wave of revolution started to ravage the region, the US secretary of state, Hillary Clinton, caused a surprise when she had a long lunch with Saleh. Just the previous month the US had protested Saleh's attempt to prolong his rule by amending the constitution. But he was also battling one of the strongest Al-Qaeda insurgencies in the world and, in that, he had strong US support.

Not long after Clinton left, the untenability of Saleh's rule became clear. All the main forces of Yemeni society seemed to agree that the old man had to go. The writing was on the wall on May 23, when the head of a major tribal federation turned against him. In June, Saleh flew to Saudi Arabia for medical treatment while the GCC brokered a deal that made for a peaceful transition. Al-Islah received further international legitimacy in October when one of its MPs, Tawakul Karman, became the first Yemeni, the first Arab woman, and only the second Muslim woman to win a Nobel Prize. The party was set to have a key role in the future of Yemen.

"Everybody was happy with the deal," the Al-Islah source says. "Not all the protesters but all the major parties of the opposition. The Saleh entourage was happy, we were happy, the old communists were happy, the Nasserists were happy, the Baathists were happy, the Islamists were happy. Even the Houthi rank and file were happy. Saleh was gone and we could have new elections, each get a piece of the pie, figure it out together. But Iran said no."

From the early days of the conflict, Soleimani had made it clear that Yemen represented a golden opportunity not to be missed. Here Iran could find a foothold right next to its main rival, Saudi Arabia. "Hajj Qassem knew a lot about Yemen," an Iranian Quds Force source remembers. "He always spoke about all that we could do there. I mean even before 2011."

The Yemeni Shia belonged to a small sect called Zaydi, known by others as "Four Imamis." This was because they followed only four of the twelve Shia Imams accepted by the Twelvers. Instead of Baqer, the Fifth Imam for the rest of the Shia, the Zaydis followed his half-brother Zayd Ibn Ali, who, in the tumultuous middle years of the eighth century, had died fighting the Umayyads, contributing to their eventual fall in the Abbasid revolution of 750.

By the twentieth century, Zaydis were rare outside Yemen. In this corner of the Arabian Peninsula, however, they had long maintained their fiercely autonomous domains. It was thanks to Zaydi efforts that even the Ottomans had struggled with controlling Yemen. The difficult, mountainous terrain that would come to bog down numerous regional and world powers in the twentieth and twenty-first centuries had already done the same to the Ottomans in the seventeenth. Between 1918 and 1962, the Zaydis ran an internationally recognized absolute monarchy. The Mutawakkilite Kingdom of Yemen joined the United Nations in 1947 and had actual sovereignty over much of Yemen, except for the port of Aden, which, along with some other territories, remained under British colonial rule. In the 1960s, Yemen fell into the grip of the revolutionary fervor traversing the region along with the rest of the world. In 1962, following the death of the imam-king, a group of leftist officers brought down the monarchy and founded the Yemen Arab Republic, inspired by Nasser. A civil war broke out in which the Egyptians supported the republic and the Saudis sent forces to defend the Shia kingdom. The Soviet Union helped the former whereas Iran's Shah, Jordan, and the British aided the latter. Simplistic narratives about Shia-Sunni divisions often curiously overlook this period. Before the end of the decade, the monarchy disappeared forever and the republic survived. Meanwhile, in 1967, Aden became the capital of the People's Democratic Republic of South Yemen. A British colony had been supplanted by the first Marxist-Leninist state in the history of the Arab world.

The end of the Cold War meant the end of the socialist South Yemen and brought about Saleh's united Republic of Yemen. But behind the unified maps of a seemingly sovereign territory sat many tribal and regional movements. The tribal Zaydis of the north maintained skirmishes with the forces of the central government throughout the 1990s and 2000s. They had a minuscule political party called Al-Haq ("The Truth") which had been founded in 1990 as something of a response to the powerful Al-Islah. President Saleh didn't mind Al-Haq as he welcomed any challenge to the worrisome force of the Muslim Brotherhood.

In the 1993 elections, Al-Haq elected two MPs including Hossein Badreddin Houthi. Inspired by the Iranian revolution, Hossein was unhappy with the parochial and tribal ways of the Zaydis. In 1997, he resigned from the parliament. In trips to Syria and Iran, he attempted to get support to form a Yemeni version of Hezbollah. Although full Iranian support wasn't forthcoming, Hossein was able to form Ansarallah, inspired by Hezbollah but much less of a centralized party. In 2004, Hossein died after having fomented a wide-ranging insurgency in the north of Yemen with some support from Iran. He had died shouting a war cry, in the long tradition of Arabian tribal battles. But his war cry had been a slogan that would now be emblazoned on the banner of the Houthis: "God is Great, Death to the USA, Death to Israel, Curse the Jews, Victory to Islam."

By 2011, the big tent of the Houthis was now under the control of Hossein's 32-year-old brother, Abdulmalek. The Houthis had been initially happy to go with the Riyadh-engineered transition and find a role in the future parliament of Yemen. But by the time the Turkish report got to the worried officials of Al-Islah, another decision had been made in Tehran, fully supported by the ambitious Abdulmalek. The Houthis would resist and continue their movement.

Unlike the previous Iranians in charge of relations with the Houthis, Soleimani took them seriously. He respected their tribal ways whereas previous IRGC commanders were known to have openly mocked them. He sent Hezbollah and Iraqi commanders to educate the Houthis politically.

"It was very difficult work," remembers an Iraqi commander sent to Yemen, later an advisor to the Houthi government. "The Houthis had very little religious or political understanding. We had to educate them in proper revolutionary values, against their tribal instincts. With the help of Allah the Almighty, the work was done and the Houthis are much more of a serious revolutionary and Islamic force now."

The old sages in Iranian foreign policy circles weren't happy with Tehran openly backing an armed movement in one of Saudi Arabia's neighbors. But Soleimani had been behind it—and so had his leader. In September 2014, the world was shocked to see the Yemeni capital of Sana'a fall to the Houthis. The policy had been vindicated in the most dramatic fashion. Under the leadership of the Quds Force, who dedicated significant resources to Yemen, Iran continued providing support to the Houthis. Saleh, conniving as ever, allied himself with the Houthis for a while but they fell out and, in December 2017, he was killed by a Houthi sniper, on the direct orders of Qassem Soleimani.

Yemen's civil war continues at the time of writing as Saudi Arabia, the UAE, Al-Qaeda, and the Houthis battle over the country. But for the first time in its short history, the Islamic Republic of Iran now has a solid ally on the Arabian Peninsula. It has used this ally in no subtle way. The missiles fired by the Houthis ravage their Saudi targets—and there is no mistake as to their Iranian origin.

* * *

Judged by its interventions in the Arab world alone, Ayatollah Khamenei's Islamic Republic was doing well. Before long, the claim that Tehran "controlled four Arab capitals" (Beirut, Baghdad, Damascus, and Sana'a) would become as commonplace a warning in Washington as it was a boast of many a Friday prayer leader in Iran. The Iranian population had never cared much for Tehran's Arab allies. The 2009 protesters declared loudly that they were ready to give their lives for Iran but "not for Gaza or Lebanon." But amid a nationalist turn in the IRGC's rhetoric and propaganda,[9] the Iranian interventions in the region were now classified as national, not necessarily Islamist, achievements every Iranian could be proud of. Who didn't like a Persian military hero conquering the faraway Arab lands?

But while Soleimani scored military-diplomatic victories in the Middle East, the Islamic Republic found itself ever more isolated for one major reason: its nuclear program. With the consent of Khamenei, Ahmadinejad had made the program a flagship part of his campaign of defiance while insisting that it was peaceful. Provoking the ire of Iranian progressives, the conservative president compared the program to the oil industry nationalized by Mohammad Mossadeq in the 1950s. Enjoying the astronomically high prices of oil, Iran seemed to be able to afford to put up with the UN-led sanctions imposed on it for its nuclear program, even amid the destruction of its middle class.

The campaign to thwart the growing nuclear program wasn't limited to economic pressure. Between 2010 and 2012, at least four Iranian nuclear scientists were assassinated in broad daylight. A fifth survived an attempt. Cyber-attacks sabotaged the nuclear enrichment facilities at Natanz. In all these incidents, fingers were pointed at the country most willing to engage in such activities: Israel under Prime Minister Benjamin Netanyahu, who made "the Iranian threat" a household expression in his country. Netanyahu made opposition to Iran's nuclear program the defining issue of his foreign policy. More than once, he came close to ordering airstrikes on Iran.

At the same time as Soleimani plotted Iran's moves in the region, his Quds Force took careful and asymmetrical actions against the Israelis and Americans. Not enough time has passed for us to have a full account of these actions. But despite Iran's strenuous denials, Soleimani's fingerprints were visible in many actions of 2011 and 2012. In October 2011, US officials alleged that the Iranians had wanted to assassinate Adel al-Jubeir, the Saudi ambassador in Washington, with a joint attack on the Saudi and Israeli embassies. A few months earlier, a Quds Force official had met with a drug cartel member in Mexico who turned out to be a source for the US Drug Enforcement Administration, leading to the unraveling of the plan. In February 2012, a car belonging to an Israeli diplomat exploded in New Delhi, injuring four people. Netanyahu quickly blamed Iran and the Delhi police investigation confirmed the IRGC's complicity. Israel's mission in Georgia was attacked on the very same day. In July, a Hezbollah suicide bomber attacked a bus full of Israeli tourists in Burgas, Bulgaria, killing the Bulgarian driver and five of the tourists.

Iran had no intention of stopping such actions. But its survival kit included more than suicide bombings and assassinations. The soldiers and diplomats had always worked in tandem. It was time for the diplomats to play their role.

Internationally isolated, regionally threatened by Israel, and with a population restive after years of repression and falling living standards, the Islamic Republic changed tack in 2013. Approaching the pinnacle of his power, Hajj Qassem would maintain a leading role in the next period.

Chapter 12

Black Flags, White Flags

The serene shores of Lake Geneva in the westernmost part of Switzerland are quite unlike any other place on earth. On clear days, you can gasp at the sight of Mont Blanc, the Alps' highest peak and a symbol of Europe. The city of Geneva itself and its picturesque little neighbors on the lakeside have a long history of hosting those in search of peace and calm: Here Edward Gibbon wrote his history of the Roman Empire; here Mary Shelley devised her *Frankenstein*; here Vladimir Nabokov spent the fortune he made from *Lolita* by moving into a luxurious hotel for the rest of his life; and here, too, Middle Eastern elites love to escape when there is too much trouble at home. It helps that Switzerland doesn't ask too many questions and hosts a UN premises more welcoming than any other. You come to Geneva if you want to make a deal. If the shores of the lake were bugged, they would pick up no end of plots, arms deals, and conspiracies.

Lacking such devices, few people know what Iran's foreign minister Javad Zarif and the US secretary of state John Kerry talked about when they took a casual stroll in January 2015 along the idyllic lakeshore. Zarif had arrived in Geneva on a commercial flight from Tehran, after a stop in Frankfurt. Heading straight to the negotiation room, he was exhausted.

He wanted some exercise and the city was tempting. But his and Kerry's simple lakeside walk was a step too far for the Iranian conservatives. From his pulpit as Tehran's Friday prayer leader, Kazem Sediqi attacked Tehran's top diplomat: "People didn't like what you did." Mohammadreza Naqdi, the old IRGC commander who had once led the force's efforts in Bosnia and was now head of the Basij, asked Zarif to "apologize to the Iranian nation" for "having trampled upon the blood of the martyrs." A conservative MP said Zarif and Kerry looked like "two lovers on their honeymoon."

That the foreign ministers of the US and Iran had been engaged in countless hours of negotiations for months, and that they could even go for a little wander by the lake, would have been inconceivable only shortly before. But as often happens in the Middle East, things had changed quickly. The conservatives in Tehran were hysterically lashing out at Zarif, not because of a harmless walk but for what it had come to symbolize: the road to amity with the Great Satan.

How had the inconceivable become reality?

Barack Obama had come to power in 2009 wanting to extract the US from the mess of the Middle East. He wanted to get out of Iraq, get the job done in Afghanistan, and use drone technology to kill the Al-Qaeda leaders from afar instead of spending trillions of dollars on what had come to be derisively called "nation-building". In May 2011, Obama's CIA achieved a feat his predecessor would have dreamed of: the killing of Al-Qaeda's top leader, Osama Bin Laden.

As Obama was re-elected in November 2012, his diplomats dreamed of realizing his declared "pivot" to east Asia. They wanted a State Department worried less about Tora Bora and Fallujah and focused more on Tokyo and Shanghai. The events of the years to come would dash such dreams. The wave of Arab revolutions led not to liberal democracies or the rule of established forces like the Muslim Brotherhood (with which the Obama administration was more than prepared to deal) but civil wars and sectarian conflicts. The United States couldn't easily get out. Despite some foreign policy achievements outside the region, the most important of which was normalization of relations with Cuba, Obama's legacy would be tarnished as much as his predecessor's by his engagements in the Middle East.

In 2013, as the re-elected president started his second term, countering Iran's nuclear program became a top priority. As detailed by Trita Parsi in his account of the process, Obama's State Department had already rejigged its Iran policy in his first term. From his very first year in office, he started a tradition of sending a video message to the Iranians on the occasion of Nowrooz, the Iranian New Year. The message was addressed to the "people and leaders of the Islamic Republic of Iran," an unmistakable recognition of the regime in Tehran. Simple rhetorical moves such as this might have been overlooked by many observers but they mattered hugely in Tehran.

In June 2013, the Iranians went to the polls to elect a new president. The 2009 movement had been shattered entirely and a few weeks before the elections, it appeared that few people would have the appetite to come to the voting booths. This could mean an easy victory for Qassem Soleimani's old comrade Mohammad Baqer Qalibaf, who had thrown his hat into the ring for the second time. He had Soleimani's solid support. On the reformist side, the main candidate was Mohammadreza Aref, Mohammad Khatami's vice-president in his second term, who was as boring and as uncharismatic a candidate as one could possibly imagine.

A man who could be classified as neither a reformist nor a conservative was also running. The West knew the man very well. When the nuclear crisis first broke out in 2002, he led Iran's negotiation team: a cleric with chubby cheeks forever inflated due to his constant grin, Hassan Rouhani could hardly have been more different from Mahmoud Ahmadinejad. In his negotiations with the West, Rouhani had agreed to cease uranium enrichment before Ahmadinejad took over and reversed the decision. A protégé of Hashemi Rafsanjani, Rouhani was the ultimate technocrat produced by the Islamic Republic. During the 1980s, he had led an informal "Assembly of the Wise" in the parliament, which argued for ending the war. This angered Ayatollah Khomeini, who ordered an end to the forum. Rouhani had spent his post-revolutionary career in the Islamic Republic's security establishment, penning books that argued for tough but effective policies that ensured the survival of the regime. Unlike Khatami, he wasn't much interested in democratic reform for its own sake. The ultimate pragmatist, he is perhaps best compared to China's Deng Xiaoping. Although he wouldn't say it out loud, Rouhani believed it didn't matter how "Islamic" the republic was so long as it could run a decent economy. In the presidential debates, he promised to end Iran's international isolation by engaging in nuclear talks with the West. Just as Iran's enrichment centrifuges were spinning, the wheels of its economy should also spin, Rouhani quipped.

Promise of a move toward normalcy struck a chord with the population. Following his endorsement by the still-popular Khatami, Rouhani went on to win the presidential election with 50.71 percent of the vote on a 72.71 percent turnout. The Iranian people had surprised the world again by playing an active role in determining their own future. For Ayatollah Khamenei, this wasn't necessarily a bad result. Constantly performing a balancing act between different factions of the regime, he had used Ahmadinejad to put down the mass reformist movement in blood. He could now use a pragmatic diplomat.

In Washington, Obama welcomed Rouhani's election. It had shown that the "Iranian people want to move in a different direction," the American president said. They had "rebuffed the hardliners and the clerics ... who were counseling no compromise on anything anytime anywhere."

"Clearly you have a hunger within Iran to engage with the international community in a more positive way," Obama added, making it clear that the nuclear talks could be resumed so long as "there's an understanding about the basis of the conversation."

Throughout the Ahmadinejad years, the nuclear talks had never come to a complete pause. They had been led by Rouhani's successor as secretary of the Supreme National Security Council, Saeed Jalili. A graduate of the regime's cadre-building Imam Sadeq University, Jalili wrote his MA thesis on the Prophet Mohammad's foreign policy and his PhD thesis on Islamic political thought in the Quran. He was known to give long lectures on similar topics to Western diplomats, who were in turn horrified and bored.

Rouhani's election signaled a change in Iran's approach to the talks. An even surer sign arrived shortly thereafter. Rouhani pulled Zarif out of six years of retirement and appointed him foreign minister, tasking him with leading the nuclear negotiations. No other diplomat of the Islamic

Republic had a better reputation in Washington, DC. Not only did he speak English and hold degrees from American universities, Zarif was also known for pioneering an approach that prioritized outreach to the West.

Change was immediate. The close ties built by Ahmadinejad with Hugo Chávez's Venezuela and other left-wing states in Latin America were quickly deprioritized. Iran vigorously re-entered the nuclear talks, and for the first time since 1979, Iran's foreign minister sat down with his American counterpart. Zarif and Kerry spent dozens of hours in negotiation rooms around the world. In September 2013, while attending the UN's General Assembly in New York, Rouhani took a phone call from Obama—the highest level of contact between the two countries since 1979.

The nuclear talks now became the top diplomatic story worldwide. For reporters covering the excruciatingly long talks, they appeared to be going painfully slowly. The chance of them collapsing was considered very real—as was the threat of escalation that could follow. But the talks progressed and achieved clear results. In November 2013 in Geneva, a general framework was agreed upon between Iran and P5+1, a group of six powerful countries consisting of the five permanent members of the UN Security Council (the US, Britain, France, Russia, and China) plus Germany. In April 2015 in nearby Lausanne, a preliminary deal was agreed. At last, on July 14, 2015, in Vienna, the final deal was signed: The Joint Comprehensive Plan of Action (JCPOA) was hailed globally as a diplomatic breakthrough. In exchange for heavy restrictions on its nuclear activities, Iran would see the lifting of most (though not all) sanctions.

As the talks were going on, many regional states, as well as conservatives in both Tehran and Washington, had opposed the deal. But when the actual deal was reached, almost all acquiesced. In September, when world leaders gathered in New York for their annual jamboree at the UN, the only leader opposing the Iran deal was the increasingly marginalized Benjamin Netanyahu. Even in Israel, much of the security establishment was in favor of the deal, seeing as it helped neutralize Iran's chances of acquiring nuclear weapons. The economic bonanza followed immediately. Iran jumped out of recession. Many obstacles remained but the buzz in Tehran was unmistakable. Many Western firms wanted to invest in a country whose opening could be the biggest economic story since the fall of the Berlin Wall in 1989. French businessmen and German backpackers flooded into Tehran airport.

What would be the place of Soleimani in this new world? Were men like him on the verge of marginalization? Did his sympathies lie with the anti-Zarif conservatives who led a campaign with the telling slogan "We Are Concerned"? Rouhani had openly clashed with the IRGC, and many of its leaders had spoken against the president and his foreign minister in no uncertain terms. The conservative press attacked Rouhani and his "New York Boys" on a daily basis. At the same time, Khamenei was in full support of the diplomatic team and affirmed his backing of Zarif.

The structures of the Islamic Republic perplexed Western diplomats and observers. Who truly spoke for Iran, the smiling duo of Rouhani and Zarif or the stern Khamenei and his soldier Soleimani? Was Iran after a "win-win agreement" with the West, as Zarif never got tired of claiming? And if so, why did it continue to jail opponents, why did it burn the US flag annually? Why did its forces instigate violence against Americans in Iraq, why did it uphold the Assad dictatorship?

Ever in search of heroes, the Western press helped catapult Soleimani to global prominence. In September 2013, a long-form piece by Dexter Filkins on the "Shadow Commander" appeared in the New Yorker. Filkins spoke of a commander who had made life hell for Americans in Iraq and was now "directing Assad's war in Syria," thus linking the Islamic Republic to the world's top story of the time, the brutal civil war in Syria.

As Zarif and his fellow Iranian diplomats, with their signature collarless shirts buttoned up to the top, negotiated with their American and Western counterparts in European hubs, Soleimani's men ran Iran's operation to save Bashar al-Assad at all costs. In public, there was no confrontation. Zarif and Soleimani paid regular tribute to each other. In private, a fierce rivalry took shape. For years, Soleimani had effectively acted as Iran's top diplomat for the region. This didn't sit well with Rouhani and Zarif, who even tried to lobby inside Hezbollah to counter Soleimani's influence. Rouhani's intelligence ministry kept a tab on the

Quds Force and complained about the brutality with which Soleimani had conducted his sectarian efforts.

No complaint about the shadow commander would get anywhere. His relationship with Rouhani's administration was to be different than with Ahmadinejad's. Months before Rouhani came to power, Soleimani had saddled Ahmadinejad's vice-president, Hamid Baqai, with millions of dollars that the latter would personally disburse among Iran's allies in Africa. Such behavior would be unacceptable to Rouhani's more professional government. But Soleimani had the absolute and ironclad support of Khamenei, the credit that came with a now-global profile and an irreplaceable presence on the battleground. At Khamenei's insistence, the Zarif-led negotiations were laser-focused on the nuclear file. The two other subjects of regular criticism in the West (coming with their own designated sanctions) were loudly and routinely declared to be outside the remit of Zarif and his men: Iran's interventions in the region and its missile program. These programs were led not by Rouhani but by the IRGC, a shadow government whose domineering attitude in Tehran was not shadowy at all.

The Americans accepted this separation of domains. They mainly cared about neutralizing Iran's nuclear arms ambitions anyway. In 2014, a cataclysmic series of events in the region made Soleimani even more famous, and placed him once more squarely on the side of the Americans, thus helping the amicable modus operandi taking shape between the Islamic Republic and the Great Satan. Tehran and Washington were now not only diplomatic partners in Lausanne and Vienna; they were to be effective military allies in Iraq and Syria.

* * *

The year 2014 started very differently for Zarif and for Soleimani. On January 20, the Geneva interim agreement reached in November 2013 officially went into implementation. In plain speech, the two sides now had to conduct another round of talks to reach a final deal. The P5+1 was to be represented by Britain's Catherine Ashton, a Labour Party member of the House of Lords and the European Union's foreign policy chief. Zarif and Ashton had to reach a level of consensus before the foreign ministers of all six powers, including Kerry, could fly in to finalize the agreement. The Austrian government agreed to host the new round of marathon talks. Millions of Iranians, and others around the globe, now turned their eyes to Vienna, perhaps the most diplomatically symbolic city in the world. Here, in 1815, all the powers of the ancient world had helped construct a reactionary world order in the aftermath of Napoleon's defeat. The Islamist diplomat and the British baroness representing the world powers now met not far from where Prince Metternich, the legendary conservative of Austria, had gone head-to-head with Count Karl Robert Nesselrode, an emissary of Russia's Tsar Alexander I.

As Zarif and Ashton led the tough talks in Vienna, Soleimani spent more and more of his time between Iraq and Syria. His personal driver, an old comrade from the war years, remembers not seeing his family for long periods of time since he had to accompany Hajj Qassem on many of these trips. The most worrying news came from Iraq.

In 2013, a crucial development had taken place in Iraq's Salafi-Jihadist scene: a split led by a new leader. Ibrahim Awad al-Samarrai, better known by his *nom de guerre* Abu Bakr al-Baghdadi, was leaving the global ranks of Al-Qaeda to establish a new organization with its area of operations straddling the Iraqi-Syrian border. Since 2010, Baghdadi had sat at the head of the "Islamic State of Iraq," which controlled small pockets in the west of the country. The "state" had been founded in 2006, shortly following the killing of Abu Musab al-Zarqawi, whose fanatical anti-Shia ethos Baghdadi inherited. But the US's 2007 "surge" policy, which saw many Sunni tribal leaders collaborate with the Americans, had brought the group to the brink of extinction. Baghdadi had started work in very difficult conditions. But in his three years at the helm, everything had gone in his favor.

First, the US troops left in 2011 and the emboldened Nuri al-Maliki, encouraged by Soleimani, set out on a triumphalist Shia path. He kicked out the top Sunni in the central government; Baghdad now looked like not an inclusive government for all Iraqis but a Shia revanchist state backed by Tehran. Second, Baghdadi recruited many unlikely but very useful leaders to his ranks. These were military and intelligence officials from Saddam's regime, many of whom he had met when they served together as prisoners in the US's Camp Bucca around 2005. The Baath

Party had once been seen by many, not least its friends in the French Socialist Party, as spearheading a progressive, secular movement. Deposed from power, humiliated by the Americans and Iranians, and without even the most basic jobs in the new Iraq, many of Baath's former adherents now joined Baghdadi's militia. Third, the civil war in Syria made for a magnificent opening for Salafi-Jihadists. The Sunni majority of the country now saw itself suppressed by a government controlled by a family of Alawites, a small Shia offshoot sect which comprised around 11.5 percent of Syria, backed by Iran's Shia republic. They became a willing constituency for all shades of Islamism. The relatively moderate Islamism of Syria's Muslim Brotherhood soon gave place to groups with much better funding and more vicious tactics. Assad helped by freeing many Salafi-Jihadist prisoners, so that he could legitimize his policy of a brutal crackdown as anti-terrorism.

In April 2013, an emboldened Baghdadi declared a new Islamic State of Iraq and al-Sham (ISIS).[1] He had claimed to have the loyalty of Al-Qaeda's successful franchise in Syria, known as the Al-Nusra Front. But the latter's leader, Abu Mohammad al-Julani, opposed the merger, as did Bin Laden's successor as the global emir of Al-Qaeda, the Egyptian Ayman al-Zawahiri. Throughout early and mid-2013, Zawahiri attempted to arbitrate between the two. But the effort would go nowhere. By October, he ordered the disbandment of ISIS. But drunk with his growing success, Baghdadi paid no heed to the old emir issuing orders from his base in the caves on the Afghan-Pakistani border. A few months prior, ISIS had led a raid on Abu Ghraib prison outside Baghdad, freeing hundreds of men who could now join his movement. The prison is infamous as the site at which the US forces raped, sodomized, tortured, murdered, and otherwise abused prisoners in the early years following 2003. Its falling to ISIS was an important symbolic victory.

The forward march of ISIS sped up in 2014 as the group was clear it wouldn't respect the lines on the hot sands of the Syrian Desert demarcating the borders of Iraq, Syria, and Jordan. By February, key Sunni towns in the west such as Fallujah and Ramadi fell to ISIS, which now controlled much of the Iraqi-Syrian border.

Still, the areas controlled by the group were too marginal for this to seem like a world-historic occurrence. The "ISIS land" in eastern Syria and western Iraq could be added to the long list of areas suffering from insurgencies, like large swathes of Afghanistan or parts of the Philippines and Thailand. But in early June, ISIS proved to be no low-level insurgency. On June 10, the city of Mosul, the unofficial capital of northern Iraq, fell to ISIS. This was no little tribal town but a metropolis with Iraq's second biggest university and a population of more than a million. Across the Tigris from the ancient Assyrian biblical city of Nineveh, Mosul had long been a proud symbol of Iraq's multiethnic character. Here Sunni Arabs socialized with Armenians, Kurds, Christians, Yazidis, and thousands who came to one of the best universities in the Middle East. The black flag of ISIS now adorned Mosul's Grand Mosque of Al-Nuri, where Baghdadi declared a new global caliphate in July, asking the world's Muslims to come and serve him.

In the 1980s, Al-Qaeda had invited Muslims from around the world to come and fight the Soviets in Afghanistan, but by no means all Muslims had what it took to accept that offer. The austere life in the mountains of Afghanistan tested even the most battle-ready. Things were very different in Baghdadi's brutal caliphate of 2014. This was an urban place easily linked to Europe via the long borders that Syria and Iraq shared with Turkey. Many young Muslims of Europe, in search of meaning for their lives, could now come and join ISIS. All it took was a simple flight to Istanbul, a short trip down to the border and an easy ride to the lands of the caliphate which now controlled the major highways linking Iraq and Syria. This was a threat like no other before, evidenced in the long line of attacks soon visited on European cities, all directed from ISIS territory.

In Tehran, some of the old hands of the Iraqi foreign policy and intelligence establishment privately accused Soleimani of being responsible for this state of affairs. He had responded to Zarqawi's murderous sectarianism with a version of his own. He had fully backed Maliki as he went on his own sectarian rampage. Iraq was now paying the price. Such criticism never came anywhere near daylight. Even in Tehran it was whispered carefully.

Whoever bore the responsibility, Iraq now faced an existential threat. Just a few days after the fall of Mosul, the most consequential response to ISIS's rise came from Najaf, the holy seat of the Shia. Ayatollah Sistani, Iraq's authoritative Shia cleric, issued a fatwa. All citizens of the country, not just the Shia, were called upon to join the fight against ISIS. "Iraq and the Iraqi nation now face threats that require us to defend this land and the lives and honor of its people," Sistani's fatwa read. "This is a collective obligation for all citizens. Citizens who are able to carry weapons, fight terrorists, and defend their country, nation, and its sacralities must join the military volunteer forces."

Sistani was seen as above Iranian influence and internal Shia politick-ings. He had, after all, been a disciple not of Khomeini but of his arch-rival Abolqasem al-Khoei, who never endorsed the Islamic Republic's claims to Shia governance. His fatwa resonated as a broad call for the Shia to rise up and defeat a monstrous force that had bewildered the world with its gratuitous display of violence.

But the fatwa couldn't mobilize men on its own. Nor could it immedi-ately overcome the extreme demoralization that had gripped the Iraqi Shia following the rapid march of ISIS. Tens of thousands of Iraqi soldiers and federal police had left their state-of-the-art American-supplied equipment and fled in the face of an armed gang. What could change now? Who were the men who would respond to the fatwa and fight ISIS?

Onto the scene stepped Qassem Soleimani. This was the most impor-tant assignment of his life. Gathering the Iraqi militias, he helped form Al-Hashd al-Shaabi or the Popular Mobilization Force. Bringing together dozens of disparate Shia militias that had worked as the praetorian guards of discordant Shia personalities, Soleimani dreamed of turning Al-Hashd into a centralized force like the IRGC. Its commanders increas-ingly came to refer to themselves as the Iraqi IRGC.

Not all Soleimani's major anti-ISIS operations had a Shia basis. Finding their capital, Erbil, surrounded by ISIS forces, the leaders of Iraq's Kurdish Regional Government (KRG) asked Iran for help. The Iranian consulate in Erbil contacted Zarif's deputy in charge of Arab and African affairs, Hossein Amirabdollahian, who happened to be the Quds Force's unofficial liaison with the foreign ministry. His opponents called him Soleimani's mole to watch Zarif. The old Kurdish leader Masoud Barzani was now faced with a task that had often fallen to his people's leaders: defending them against genocide.

Barzani was simply told to call Soleimani. The Iranian commander didn't disappoint. He arrived at Erbil airport with dozens of field commanders. He promised not only men but Iran's small fleet of Sukhoi jets. The bravery that it took to fly to a city besieged by ISIS wasn't lost on anyone. Soleimani's old habit of being on the scene had proved crucial. Even more crucial were his old links with the Iraqi Kurds. Soleimani's closest ties were with Jalal Talabani, about to end his term as Iraq's president. Talabani remained the leader of the Patriotic Union of Kurdistan, a rival of Barzani's which effectively controlled a part of the KRG's territory centered on the city of Sulaymaniyah. The Quds Force also had close ties to the Kurdistan Socialist Democratic Party, a split from Barzani's camp in 1976. It remained a minuscule force but it supplied military forces that would fight under Soleimani's command.

Soleimani's rushing to the scene brought him praise at home and abroad. Not only had the Quds Force dedicated itself to the fight against ISIS, it had done so in alliance not just with the Shia but with the Kurds, whose regional government also counted Israel as an ally. Soleimani's profile rose. Many young people in Iran who would have never gone anywhere near an IRGC figure now loved to share the heroic images of his presence in the battleground. With its crafty videos depicting brutal scenes of beheading with Hollywood-level production values, ISIS disgusted the entire world. People were ready to praise anyone who fought this evil force. Even anti-regime Iranians couldn't sometimes help but marvel at the man who was fighting to defend basic civility.

When the Shia Turkmen town of Amerli, 170 kilometers north of Baghdad, came under siege from ISIS, the entire world watched in horror. More than 40,000 residents of Iraq's largest Turkmen-majority town were under imminent threat of extermination. The UN warned about an impending catastrophe. The long siege started in June and throughout the summer, the city seemed to be on the brink of falling to ISIS.

Amerli was barely 100 kilometers from the Iranian border but it wasn't easy to get help to a city under siege from every side. Soleimani still wouldn't stay back. He made a daring landing in the city with a helicopter and played a key role in organizing local Shia militias and the Kurdish Peshmerga forces. They fought to break the siege and force ISIS back. By the end of August, the road to Baghdad was opened. Victory had been achieved by Soleimani working closely with the Iraqis while also getting air support from the United States and aid from other Western countries such as the UK, France, and Australia. Just as Zarif sat down in the diplomatic halls of Vienna with the US undersecretary of state Wendy Sherman, the American and Iranian militaries were now allies on the ground.

Years later, when Khamenei wanted to eulogize Soleimani in a Friday prayer sermon, he recalled the siege of Amerli. Without naming the town, the Supreme Leader said: "Which commander lands in a helicopter in a region under total siege by the enemy? There were good youth in the region but they were alone and without a commander. When they saw Hajj Qassem, they gained a new life."

Back in 2014, stories of Soleimani's heroism in Amerli now filled Arab, Iranian, and Western media. By September, his pictures were being circulated on social media. The brave shadow commander had come into the limelight.

Two of the most trusted acolytes of Ayatollah Khamenei, Javad Zarif and Qassem Soleimani, were now media darlings in Iran and around the world. In October, the Tehran daily *Hafte Sobh* spoke for many when it ran a cover story about the two men as "Iran's greatest sources of trust," "two key men whose greatest capital is the trust of a nation."

In December, the US's *Newsweek* magazine put Soleimani on the cover, his piercing eyes capturing audiences across America. "First he fought America, now he's crushing ISIS," said the big white block letters. Stories inside the magazine introduced Soleimani-led Shia militias as the only chance the world had of defeating ISIS. In March 2015, the British-American publication *The Week* took things a step further with a cartoon cover that depicted Soleimani in bed with Uncle Sam. "Strange bedfellows," the cover headline read, pointing to the de facto military alliance between Tehran and Washington in the fight against ISIS.

By the time *The Week's* cover went to print, Soleimani had helped liberate Tikrit, the hometown of Saddam Hussein. Once more, he had been there in person. Once more the US and Iran had effectively worked together on the ground. In January 2015, when Iraq's new prime minister, Haydar al-Abadi, spoke in the World Economic Forum in Davos, he profusely thanked both the West and Iran for their help in the fight against ISIS, making a special mention of Soleimani. "We have respect for him," Abadi said. It was common knowledge that Abadi, who had replaced Maliki the previous September, owed his position to negotiations between the US and Soleimani's men. Iran and America were not only collaborating on the battlefronts, they were now coordinating politically.

What could possibly go wrong?

* * *

"My heart won't stop wanting you, even if I lose my head," bellowed Hossein Taheri into the microphone as hundreds of people in the audience beat their chests, chanting the name "Hossein," seemingly in a trance. It was the eighth day of the month of Muharram, two days before the mourning ceremonies of Ashura peaked. The mourners in Chizar, this corner of leafy and wealthy northern Tehran, were as lively as anywhere in the rest of the Shia world.

The Shia had been performing Ashura mournings for centuries but the lyrics used by Taheri, in this ceremony in October 2015, were new and different. Taheri was no ordinary panegyrist. His father, Mohammadreza, had been in the profession, as had his grandfather. Having fought in the war with Iraq, Mohammadreza had been among the stars of the Ashura ceremonies of the 1990s, using lyrics that tied old Shia symbols to the politics of the day. Together, these religious performers arose to become celebrities, well connected to the establishment. When Ahmadinejad declared victory in the 2009 elections, Taheri the father attended his victory party just as millions of Iranians got ready to decry rigging of the elections. When his mother died in 2017, Mohsen Rezayi attended the funeral, as did Parviz Fattah, head of the Imam Khomeini Aid Committee, a massive parastatal charity that helped funnel funds to Soleimani's forces in Syria. Hossein had assumed the mantle from his father and the lyrics he performed spoke to the pressing issue of the day: the Shia-Sunni conflict in the region.

Just as Soleimani emblazoned the cover of Western magazines and added to his popularity in Iran, his forces helped advance the sectarianization of the region's conflicts. The process that had started in post-2003 Iraq reached new heights in the post-2011 Middle East. In Iraq, Soleimani had made "the defense of the shrines" a centerpiece of his intervention efforts. Now he would assist in elevating the concept across the region. The Shia had to be organized as Defenders of the Shrine, whether this referred to the Imams buried in Iraq or Zeynab and Ruqaya, respectively sister and daughter of Imam Hossein, buried in Damascus.

"I won't let your enemy get close to the shrines," the young Taheri sang that October night in 2015. "If they get to Karbala, Master, we will do our morning prayers in Baqi." Karbala hosted the final resting place of Imam Hossein, while Baqi Cemetery in Medina, Saudi Arabia, held the graves of most of the Prophet Mohammad's family.[2] The Saudi rulers had long considered any veneration of shrines to be a form of idol worship and denied any access to the tombs of the Prophet's family in Baqi. The lyrics thus intensified the sectarian conflict by threatening Saudi Arabia. "One of these days," Taheri sang, "the Shia will build a shrine for Imam Hassan in Medina."

At least one of the men in the audience that day was among the students who ransacked the Saudi embassy in Tehran a few months later, on January 2, 2016. The action followed the Saudis' execution of a prominent Shia cleric hailing from the Shia-majority Eastern Province. The embassy attack heightened the cold war between Tehran and Riyadh. The Saudis swiftly broke diplomatic relations with Tehran, as did Bahrain, Somalia, Sudan, and the small but strategically located African country of Djibouti.

Two other men in the audience went far beyond attacking embassies. They signed up to fight in Syria, just like the lyrics had enjoined them to. Taheri sang:

> I am waiting for the permission of Jihad. Me and all my family.
> No, I am not being sentimental! Does the world not know the Shia by
>   now?
> My wish is to die for you, Hossein; the Defenders of Your Shrine are
>   an army who beat their chests.
> Look at our mosques, full of soldiers! Look at our mouths, singing
>   this song.
> Look at an army, Master, ready to lose their lives; they are in
>   Samarra, they are in Kazemein.

Soleimani was indeed in Samarra. Once the capital of the medieval Abbasid caliphate, Samarra sat in the so-called Sunni Triangle: areas north and west of Baghdad which were Sunni-majority and known as a strong base for Saddam. It was the hometown of ISIS's leader Baghdadi. But the city also contained the shrines for the Tenth and Eleventh Shia Imams. In 2006, an Al-Qaeda attack on the shrines helped intensify the sectarian onslaught. In 2014, as the forces of ISIS ravaged Iraq, Samarra was a point of attack.

Soleimani loved Samarra perhaps more than any other Iraqi city. The attacked shrines were for him a symbol of Shia oppression. What could be more symbolic than Shia shrines engulfed in the midst of Sunnis who had attacked them? He would help acquire funds in trying to rebuild them. He loved staying overnight in the Samarra shrine, overcoming security complaints. Such moves were characteristic of an increasingly sectarian commander who spoke in ever more inflammatory terms.

Traditionally, the leaders of the Islamic Republic had been careful to not fan too much sectarianism. Extremist anti-Sunni Shia were suppressed by the Iranian government and practices such as celebrating the death of the caliph Omar were discouraged. Soleimani would also not use such blatantly hateful language. In Syria there was even a small contingent of Iranian Sunnis, mostly from the province of Sistan and Balochistan, who fought on Assad's side. They were called Navabioon, the People of the Prophet, and their best-known face was perhaps Salman Barjeste, a 22-year-old African-Iranian who fell fighting for Assad's Syria in January 2016. Salman's father had fought by his side.

But there was no mistaking Soleimani's increasingly sectarian narrative. In a speech in Kerman in 2014, he spoke of the so-called Shia Crescent as an economic powerhouse that could help Iran. "Led by Iran, the Shia revival will give Iran political, security, and economic power," he said. "Seventy percent of the world's oil sits in the three countries of Iran, Iraq, and Saudi Arabia. All of it is in the Shia areas."

In Syria, the Islamist "Army of Islam," known to receive funding from Saudi Arabia and Turkey, attacked the "Safavid" Iranians, linking the men of Soleimani to the sixteenth-century dynasty of Iran. The Safavids had helped turn Sunni-majority Iran into a Shia powerhouse just as they clashed with the caliphate of their day, the main Muslim power, the

Ottoman Empire. Soleimani now spoke of a long dark night of Islam that had only come to an end with Khomeini. The long history of Islam before 1979, from the Umayyads in the seventh century to the Ottomans in the twentieth, was "a long decline" only halted by Khomeini. In the Ottoman parliament, he quipped, even the Jews had MPs, but not the Shia. Now twenty million Shia marched on Arbaeen, "right next to the Saudis."

With such words, Soleimani mobilized the Shia from Iran, Pakistan, Afghanistan, and Iraq. They went to die in Syria, to defend the oppressive government of one of the world's most hated dictators, whose affinity with Iran had much to do with crude politics and little to do with the incidental fact that the Alawites were an offshoot of the Shia.

Meeting Assad in his presidential palace in 2012, Soleimani asked him a simple question. Did he want to stay and fight or did he want to flee to Iran? Iran would welcome him if he chose the latter. But if he wanted the former, he needed to listen. Soleimani would take on much of the effort but he needed to follow. In the years to come, Assad remained intimidated by the Iranian general.

* * *

Soleimani liked to focus his forces in one area, win the battle, and then move on. A testament to this strategy is the moving itineraries of men like Abu Baqer, *nom de guerre* of Mohammadreza Falahzade, a comrade of Soleimani's from the 1980s war with Iraq who moved from Damascus to Aleppo as the war in Syria went ahead. Abu Baqer was little known to the international media despite playing a key role on the battlefront.

When Abu Baqer first entered Syria, Assad controlled around 16 percent of the country's territory. Most importantly, he had lost every single land border and the only way into the country was now via the Mediterranean. The capital itself was under partial siege. When Iranians went to the shrine of Zeynab to pray, they could hear the rebels' guns. Soleimani first secured Damascus airport with a wall of concrete. If this war was going to be won, he had to fly his forces into Damascus.

In the spring of 2013, Soleimani won over the skeptics by showing how fruitful his international approach could be. Thousands of Hezbollah fighters flocked to the battleground and helped take back the district of al-Qusayr from the rebels. Lying right on the Lebanese border, the city was relatively easy to infiltrate for the Hezbollah. After two weeks of intense fighting, by June 5, Hezbollah and the Syrian army reached a decisive victory. The district was in the province of Homs and lay on the road that connected Damascus to Assad's stronghold on the Alawite-heavy Mediterranean coast. At this early stage, Iran all but denied any involvement in the civil war. The vast extent of Soleimani's role in securing the Hezbollah fighters and in military planning for the victory became clear later.

In 2015, Abu Baqer moved to Idlib with many Shia fighters. Things weren't going well. The area continued to be held by rebels who were killing an increasing number of the Shia fighters. In a key meeting at Latakia airport, Soleimani convinced Assad that only one thing could turn things around: a serious intervention by Russia.

He was prepared to secure it himself.

* * *

In July 2015, Qassem Soleimani went to the Kremlin. The sight of the Shia general walking the halls of power in the capital of a great power was unforgettable for the men who were with him.

Back in Damascus, an Afghan Shia fighter received the news with joy. "We heard of Putin having respected the Hajji so much," he says. "We heard they had talked for more than two hours. We heard that the Hajji had interrupted the meeting to say his prayers right there. This was Moscow! The center of atheism."

Such stories soon went around the Shia fighters. For the Afghans who still looked nostalgically to the Islamist struggle that had kicked the Soviet forces out of their country, the meeting held a deeper meaning.

By all accounts, including those from the Russian side, the Russian president was impressed with Soleimani. "To say Soleimani convinced our president to intervene in Syria is obviously silly," a Russian analyst who was present in the Kremlin on the day of the meeting says. "Putin doesn't take grand decisions based on one person. But there is no doubt that he had respect for Soleimani and considered him way more reliable than anyone he had met from the Syrian government. I can even say that without the meeting, he wouldn't have committed to Assad the same way."

By September, the Russian forces intervened, filling Syrian airspace with their presence and striking a decisive blow against the opposition, which had gotten next to no serious military help from the United States. It would never get the no-fly zone it asked for. Action-averse after the disaster of Iraq, and having already burnt his fingers on the bungled intervention in Libya in 2011, Obama didn't even respect a "red line" he had declared himself. In 2012, he had said that Syria's use of chemical weapons would force him to intervene. In 2013, US intelligence found strong evidence of Assad using a chemical agent that had killed more than 1,000 people. But Obama conditioned intervention on permission from Congress. Seeing how hesitant to act the president was, Congress didn't give the go-ahead, especially when the British parliament rejected intervention after a maneuver by the opposition leader, Labour's Ed Miliband. "Red Ed" convinced enough rebels in the Tory camp to defeat a government motion clamoring for intervention.[3]

Without American intervention and with Russian support, Soleimani's men were able to boost Assad up. Hundreds of thousands of Syrians would die at the hands of the forces of Assad, Putin, and Soleimani, but the dictator would survive.

In December 2016, following four years and five months of battle, the grand city of Aleppo in the north fell to government forces. It had been the bloodiest battle of the war and one of the longest sieges in military history. The hopes of freedom ignited by the 2011 revolution were now deeply buried in the rubble of Aleppo.

* * *

In March 2017, Soleimani was with his father in Qanat Molk. His son might have been a global celebrity, but the father still lived in their little village. Qassem loved to visit for Nowrooz, which they celebrated together on March 21. A day later, Soleimani spoke to his field commanders in Syria. Things were not going well. Hama was about to fall to the onslaught of Hayat Tahrir al-Sham (Al-Qaeda's Syrian franchise, which had now left the mother organization) and the Assad-held Syria would become not a contiguous whole but split in two: a besieged Damascus and the coastal area.

Soleimani knew what the alarmist reports were intended to provoke. "Do you want me to come there?" he asked.[4] He already knew the answer. In less than twenty-four hours, Soleimani was on the battlefront in Hama, the infamous site of the 1982 massacre by Hafez al-Assad.

Iran's base was on the Zayn al-Abidin mountain north of Hama, named after the Fourth Shia Imam and a minor site of pilgrimage (the Imam himself was buried in Medina). Looking at the Orontes, the chief river of the Levant that passed through the city, Soleimani predicted that the enemy was to come from the west bank. "They like to come from the side where they can see Hama with their own eyes," he said. "Just like we once approached Khorramshahr from a side where we could see its walls and palms." The old commander hadn't forgotten his historic battle of thirty-five years ago.

The month-long battle illustrated the internationalized nature of the war. On the rebel side, the Al-Qaeda groups boasted volunteers from across the region and beyond. There were even a small number of Iranian Sunnis who had joined Al-Qaeda and made it to Syria. A Salafi-Jihadist party claimed to represent the Uyghur of China.

On the side of Assad's forces, Soleimani had a collection of his Afghan, Iranian, and Pakistani volunteers. The Fatemiyoon Brigade consisted of the Afghan volunteers. In Hama they fought in the memory of their founder, Alireza Tavasoli. He had moved to Iran in 1984, working in construction and studying in the seminaries of Isfahan and Qom. Tavasoli had been among the Shia volunteers in the Abudhar Brigade, which helped fight Saddam in the war with Iraq. He had then gone to fight the Soviets in Afghanistan and had returned there in the 1990s to fight the Taliban. When the Iranian intervention in Syria started, Soleimani recruited Tavasoli for a simple task: organizing the Afghan migrants in Iran and sending them to fight in Syria. Tavasoli proved more than capable. He used religious groups based in Mashhad to rapidly recruit hundreds of Afghans. He housed them around Zeynab's shrine in Damascus and they would soon become respected as a valiant fighting force. On February 28, 2015, under the *nom de guerre* Abu Hamed, Tavasoli fell while fighting the Al-Qaeda affiliates in southern Syria.

Also present in the fields was a small contingent of Zeynabioon, the Pakistani Shia. They carried pictures of Seyyed Ali Shah, a young cleric from Qom who had fought for two years in the Syrian battlegrounds before falling in January 2016. Iraqis were there too, fighting under the banner of Heydarioon.

Alongside the Syrian army, Hezbollah, and the Iranians fought the brigades of Fatemioon, Zeynabioon, and Heydarioon, respectively named after Fatima, Zeynab, and Ali (Heydar was one of his many titles). After five weeks, victory came to the Shia and the rebels were driven back.

The advances of the Shia army pushed forward in both Iraq and Syria. In 2017, the Iranian and Syrian forces, together with Fatemioon and Zeynabioon, won battle after battle and finally reached Syria's borders with Jordan and Iraq. Iraq's Al-Hashd al-Shaabi joined them from the other side.

In November 2017, Soleimani was on the scene when Hezbollah, Heydarioon, Fatemiyoon, Zeynabioon, and Al-Hashd fought together to free the Iraqi border city of al-Qaim from ISIS. A few days before, on October 31, the shadow commander had lost his father. He flew home, attended the funeral, and made it back to be there in time for the victory. Immediately after, he moved to the front at the nearby Syrian city of Abu Kamal which, after changing hands three times in a month, finally fell to the Syrian army on November 19. With ISIS having lost all its strong-holds, the world could now celebrate its demise.

On November 21, Soleimani wrote a letter to Khamenei to congratu-late him. "Having brought down the flag of this American-Zionist group, I declare an end to the domination of this cursed group," Soleimani wrote. He congratulated Khamenei "on behalf of all the commanders and the unknown Mojaheds on the field, and the thousands of Iranian, Iraqi, Syrian, Lebanese, Afghan, and Pakistani martyred and injured Defenders of the Shrine."

He signed off simply as "Your son and soldier."

Epilogue
The Endgame

On July 14, 2015, shortly following the signing of the Iranian nuclear deal in Vienna, the US's top diplomat, John Kerry, took questions from reporters. Being the only Iranian reporter scheduled to ask a question, I had a simple one for him. The deal was great. But what if the Democrats lost next year's presidential elections?

"I am convinced that whoever is our next president will see the wisdom of this agreement and they will leave it in place," Kerry told me.

All the experts agreed with him. Even if a Republican won the 2016 elections, it was quite unlikely that he or she would quit the deal. It was one thing to oppose the talks when they were ongoing; quite another to withdraw from a deal once agreed.

But the next American president was unlike any in recent memory. Perhaps unlike any in the country's entire history.

Donald J. Trump made the repeal of the Iran deal a centerpiece of his foreign policy. He mentioned it in every single one of his presidential debates with the Democratic nominee, Hillary Clinton. Still, as he took office in January 2017, it was not clear what Trump's actual Iran policy would be. He had, after all, repeatedly spoken against the American

interventions in the Middle East. His first year in office was characterized by equivocation and zigzag policies on many fronts. But the direction toward increasingly harsh policies on Iran was clear. In the second
year, Trump's Iran policy became even clearer. In April 2018, he appointed
his former CIA chief, Mike Pompeo, as the new secretary of state and
John Bolton, easily the most hawkish anti-Iran figure in Washington, as
his national security advisor. A month later, Trump formally withdrew
from the Iran deal. His dangerously escalating course of action included
imposing the toughest sanctions in history on Iran. Trump's "maximum
pressure" policy had the declared goal of bringing Iran back to the negotiating table. It explicitly disavowed regime change. The regime-change
enthusiast Bolton would lose his job in September 2019 and enter a very
public feud with the president.

Qassem Soleimani was at the height of his power just as Trump
started his high-risk battle with the Islamic Republic. The American
president also emboldened Benjamin Netanyahu. The right-wing Israeli
prime minister had openly clashed with Barack Obama, speaking to the
Republican-dominated Congress in criticism of his Iran policy. With
tables now turned, he had an ally at the White House that would go the
extra mile for him. Trump's White House would be filled with politicians of the same hue—chief among them was Jared Kushner, the president's senior advisor who, to make everything better, was also friendly
with Mohammad bin Salman, the assertive son of the Saudi king who
pushed out his rivals to become crown prince (and de facto ruler) in
June 2017.

The assertive presence of Soleimani's men in Syria obviously worried
the Israelis. The Quds Force often got too close for comfort to the actual
Quds. Since 2015, Israel's army had been led by Gadi Eizenkot, the
Moroccan-born general who, as the IDF's northern commander, battled
Soleimani and his men in the Second Lebanon War of 2006. Eizenkot
remembered his enemies well from that war. Imad Muqniyah's 23-year-
old son, Jihad, who had been photographed with Soleimani in Iran, was
killed in January 2015 by an airstrike in the Golan Heights. Killed alongside him was an Iranian IRGC commander, Mohammad Ali Allahdadi,
who hailed from Soleimani's Kerman province and was particularly
close to him. Samir Kuntar, whose imprisonment had been Hezbollah's

casus belli in the 2006 war, was killed in the suburbs of Damascus when a six-story building he was in got destroyed in an Israeli strike. Additionally, Mostafa Badreddin was killed in May 2016 in a mysterious operation at Damascus airport. Hezbollah's unconvincing statement said he had been killed by "Takfiri groups," but none of these groups came forward to accept responsibility for such a grand hit. Saudi Arabia's Al-Arabiya TV claimed Hassan Nasrallah and Soleimani had ordered the man killed and, on March 2017, Eizenkot confirmed the news. In May 2020, the venerable Israeli columnist Yossi Melman gave a full account of how Soleimani had killed Badreddin because he had "dared to say no."

Whether the story is true or not, it seems in character with Soleimani's increasing hubris, now visible for all to see. The Israelis complained to Russia, which agreed not to let the Iranians get too close to the Israeli border. With permission from the emboldened Netanyahu, Eizenkot took the gloves off in 2017. Israel now hit the Iranians on an almost daily basis. In 2018 alone, it dropped 2,000 bombs on Syria, almost all of them targeting the Iranians or their allies. Soleimani didn't just sit and watch. He occasionally fired rockets at Israel. When Eizenkot left his post, he boasted about having taken Soleimani down a notch in an exit interview with Bret Stephens of the *New York Times*. The American newspaper of record bade farewell to Gadi Eizenkot as "the man who humbled Qassem Soleimani."[1]

Soleimani's actions showed no such supposed humility. Shortly after Trump was elected, Pompeo attempted to get a letter to Soleimani, but he refused to read it. Previously, in June 2016, he had published a stern warning against Bahrain and warned its rulers he'd overthrow them in a "bloody intifada" if they continued harassing the Shia cleric Isa Qassem. He spoke with increasing confidence if not outright arrogance.

In February 2018, as he gave his habitual speech in Kerman on the anniversary of the revolution, Soleimani made a rare dip into the country's domestic politics, implicitly criticizing the leader of the Green Movement, Mehdi Karoubi, who was under house arrest and had dared write an open letter to Khamenei. In the same year, the former president Mahmoud Ahmadinejad, who had now entered an embittered row with Khamenei and the establishment of the Islamic Republic, wrote to Soleimani and threatened to bring skeletons out of the closet. Ahmadinejad's vice-president, Hamid Baqai, was undergoing trial and the charges against him included receiving "millions of dollars" from Soleimani. Ahmadinejad wanted the commander to come clean and save Baqai.[2] The former president, one of the few people in Iran brave enough to counter Soleimani at the height of his power, wrote again in a few months to criticize him for having helped secure the release of the banker Mehdi Jahangiri, whose brother was Hassan Rouhani's vice-president.

Soleimani now often spoke in a threatening fashion to all and sundry. In January 2019, after an attack on an IRGC bus in Zahedan by a Sunni group which was known to shelter in Pakistan, the commander warned Islamabad to guard its borders properly or face the consequences. In February, when Syria's President Assad visited Iran, Mohammad Javad Zarif failed to be invited to his meetings with Rouhani and Khamenei. The whole thing had been arranged by Soleimani as if Iran didn't have a foreign ministry anymore. The offended foreign minister announced his resignation on Instagram, only taking it back after intervention by the Supreme Leader. Soleimani publicly praised Zarif, but there was no mistaking the growing rift between the frustrated diplomat and the increasingly powerful commander. A month later, Soleimani was awarded the military Order of Zolfaqar, named for the storied twin-pronged sword of Imam Ali. Technically founded in 1922, the Order of Zolfaqar had never been given to anyone in the Islamic Republic. No one could remember the last time it was awarded.

* * *

Soleimani's progressively boastful rhetoric matched Trump's hyperbole. The tit-for-tat between the two men made great TV in both Iran and the US. In a speech in July 2018 in Hamedan, Soleimani attacked the American president. Trump hadn't quit his casino-building days, the Iranian commander quipped.

"Mr. Trump, you gambler!" Soleimani boasted. "You have to deal with me. Have you forgotten you used to put your adult soldiers in Pampers?" He went on to list all the instances in Afghanistan, Iraq, Lebanon, and

Yemen when the Americans had been allegedly humbled by Soleimani's allies.

"There is no night when we go to sleep and do not think of you," the Iranian commander added in a menacing threat. "We are closer to you than you think. If a war breaks out, it will end with the destruction of all your capabilities and our victory. Start the war. The rest is with us."

Later in the year, when Trump tweeted a *Game of Thrones*–style image to warn Iran that "Sanctions Are Coming," Soleimani, increasingly adept at social media, responded with a similarly styled image of his own carrying another message: "I Will Stand Against You." This was 2018: Soleimani tweeting back at Trump using the tropes of an American TV show. HBO openly complained about this use of its products by Trump.

The threats weren't simply rhetorical. Soleimani's men in Iraq grew increasingly restive and audacious, striking the Americans more than ever before. In 2019, Israel started attacks on Al-Hashd and Iranian bases in Iraq, killing dozens of personnel, including Abolfazl Sarabian, buried in his hometown of Kermanshah as the sixteenth citizen to be killed as a Defender of the Shrines.[3] These were the first Israeli attacks on Iraq in thirty-eight years; the previous attacks had been in 1981, against Saddam's nuclear plans and in line with the goals of the then nascent Islamic Republic.

In a strange threat in August, Israel's former prime minister Ehud Olmert spoke of his old adversary Soleimani in a radio interview: "There is something that he knows, that he knows I know, that I know he knows, and both of us know what that something is." He paused for a moment and added: "What that is, that's another story."

Undeterred, the Quds Force kept expanding its operations. In September, the Houthis attacked oil installations in eastern Saudi Arabia, the largest such attacks in modern history. A UN investigation confirmed Saudi allegations of Iranian complicity. As Trump's maximum-pressure policy squeezed Iran, the Islamic Republic used its shadow commander to respond in bewildering, unpredictable ways.

There was resistance from people who didn't want their countries to be a scene of proxy confrontation. In the fall of 2019, mass movements broke out in Lebanon and Iraq against government incompetence. Iran had boasted about "controlling" Baghdad and Beirut, and the chickens now came home to roost. Lebanese and Iraqi citizens attacked their governments as beholden to Iran and asked for an end to Tehran's interference. Soleimani was on the scene in Iraq, conferring with his old comrade Hadi al-Ameri on how best to suppress the movement.

But Soleimani's men now went far beyond Iraq and Lebanon. They took part in the tricontinental drug trade based in Shia communities in west Africa, Latin America, and Europe. In Eritrea, they had bases not far from Israel's listening posts in the Dahlak Archipelago. They intervened in the civil wars of the Central African Republic. They helped liaise with the Islamic Movement in Nigeria (IMN), a strong Shia movement that followed Iran's commands. In 2014, the IMN's attempt to organize a Quds Day rally in the northern city of Zaria, Kaduna State, led to a confrontation with the army and the deaths of thirty-five people. Jumai Karoofi, a surviving woman who was sent to Iran to get medical help, met with Soleimani. On his encouragement, she had already helped organize a network of women leaders including Batool Mousavi, daughter of Hezbollah's assassinated secretary-general; Hoora Ragheb Harb, daughter of another slain Hezbollah figure; and Nasin Singh Wing, a Shia activist in Thailand.

Soleimani's last year didn't merely consist of threats and military bluster. This man had plans. He increased his media activities, and his social media accounts clearly attempted to portray him as a national figure above all the politickings of the hated ruling caste in the Islamic Republic. Using a well-known cliché, he reminded Iranians that "the girl who is not wearing her hijab very well is also our daughter," to curry favor with average Iranians, sick of the regime's compulsory-hijab policy. In March 2019, when officials showed incompetence in dealing with floods in the southwestern province of Khuzestan, Soleimani joined other IRGC commanders who went to the area to help. The province he had spent eight years defending against Saddam's Iraq still contained some of Iran's most marginalized areas, mired with unemployment and poverty. When nationwide protests against economic destitution and the regime's incompetence hit Iran in January 2018 and, again, in November 2019, Khuzestan was a center.

In what turned out to be the last months of his life, Soleimani even started thinking the unthinkable: of running for president in 2021. Previously, he had rejected all such requests, often shaking his head in

jest when the idea came up. He was a humble soldier of the Supreme
Leader and nothing more, he'd say. But in November 2019, he asked
some of his men to look into a presidential run as a possibility.[4] Unable
to do much to help people in the crisis-ridden and economically collapsing Iran, the aloof Rouhani had become ever more hated. His diplomatic
dividends had come to naught and he had failed to seriously counter
Khamenei. If there was one regime figure who could have changed the
calculus of the Iranian people, it could have only been Soleimani, the
brave general of faraway lands. But he would find no such opportunity.

The escalation with the US cost him dearly. On December 27, 2019,
Iraq's Kataeb Hezbollah, conceived by Soleimani and his Iraqi friend and
comrade Abu Mahdi Muhandis, killed a 33-year-old Iraqi-born
American defense contractor named Nawres Hamid when it fired rockets at a base near Kirkuk, little imagining the sequence of events that
would follow. Two days later, the US responded vigorously with strikes
on five Iranian-supported militia sites in Iraq and Syria. Twenty-five
Shia soldiers were killed. One would now expect Soleimani to back off.
But he had no such intentions. On his direct order, Kataeb Hezbollah
supporters marched on the US embassy in Baghdad, putting it under
effective siege. The shadow commander had played his hand badly. In
less than twenty-four hours, Donald Trump ordered his assassination.
On January 3, 2020, Qassem Soleimani was killed by an American drone
strike. With him were Muhandis and eight other Iranian and Iraqi
soldiers, including Hossein Poorjafari, a fellow Kermani and close family
friend.

The entire machinery of the empire he had built would soon start a
massive campaign to eulogize him. Backed by the might of the Iranian
state, millions thronged the streets in cities of Iran and Iraq to mourn
Soleimani. In Kerman, soon to be his eternal home, dozens died in a
stampede.

But as the airwaves were filled with a chorus of voices singing
Soleimani's praise, the most accurate reading perhaps came from an old
American diplomat, both partner and adversary to Soleimani:
Ambassador Ryan Crocker, who had negotiated with Soleimani's men
over Afghanistan and Iraq. Writing in the *New York Times*, Crocker said
Soleimani had "allowed his ego to overcome his judgment."

"The shadow commander came out of the shadows," Crocker quipped. He did not live long beyond that world of shadows.[5]

* * *

In Idlib, Syria, the last major city held by the opposition, Soleimani's death was greeted with open jubilation. Candy was distributed to celebrate. A young man who had fled to Idlib from Damascus's suburbs ate the candy as he remembered the days of siege under Soleimani's men, when he had had to eat cats to survive, when people exchanged their vehicle for a bag of rice.[6]

In the United States, as the community of Middle East experts started fierce debates around Soleimani's legacy, Syrians displaced by Soleimani's wars could hardly hide their joy. Omar Andron, a young man from Latakia now studying in New York, took to Facebook to commemorate the countless numbers killed by Soleimani's men in Aleppo and Deraa. In Chicago, Sarah Hunaidi, a writer from Suwaida, texted all night with family in Syria, discovering a gap in her world: her people in Syria celebrating Soleimani's demise, just as those in the US debated its legality. She was determined to fill the gap by telling the world about the voices from the Middle East, the men and women whose lives Soleimani helped destroy. Memories of a photojournalist from Aleppo stood out. Basem Ayoubi told Sarah about a distinct memory of Soleimani following the 2016 fall of Aleppo: seeing a picture of him walking in the rubble of the very house Ayoubi had grown up in.[7] He said he now felt "a sense of relief, a sense of divine revenge."

* * *

According to his wishes, Soleimani's body was washed in an Islamic ritual by Mahmood Khaleqi, a fellow Kermani and old friend. The commander had known Khaleqi since they'd fought against Iraq together in Operation Dawn VIII of 1986. They had spent forty days together on the Haj pilgrimage in 1992. They had also become family friends, their children playing together when Khaleqi ran a female Shia seminary in Kerman in the 1990s.

Soleimani had wished to be buried next to Hossein Yousefelahi, another fellow Kermani who ran the Blood of Allah Division's intelligence operation in the war before he was killed in 1986, at the age of twenty-four, from injuries sustained during Operation Dawn VIII. Yousefelahi had an ordinary grave in Kerman's main cemetery which bore the typical name of Iranian cemeteries, the Paradise of Zahra, Zahra being another name for Fatima.

Soleimani's grave may have been a simple one. But nothing was simple about the aftermath of his death. Khamenei swiftly promised a "Hard Revenge." The world held its breath in anticipation of the shape of the Iranian revenge, which arrived in a few days. Iran rained missiles on Ain al-Assad, a base in Iraq that held US and Iraqi soldiers. Khamenei was praised by many for his prudence. He had attacked an American base and yet no US soldiers had died. Trump and Khamenei seemed to have temporarily stepped back from the brink of a brutal confrontation. The praise evaporated when it became clear that, on the same night as the Eyn Assad attacks, the IRGC had mistakenly shot down a Ukrainian airliner, killing all 176 people on board, the vast majority of whom were Iranians heading to Canada, one of the main destinations of the country's "brain drain." Iran's dangerous incompetence continued to cost the lives of its citizens.

* * *

As Quds Force commander, Soleimani was replaced by his deputy, Esmayil Qaani, the man from Mashhad whose focus had been on Iran's relations with its eastern neighbors as Soleimani focused on the Arab countries to the west. A more unlikely successor to the slain commander was his 28-year-old daughter, Zeynab. Qassem's two sons, Hossein and Mohammadreza, were seen sobbing in pictures but it was Zeynab who appeared to don her father's political mantle.

It was rare for Soleimani's family to play any public roles. Throughout his lifetime, Soleimani's private life had been carefully shielded from the public. The name of his wife, whom he married in the early 1980s,[8] was never published. Nor was the news that he lost a son to an illness in the 1990s. With his family, he lived in Tehran's desirable northeastern Shiyan neighborhood, right next to the Lavizan Jungle Park. They were residents of the exclusive Martyr Daqayeqi gated complex, where only the top figures of the regime lived, including old IRGC comrades Mohsen Rezayi and Mohammad Baqer Qalibaf.[9] Soleimani often spoke with nostalgia of the days when there was complete equality on the battlefront, when the IRGC didn't even have military ranks and everyone was simply called a brother. But his family now lived in elite housing in the very area that was once home to Qajar and Pahlavi royals.

Zeynab didn't want to be royalty. Born in 1991 and a student of humanities, she had often accompanied her father on trips to Syria, Iraq, and Lebanon. They called her the little guerrilla. She spent months in Beirut, spoke excellent Arabic, and developed close relations with the Muqniyah family.

Prior to Soleimani's death, Zeynab had had little public profile except for an Instagram spat with an Iranian actress. Following his assassination, a clear strategic decision was made to put Zeynab forward as the public face of the family. Imam Hossein's martyrdom had followed the oratory of his sister, Zeynab, who spoke truth to power. There could be no stronger Shia symbolism than for Soleimani's demise to be followed by an eloquent Zeynab.

And eloquent she was. On live TV she asked her "uncle" Hassan Nasrallah to take revenge for his father's death. Her searing ten-minute speech at her father's memorial in Tehran became a global sensation. Other speeches followed in Friday prayers in Kerman and at a memorial in Beirut, this one in fluent Lebanese Arabic, albeit in a heavy Persian accent, just like that of her father or more prominent Iranians of Lebanon such as Imam Musa Sadr.

Zeynab's links to Lebanon and to the Axis of Resistance were soon to be solidified further. In summer 2020, she married Reza Saffiedin, son of a top Hezbollah official. The news was first published on Instagram by Zeynab Muqniyah, sister of Imad. She was also appointed the head of the Qassem Soleimani Foundation, whose logo makes clear the legacy of her father. It shows her father's hand, with his signature ring, over Jerusalem's Dome of the Rock, emblazoned with a simple slogan: "Quds will be your blood money."

On May 20, the first annual Quds Day following Soleimani's demise, his family published a statement with a familiar promise:

On the path of the blood shed by our martyred father, we declare to the whole world: To the last drop of our blood, we will struggle. We will stand with the freedom-loving nations of the world until the complete destruction of the child-killing Zionist regime.[10]

As Soleimani's successors continued to promise the elusive destruction of their old foe, the Quds Force struggled on the ground. In his first few months at the job, Qaani didn't even come close to filling the shoes of his predecessor. Not only did he not speak Arabic, not only did he lack the charisma of Soleimani or his personal connections across the field, he was also dealt a very bad hand. With the Iranian coffers empty, Tehran could no longer bestow largesse on its army of soldiers without borders. In Iraq, the new prime minister, Mustafa al-Kadhimi, in power since May 2020, seems determined to curb Iranian influence at all costs. The Iraqis, like other people of the Middle East, do not wish to be ruled by shadow commanders.

Timeline

March 21, 1956
Qassem Soleimani is born in the village of Qanat Molk, Kerman province, Iran.

1970
Soleimani finishes primary school.

1975
Soleimani moves to Kerman, the provincial center.

1977
Reza Kamyab gives a memorable anti-Shah speech in Kerman. Soleimani is in the audience and this prompts him to join the revolution.

1979
Iranian revolution.

May 22, 1980
Soleimani is allowed to join the IRGC, his earlier application having been rejected.

September 22, 1980
Iraq's Saddam Hussein attacks Iran. Soleimani is initially in charge of guarding the airport in Kerman.

1981
Soleimani moves up the ranks and is appointed head of the Blood of Allah battalion.

September 27–29, 1981
Soleimani's force helps break the siege of Abadan in Operation Eighth Imam.

November 29–December 6, 1981
Soleimani badly injured while taking part in the successful Operation Path to Jerusalem as a battalion commander.

March 22–April 1, 1982
Operation Manifest Victory, Soleimani's first battle as a brigade commander. He would later call it the best operation of his life.

May 24, 1982
Victory of Operation Beit-ol-Moqaddas, which liberates the city of Khorramshahr. Blood of Allah is turned into a division later.

1983
Iran's failures on the front in the war with Iraq.

October 1983
Beirut barracks bombings, in which Imad Muqniyah has a key role.

1986
Iran experiences some victories in the war with Iraq and occupies Iraq's al-Faw peninsula.

January–March 1987
Iran stages Operation Karbala V, its biggest in the war. It fails to take Basra.

June–July 1987
Soleimani fights in Operation Nasr IV in Iraqi Kurdistan, suffering chemical attacks by Saddam.

July 20, 1987
United Nations Security Council issues Resolution 598, asking for a ceasefire in the Iran-Iraq War. Iran refuses to accept.

1988
Quds Force founded, tasked with the IRGC's operations abroad.

July 18, 1988
Iran accepts UNSCR 598, bringing the war with Iraq to an end.

1992
Soleimani makes the Haj pilgrimage.

January 1998
Soleimani is appointed the head of the Quds Force.

January 1999
Soleimani visits Tajikistan at head of military delegation, helping to organize the Afghan opposition to the Taliban.

July 1999
IRGC commanders including Soleimani write a letter to Khatami, threatening to put down student protests if he doesn't do so himself.

2001
Soleimani helps lead Iran's collaboration with the US against the Taliban in Afghanistan. He refuses Al-Qaeda's offer of allying against America.

January 2002
President Bush declares Iran to be part of the "Axis of Evil."

2003
Invasion of Iraq.

2006
Nuri al-Maliki becomes prime minister of Iraq.

July 12–August 14, 2006
Soleimani is in Lebanon for the Hezbollah-Israel War.

March 2007
United Nations Security Council applies sanctions to Soleimani.

2008
Soleimani helps achieve a ceasefire between the Iraqi army and Muqtada al-Sadr's Mahdi Army.

2011
Arab Spring breaks out. US starts withdrawing from Iraq. Soleimani is made a major general (*sarlashkar*).

2013
Hassan Rouhani wins Iranian presidential elections and nuclear negotiations with the West start. Soleimani backed Rouhani's conservative rival, his old comrade Mohammad Baqer Qalibaf.

June 2014
ISIS captures Mosul.

September 2014
Yemen's capital, Sana'a, falls to an alliance led by Iran-supported Houthis.

2015
Iran and the United States are once more on the same side as Soleimani helps battle ISIS.

July–September 2015
Soleimani meets Vladimir Putin in Moscow. Russia starts intervention in Syria.

September–October 2015
Iran increases its presence in Syria. Soleimani commands the offensive in the northwest.

December 2016
Soleimani is in Aleppo as Bashar al-Assad's army retakes the city.

Early 2018
Soleimani attacks reformists in a speech. Mahmoud Ahmadinejad writes a letter to him, threatening to reveal secrets.

July 2018
Soleimani gives a speech in Hamedan, threatening President Trump.

Early 2019
Following an attack on an IRGC bus in southeastern Iran, Soleimani gives stern warnings to the Pakistani government.

February 2019
Iran's foreign minister, Mohammad Javad Zarif, resigns in protest at Soleimani not inviting him to a meeting with Assad in Tehran.

March 2019
Floods in Khuzestan. Soleimani and other IRGC leaders go to help.

January 3, 2020
US drone assassinates Qassem Soleimani and a group of his fellow soldiers.

Acknowledgments

Sometime in the fall of 2018, publisher Novin Doostdar asked me if I knew someone who could write a book on Qassem Soleimani. I jumped at the question. The life of the Iranian general had long fascinated me. It had obvious relevance to my prime area of interest and scholarship, the ties that bind Iran to the Arab world. This had been my beat as a journalist and it was the subject of my doctoral studies. I wanted to write this book.

It helped that I already had copious files and notes on Soleimani and his Quds Force as well as contacts in the world of multinational Shia soldiers he commanded. I continued to discuss the idea of a book with Novin over several lunches and dinners in London and New York. In May 2019, I committed to writing the book but this was still slow work. Then, on January 3, 2020, Qassem Soleimani was killed. I knew his story had to be told now. The result is the book you now hold in your hands.

My gratitude goes to a long list of men and women without whom I would have been nowhere near the position of writing this book. My mother Mitra Mansouri was not only my first feminist hero but inspired me to look at the world with a creative eye and has been a constant rock of support my entire life.

In the Tehran of my early teen years, Marxist publisher Parviz Shahriari trusted a kid who loved Lenin and was into computers with writing for the esteemed journals he edited. Later on, the great Alireza Rajayi published a book I had translated and mentored me over unforgettable Cholo Kabab lunches. The leading light of journalism in the Iran of my youth, Rajayi could have been a great member of parliament if he hadn't been robbed of an obvious victory in 2000. It pains me that he has been robbed of much more since, while heroically standing up to years of prison and torture. I will be forever grateful to him.

Mohammad Qoochani and Hadi Khosrow Shahin were my first real editors. When I was an awkward teenager with radically different politics than theirs, they gave me writing positions I could only dream of. The years of writing for *Shahrvande Emrooz* are still among my sweetest and I continue to believe that its quality rivaled the best of current affairs journals anywhere in the world. Matin Ghaffarian was much more than another editor. Not only did he entrust me with the international editor position at the newspaper *Kargozaran* at the age of nineteen, he taught me more than I could ever recount.

I am grateful to Qoqnoos Publications' boss Amir Hosseinzadegan for publishing my first books of translation in Persian. The amazing chief editor at Qoqnoos, Arslan Fasihi, taught me how to respect prose. To this day, he is my *ostaad* and not only in prose. In those good days of Tehran, Kamran Malakmotiee patiently tolerated my questions by telling me what to read, what to watch, and where to visit in Tehran and the world. I hope he knows how much I'll owe him for the rest of my life.

In Toronto, I was fresh off the plane when Michael Petrou generously opened my eyes to the world of Western journalism. I wish to learn from his kindness and good spirits. The unforgettable duo of Hassan Zerehi and Nasrin Almasi, publishers of Toronto's *Shahrvand*, gave me hope that exilic Persian journalism can be of the highest quality.

I met Constance Dilley in Toronto during a local film festival but I can't imagine I once lived without her friendship and advice. I couldn't teach her Persian very well but she has taught me endlessly not only about journalism and scholarship but simply about being a good person. Every chapter of this book owes something to her.

At BBC Monitoring, I learnt so much from the talented men and women who lived and breathed the world of news. As many of them work away from the public eye, I won't name them for fear of prejudicing their situation. You know who you are.

At Manoto, Kayvan Abbasi trusted a young man with next to no broadcasting experience to fly around the world and cover the most important stories of our time while giving me full autonomy. I will always be grateful to him, to my editor there, Pouria Zeraati, and to my newsroom colleagues Pantea Modiri, Armin Qobadi Pasha, Shabnam Shabani, Sheyda Hooshmandi, and Sanaz Qaziadeh.

In the world of academia, I've been immensely lucky to learn from some of the best scholars in the world. At the University of Toronto, Ato Quayson, Anna Shternshis, and Antonela Arhin opened my eyes to a world beyond methodological nationalism. I was blessed to again overlap with Professor Quayson years later at New York University. He remains a primary role model. At the Free University of Berlin, Sebastian Conrad showed me how to think about history magisterially. His answer to "what is history about," given to me in a crowded coffee shop near the New School in New York, remains a guide to my scholarly life. Khodadad Rezakhani taught me how to read texts with the patience of a scholar of centuries past. Joseph Ben Prestel made me see Europe and the Middle East in a single frame. Nora Lafi's passionate yet erudite lessons helped me see the Ottoman legacies that shape our current world. Nadin Heé was the best professor, advisor, and mentor I could dream of. Her serious erudition on topics as diverse as Japanese fascism and German environmentalism comes with a *joie de vivre* that I wish we could all replicate.

Without working as an assistant for Lior Sternfeld, I would have never started a PhD. On some days, I am even grateful to him for this. I hope I can make him proud one day.

At NYU, I've benefited from a galaxy of scholars who sometimes also allow me to call them comrades. Zachary Lockman, Arang Keshavarzian, Sara Pursley, Ali Mirsepassi, and Ayse Baltacioglu-Brammer are as formidable a team of Middle East scholars as anyone could imagine. This is where Murphy's Law goes to die since it's definitely too good to be true. Whether it is the art of social-relational history, the significance of borderlands, legacies of nativism, or the roots of sectarianism, I've learnt from them so much of what little I know. Outside my core department, Mary Nolan taught me the very basics of history, Frederick Cooper and Jane Burbank showed me how to work with flexible historical categories, Chen Jian rekindled my passion for the study of the Cold War, and Pedro Monaville's class on the Global Sixties forever changed my view of twentieth-century history. I am also grateful to Olga Verlato, Zavier Wingham, and Gabriel Young, my lovely cohort; we held hands as we passed through the storm of doctoral studies together. The same is true about Amy Fallas, Arran Robert Walshe, Zachary Cuyler, and Professor Golbarg Rekabtalaei, who never left me alone on this journey.

That I can directly learn from some of the giants of Iranian studies is still surreal to me but I've come to believe it is real. Even if I can never write as gracefully as Negar Mottahedeh, I will continue to learn from her. My inspiration from Roham Alvandi's joyful love for Cold War history is only surpassed by his unapologetic love for our common homeland Iran. Ervand Abrahamian might be the grand scholar on whose history books we all grew up; but he is also forever as curious and engaging an interlocutor as anyone can dream of.

My grandmothers Sediqe Paki and Hajbibi Mesdaqi and late grandfathers Hajj Seyyed Morteza Azizi and Asghar Mansoori taught me the stories of Iranian and Shia lore from before I could read. The vivid mark they left on my imagination will never leave. That my mother's family hails from Kerman gave me a strong personal connection to the story and a resource for reconstructing the Kerman of the old days. I am indebted to my aforementioned mother, Mitra, and to her sisters, Soheila and Simin Mansoori, for the wondrous tales of their hometown.

On the other side of the family, Parastoo, Omid, Afsane, Elahe, and Hanie Azizi; Fariba Mohajerani; Tofigh and Elnoor Torabi; and Mohammad, Zeynab, Sepide, and Amir Mohammad Salarvand are not only an awesome paternal family cabal. They make me feel like I've never left the Tehran of my birth.

* * *

Much of the work done on this book first developed in stories I wrote for Maziar Bahari, IranWire's founder and editor. His good humor is as much a guiding principle as is his endless love for Iran and its arts, culture, and history. Throughout writing the book, I also had the support of Camelia Entekhabifard, my editor at *Independent Persian*.

Most writers rely on their close writer-friend circles more than they care to admit. In New York, Didi Tal and Etan Nechin are forever my sounding board, not afraid to tell me off when they need to. From afar, I am sustained by the unrepeatable friendship and advice of Loubna Mrie, Rohan Advani, and Verena Walther. Writing this book, I never ceased to dream about the Middle East as seen through the eyes of these five friends and their words. Loubna also brought Shane Bauer into our lives and mine is now all the more richer for it.

In Paris, Tinouche Nazmjoo and his publishing house Naakoja found me even the most obscure titles published in Iran. In London, Holly Dagres encouraged me no end to keep on with the writing. I am grateful to her also for bringing Ian Lee into our lives. Saleem Vaillancourt and Simin Fahandej are two other Londoners who stood by me as I wrote, even if that meant hanging out in cafes past midnight. I sometimes forget Mahsa Alimardani is also now a Londoner as our friendship passed through Toronto and Amsterdam before she settled there. I am forever grateful for her wisdom and friendship and for bringing us her lovely Mr. Alef. In addition to all these old friends, I was lucky to meet Tanya Efremova in London, even if it turned out she was my neighbor in the East Village, New York. As the world entered the nightmare of a global pandemic, she helped me keep my sanity—and even brought me a thermometer when I got the virus.

The sample chapters of this book were written at the Santa Barbara Eco Beach Resort on the gorgeous island of São Miguel in the Azores. A writer could not have dreamed of a better setting. I am grateful to my friend Ida, who accompanied me on the trip there, discussed ideas with me while we rode horses, and read these words before anybody else. I promised Heloisa and Maria at Santa Barbara that I would mention them in the book if it ever got published. I am happy not to disappoint them.

Without Hamdi Malik's unrivaled expertise on Iraqi politics, I could never have dared write the Iraqi chapters. Without conversations with Sara Ajalyakin, Sara Dadouch, and, of course, Loubna Mrie, I'd never have allowed myself to write about Syria. Ena Muraspahić is never shy to correct me on Yugoslav and Bosnian history—or on anything else for that matter. Between New York and Warsaw, Karolina Partyga read my draft with the eye of the fine historian she is in the process of becoming. Ayse Lokmanoglu helped me understand Salafi-Jihadism and scholarly literature on modern terrorism.

There would have been, of course, no book without Novin Doostdar. To work with him and his publishing partner in crime, Juliet Mabey, is truly a dream come true. Sam Carter and Rida Vaquas gave me sharp edits on the sample chapters and their voices never left me to the end. ("No boring verbs!") Rida also did invaluable final edits. Jon Bentley-Smith kept me on track and did invaluable fact-checking. Rights director Anne Bihan advocated for the book. I am lucky that my author photo was taken by an excellent artist but also a caring friend, Zoe Prinds-Flash. Her work is so good that I wish I looked like that in real life.

I've dedicated the book first and foremost to my hometown Tehran and my maternal city of Kerman. Years of separation from my Iran casts a long shadow over my life, but in other cities of the Middle East I have found a broader homeland and many kindred spirits. The dream of our people for freedom and dignity is a light that will outshine the most shadowy of commanders. Of this, I have no doubt.

A Note on Sources

This book is written by a former journalist who consciously defected to academia. It thus bears the traces of this transition, although my utopian quest is for a space in between these two worlds. Whether I succeed or not, I shall never accept that scholarship should be written in a dull fashion and for audiences of nine people or that journalism should be empty of ideas.

Compared to the many books that cover a broadly similar period, what I hope makes this one stand out is that it squarely relies on the perspective of Iranians and other Middle Easterners. I've based myself on published material in Persian and interviews with Iraqi, Afghan, Syrian, Yemeni, Israeli, and Iranian interlocutors. They speak for themselves. I am particularly indebted to the extensive work of oral history done in Iran, especially Abbas Mirzayi's work on the Kermanis of the Iran-Iraq War period; a crucial literature that, alas, is almost never cited in English.

My visits to Cairo, Casablanca, Amman, Istanbul, Van, Beirut, Tel Aviv, Jerusalem, Haifa, Riyadh, Doha, Dubai, Manama, Tbilisi, and Baku not only helped me tell many of the stories in this book; they strengthened my love for the region in which they take place.

Bibliography

Akbari, Ali. *Chamran Mazlum Bud: Khaterat-i az Shahid Mostafa Chamran.* Tehran: Ya Zahra, 2018.

Akbari Mazdabadi, Ali. *Hajj Qassem: Jostari dar Khaterat-e Hajj Qassem Soleimani.* Tehran: Ya Zahra, 2015.

Alhasan, Hasan Tariq. "The Role of Iran in the Failed Coup of 1981: The IFLB in Bahrain." *Middle East Journal,* 65(4), 2011, pp. 603–17.

Alvandi, Roham (ed.) *The Age of Aryamehr: Late Pahlavi Iran and its Global Entanglements.* London: Gingko Library, 2018.

Alvandi, Roham. *Nixon, Kissinger, and the Shah: The United States and Iran in the Cold War.* New York: Oxford University Press, 2014.

Bastani, Hossein. "Nagoftehaye Hokomate Iran dar Parvandeye Ahamde Motavasellian." BBC Persian, July 7, 2020.

Bloom, Mia, and Ayse Lokmanoglu, "From Pawn to Knights: The Changing Role of Women's Agency in Terrorism?" *Studies in Conflict & Terrorism,* 2020, DOI: 10.1080/1057610X.2020.1759263.

Chehabi, H. E. (ed.) *Distant Relations: Iran and Lebanon in the Last 500 Years.* Oxford: Centre for Lebanese Studies, 2006.

Cockburn, Patrick. *The Rise of Islamic State: ISIS and the New Sunni Revolution,* rev. ed. London: Verso, 2015.

Dagher, Sam. *Assad or We Burn the Country: How One Family's Lust for Power Destroyed Syria.* New York: Little, Brown, 2019.

Ghazanfari, Kamran. *Raz-e Ghat'nameh: Cheray va Chegunegi-e Payan-e Jang-e Tahmili*. Tehran: Sherkat-e Entesharat-e Keyhan, 2013.

Jafarpour Rashidi, Rashed. *Mojahed-e Basir: Seyr-i dar Zendegi va Mobarezat-e Shahid Mohammad-e Montazeri*. Tehran: Intesharat-e Markaz-e Asnad-e Enghelab-e Eslami, 2013.

Knights, Michael, Hamdi Malik, and Aymenn Jawad al-Tamimi. "The Future of Iraq's Popular Mobilization Forces," Policywatch 3321. Washington Institute, May 28, 2020, https://www.washingtoninstitute.org/policy-analysis/view/the-future-of-iraqs-popular-mobilization-forces.

Lokmanoglu, Ayse Deniz. "Coin as Imagined Sovereignty: A Rhetorical Analysis of Coins as a Transhistorical Artifact and an Ideograph in Islamic State's Communication." *Studies in Conflict & Terrorism*, 2020, DOI: 10.1080/1057610X.2020.1793458.

Mirzayi, Abbas. *Hojum be Tahajom: Bahman-e 1360 ta Ordibehesht-e 1361*. Tehran: Ya Zahra, 2017.

Mirzayi, Abbas. *Nabard-e Seyyed Jaber: Ordibehesht ta Tir-e 1361*. Tehran: Ya Zahra, 2016.

Mirzayi, Abbas. *Nabardha-ye Piruz: Tarikhname-ye Defa-e Moghddas-e Ostan-e Kerman, Vol. 3*. Tehran: Soureye Mehr, 2013.

Ostovar, Afshon. *Vanguard of the Imam: Religion, Politics, and Iran's Revolutionary Guards*. New York: Oxford University Press, 2016.

Razoux, Pierre. *The Iran-Iraq War*. Cambridge, MA: Belknap Press, 2015

Richter, Paul. *The Ambassadors: America's Diplomats on the Front Lines*. New York: Simon & Schuster, 2019.

Soufan, Ali. "Qassem Soleimani and Iran's Unique Regional Strategy." *CTC Sentinel*, November 2018, pp. 1–10.

Taheri, Hojjatollah. *Shahid Montazeri be Revayat-e Asnad-e Savak*. Tehran: Intesharat-e Markaz-e Asnad-e Enghelab-e Eslami, 1999.

Veisi, Moradi. "Baazkhaniye 96 Mah Nabarde Zaminiye Iran o Aragh." BBC Persian, September 22, 2015.

Veisi, Moradi. "Iran o Araq dar Jang che Manateqi az Khake Yekdigar ra Eshqal Kardand?" BBC Persian, July 18, 2018.

Voll, John. "The Sudanese Mahdi: Frontier Fundamentalist." *International Journal of Middle East Studies*, 10(2), 1979, pp. 145–66.

Zand Razavi, Siamak. "Ilat va Ashayer-e Kerman: Pishine-ye Tarikhi va Masal-e Eskan." *Oloum-e Ejtemai Quarterly*, 1993.

Zarei, Sadollah. *Sadeq al-wa'd*. Tehran: Andisheh Sazan-e Noor Institute for Students, 2018.

Zimmt, Raz. "Portrait of Qasem Soleimani, Commander of the Iranian Islamic Revolutionary Guards Corps' Qods Force, Instigator of Iranian Subversion

and Terrorism in the Middle East and around the Globe." Meir Amit
Intelligence and Terrorism Information Center, October 29, 2015.

"Sardar-e Del'ha." *Ettelaat*, 94(27499), February 2020.

Vije'nameh-ye Maktab-e Hajj Qassem. Tehran, March 2020.

Notes

All website links were accurate at the time of writing (August 2020).

Introduction

1 https://www.newyorker.com/magazine/2020/02/10/qassem-suleimani-and
-how-nations-decide-to-kill

1 A Life on the Margins

1 I owe this anecdote to a conversation with Hamid Dabashi.
2 Abrahamian, Ervand. *Iran Between Two Revolutions*. Princeton, NJ: Princeton University Press, 1982, p. 141.
3 Zand Razani, Siamak. "Ilat o Ashayere Kerman: Pishineye Tarikhi o Masaleye Eskan." *Faslnameye Oloome Ejtemayi* 3(4), 1993, p. 167.
4 Interview with the author, August 29, 2019.
5 https://www.aparat.com/v/jmK7a
6 https://tinyurl.com/y6exnteq
7 https://tinyurl.com/yyo4mfa4
8 Atabaki, Touraj and Erik J. Zürcher (eds.) *Men of Order: Authoritarian Modernization under Atatürk and Reza Shah*. London: I.B. Tauris, 1997.

9   Kuniholm, Bruce. *The Origins of the Cold War in the Near East: Great Power Conflict and Diplomacy in Iran, Turkey, and Greece.* Princeton, NJ: Princeton University Press, 1980.

10 For most of his life, Soleimani's date of birth was noted in most sources as March 11, 1957. This is still the date on his Wikipedia page at the time of writing, August 2020. But the date on his gravestone is March 21, 1956, the very first day of the Iranian calendar year of 1335, while an official commemorative booklet published after his death claimed that Soleimani's real date of birth was March 21, 1958. My preference is the date on the gravestone.

2 A Young Man in the City

1   https://tinyurl.com/y504640d
2   https://tinyurl.com/yyo4mfa4
3   The later hagiographies would make claims about his presence in the anti-Shah movement that are rejected by other contemporaries and lack evidence.

3 To Guard a Revolution

1   Interview with the author, November 19, 2019.
2   Trotsky, Leon. *History of the Russian Revolution.* Chicago, IL: Haymarket, [1932] 2008, p. xv.
3   Mirsepassi, Ali. *Iran's Quiet Revolution: The Downfall of the Pahlavi State.* Cambridge, UK: Cambridge University Press, 2019.
4   https://www.marxist.com/marxism-and-the-state-part-one.htm
5   https://tinyurl.com/y55ffle5
6   https://tinyurl.com/y5zh2dru
7   In something of a strange compromise, it was agreed that the IRGC's banner wouldn't carry the word "Iran" but the Majlis-approved constitution would. IRGC (without any reference to Iran) is the name that stuck.

4 "A Gift from the Heavens"

1   https://history.state.gov/historicaldocuments/frus1977-80v09Ed2/d242

5 War Makes Man

1   Those who picked the name were probably not educated enough to know that "Beit-ol-Moqaddas," or "The Holy House," actually referred to the city's much longer history as a Jewish, not Muslim, site of worship.

2 Interview with the author, August 28, 2019.

3 Ibid.

4 Ibid.

5 Quoted in Akbari Mazdabadi, *Haj Qasem*.

6 Mirzayi, *Nabardha-ye Piruz*, p. 32.

7 Ibid., p. 215.

8 Ibid., p. 230.

9 https://tinyurl.com/y68l27kg

10 Mirzayi, *Nabardha-ye Piruz*, p. 245.

11 Ibid., p. 250.

12 Quoted in Akbari Mazdabadi, *Haj Qasem*, p. 15.

13 Ibid.

14 Mirzayi, *Nabardha-ye Piruz*, p. 337.

15 Quoted in Mirzayi, *Hojum be Tahajom*, p. 13.

16 Ibid., p. 29.

17 Quoted in Akbari Mazdabadi, *Haj Qasem*, p. 11.

18 Mirzayi, *Nabard-e Seyyed Jaber*.

19 https://tinyurl.com/y68l27kg.

20 Montazeri, Hosseynali. *Khaterat*. Los Angeles, CA: Ketab, p. 589.

21 Quoted in Davudabadi, Hamid. *Seyyed Aziz*, Tehran: Ya Zahra, 2016.

6 No Islamism in One Country

1 Chehabi, *Distant Relations*, p. 212.

2 Ibid.

3 Ibid., p. 151.

4 Ibid., pp. 158–9.

5 Ibid.

6 Akbari, *Chamran Mazlum Bud*.

7 Kim Ghattas follows this line of thinking in *Black Wave: Saudi Arabia, Iran, and the Forty-Year Rivalry That Unraveled Culture, Religion, and Collective Memory in the Middle East*. New York: Henry Holt, 2020.

8 https://tinyurl.com/y3f9tlt6

9 Chehabi, *Distant Relations*, p. 215.

10 Interview with the author, November 22, 2019.

11 https://www.deseret.com/1998/1/3/19355803/a-crush-on-lollobrigida-benefited-italian-troops

7 A Chalice Full of Poison

1   The details of this event have long been a point of contention between Iran and Saudi Arabia. Iran claims the pilgrims were shot at by the Saudi police. Saudis claim it was a stampede.

2   Quoted in Ghazanfari, *Raz-e Ghat'nameh*, p. 95.

3   Khomeini, Ruhollah. *Sahifeye Imam Khomeini*, vol. 21, p. 98. Tehran: Markaze Tanzim o Nashre Asare Imam Khomeini, 1999.

4   "Hokme Tarikhiye Hazrate Emam Rahmanollah Allayh Darbareye Salman Rushdie." *Golbarg Magazine*, 47, 2004.

5   Later published as a book: Mahallati, Mohammad Jafar Amir. *Ethics of War and Peace in Iran and Shi'i Islam*. Toronto: University of Toronto Press, 2016.

6   Ghazanfari, *Raz-e Ghat'nameh*, p. 62.

7   Interview with the author, May 22, 2019.

8   https://tinyurl.com/y4pcqonu

9   http://aranvabidgoldefe.mihanblog.com/post/category/18

10 https://tinyurl.com/y6sjlwx6,

8 An "Unwritten Pact"

1   With the exception of Sadeq Kharazi, who was allowed permission to sport a tie. Iran's dandy-looking ambassador to France from 2002 to 2006 and at other times deputy envoy to the UN and deputy foreign minister, Kharazi happened to be a close personal friend of Soleimani.

2   https://www.youtu.be/DqnoJ1qJTvE

3   Interview with the author, June 22, 2019.

4   Ibid.

5   https://tinyurl.com/y2febufp

6   https://moderndiplomacy.eu/2020/03/09/qassem-soleimanis-broken-dream-in-central-asia/

7   Zandie, Mostafa. "Hajj Qassem, Memare Diplomasie Jahadi." *Maktabe Hajj Qassem, Yadnameye Sardar Sepahbode Shahid, Hajj Qassem Soleimani*, spring 2020.

8   Richter, *The Ambassadors*, p. 24.

9   https://1997-2001.state.gov/statements/2000/000317.html

10 Interview with the author, April 30, 2020.

11 https://www.theatlantic.com/international/archive/2017/11/al-qaeda-iran-cia/545576/

12 https://slate.com/news-and-politics/2003/01/axis-of-evil-authorship

-settled.html; Frum, David. *The Right Man: The Surprise Presidency of George W. Bush*. New York: Random House, 2003.

13 https://www.newyorker.com/magazine/2013/09/30/the-shadow-commander

14 Richter, *The Ambassadors*, p. 27.

15 Burns, William J. *The Back Channel: A Memoir of American Diplomacy and the Case for Its Renewal*. New York: Random House, 2019, p. 165.

16 Ibid., p. 161.

9 We Protect the Shrines

1 Interview with the author, May 22, 2020.

2 Ibid.

3 Ibid.

4 The actual title did not come to use until a decade later when the Iranian intervention in Syria was justified as a response to ISIS's destruction of Shia shrines. But the symbolic centrality of shrines in Iranian foreign operations obviously has a pedigree, evident in the fact that CRSG was founded in 2003. The organization would come to play a major role in Iran's later interventions in Syria.

5 http://www.azadi-b.com/G/2017/10/post_42.html

6 Sayej, Caroleen Marji. *Patriotic Ayatollahs: Nationalism in Post-Saddam Iraq*. Ithaca, NY: Cornell University Press, 2018, p. 101; https://www.independent.co.uk/voices/commentators/ayatollah-mohammed-baqir-al-hakim-we-dont-want-an-extremist-islamic-government-in-iraq-104583.html

7 https://www.un.org/press/en/2007/sc8980.doc.htm

8 https://www.newyorker.com/magazine/2013/09/30/the-shadow-commander

10 Busy in Beirut

1 Interview with the author, April 22, 2020.

2 Interview with the author, February 21, 2020.

3 Interview with the author, May 2, 2020.

4 https://tinyurl.com/y5qu398v

5 Interview with the author, February 22, 2020.

6 Zarei, *Sadeq al-wa'd*, p. 61.

7 Interview with the author, December 22, 2019.

8 In Soleimani's version of the story, it was actually Bolton who begged Hamad

to push for a ceasefire, knocking on his door in New York, where he was staying to lead mediation efforts.

9 https://www.ynetnews.com/articles/0,7340,L-3569288,00.html
10 https://www.cfr.org/israel/second-lebanon-war/p11363
11 https://tinyurl.com/y4f335q0
12 Interview with the author, December 22, 2019.
13 https://www.radiofarda.com/a/f12_revolutionary_guards_against_ceasefire_in_gaza/24777607.html
14 Zarei, *Sadeq al-waʾd*, p. 165.

11 Islamic Awakening, Sectarian Degeneration

1 Yemen's Ali Abdullah Saleh was still technically president and Libya's Muammar Gaddafi still held his "Brotherly Leader" title but they both wielded little power by this point and would be out within months.
2 https://www.magiran.com/article/2403999
3 Ghannouchi, Rached. "From Political Islam to Muslim Democracy: The Ennahda Party and the Future of Tunisia." *Foreign Affairs*, September/October 2016.
4 https://tinyurl.com/y2rwy5ve
5 Interview with the author, July 1, 2020.
6 https://www.youtube.com/watch?v=jm-OewI-I20
7 Interview with the author, June 19, 2020.
8 Interview with the author, June 20, 2020.
9 Bajoghli, Narges. *Iran Reframed: Anxieties of Power in the Islamic Republic.* Stanford, CA: Stanford University Press, 2019.

12 Black Flags, White Flags

1 "Al-Sham" can refer both to Damascus and also to the broader region of the Levant usually denoted as "Bilad al-Sham" in Arabic.
2 The Prophet himself is buried in the Prophet's Mosque, a stone's throw from Baqi.
3 https://www.theguardian.com/commentisfree/2013/sep/02/syria-ed-miliband-david-cameron
4 Falahzade, Mohammadreza. "Hajj Qassem baa eradeye khod Jahane Eslam raa az yek Ejdeha nejaat dad." *Maktabe Hajj Qassem*.

Epilogue: The Endgame

1 https://www.nytimes.com/2019/01/11/opinion/gadi-eisenkot-israel-iran-syria.html

2 https://tinyurl.com/yxjhlynv

3 https://tinyurl.com/yxbnxedj

4 Interview with the author, May 22, 2020.

5 https://www.nytimes.com/2020/01/05/opinion/suleimani-iran-trump.html

6 https://www.middleeasteye.net/news/syrians-idlib-celebrate-qassem-soleimanis-death-sweets-and-cakes

7 Interviews with the author, July 20, 2020; https://www.buzzfeednews.com/article/sarahhunaidi/oppose-all-wars-iran-not-just-american-ones

8 The official commemorative magazine published following his death claims he was married on November 24, 1979. But in an interview he said he married his wife during the war and when he was already based in Ahvaz. This suggests a date in the early 1980s.

9 https://tinyurl.com/y38qjhu9

10 https://tinyurl.com/yxoryeom

Index